Zend Framework 1.8
Web Application Development

Design, develop, and deploy feature-rich PHP web
applications with this MVC framework

Keith Pope

BIRMINGHAM - MUMBAI

Zend Framework 1.8 Web Application Development

Copyright © 2009 Packt Publishing

All rights reserved. No part of this book may be reproduced, stored in a retrieval system, or transmitted in any form or by any means, without the prior written permission of the publisher, except in the case of brief quotations embedded in critical articles or reviews.

Every effort has been made in the preparation of this book to ensure the accuracy of the information presented. However, the information contained in this book is sold without warranty, either express or implied. Neither the author, nor Packt Publishing, and its dealers and distributors will be held liable for any damages caused or alleged to be caused directly or indirectly by this book.

Packt Publishing has endeavored to provide trademark information about all of the companies and products mentioned in this book by the appropriate use of capitals. However, Packt Publishing cannot guarantee the accuracy of this information.

First published: September 2009

Production Reference: 1160909

Published by Packt Publishing Ltd.
32 Lincoln Road
Olton
Birmingham, B27 6PA, UK.

ISBN 978-1-847194-22-0

www.packtpub.com

Cover Image by Vinayak Chittar (vinayak.chittar@gmail.com)

Credits

Author
Keith Pope

Reviewers
Wenbert Del Rosario
Md. Mahmud Ahsan

Acquisition Editor
Rashmi Phadnis

Development Editor
Ved Prakash Jha

Technical Editor
Pallavi Kachare

Copy Editor
Leonard D'Silva

Indexer
Hemangini Bari

Editorial Team Leader
Akshara Aware

Project Team Leader
Lata Basantani

Project Coordinator
Rajashree Hamine

Proofreader
Lynda Sliwosk
Jeff Orloff

Graphics
Nilesh Mohite

Production Coordinator
Shantanu Zagade

Cover Work
Shantanu Zagade

About the Author

Keith Pope has over ten years of experience in web-related industries and has had a keen interest in programming from an early age. Keith currently works in the airline industry as a technical project manager, providing entertainment systems for aircraft.

He has been working with the Zend Framework since its first preview release, using it in many of his work and personal projects.

I would like to thank my wife; without her support and patience, this book would not have been possible. I would also like to thank Matthew Weier O'Phinney who has been instrumental in the success of the Zend Framework project as well as giving lots of time to the mailing lists, answering both mine and others questions. The rest of the Zend team for all their hard work while creating a great framework that I could write about. Rob Allen and Alex Mace for general help and support. The technical reviewers and the team at Packt for their hard work in getting everything together. Derek Au for his bug reports. Big thanks to my family, the Adkins family, Phil Dunsford, Martin Williams, Tom Hoddell, Sally Hoddell, the Allpay team, Francesca Oliveri, Lucy Hughes-Martin, and Rob Whittle; you all supported me in various ways.

About the Reviewers

Wenbert Del Rosario is from Cebu, Philippines. He started his career as a web developer in college, learning PHP and Adobe Photoshop. He works with open source technologies—Zend Framework, Code Igniter, MySQL, and jQuery are some of the tools he has under his sleeve.

He likes to keep it simple and believes that being mindful of best practices in software development can be more effective than adopting every latest technology.

In his free time, he loves to work on personal projects using PHP, Javascript, and MySQL. He also does some freelance jobs and consulting from time to time.

All in all, he is very passionate about what he does and is a big fan of open source software.

Wenbert has worked for Lexmark Research and Development Corporation in Cebu. He develops in-house web-based applications using Apache, PHP, MySQL, and Linux. Some of his web applications are used in different geographc regions (USA, Europe, and Asia Pacific) by Lexmark employees, while other small but significant ones are used locally by Lexmark Cebu employees.

I would like to thank my family. My mother, Wenia, who is always very supportive and understanding. My brothers, Andrew, John, and Alberto. And my sister Jonina Mae. To my father, Luis, who passed away a few years ago and to God.

Md. Mahmud Ahsan is a freelance consultant currently working as a software engineer in Berkeley-based i2we, inc.

Mahmud received a Bachelor's degree in Computer Science and Engineering from the International Islamic University Chittagong, in Bangladesh. He is also a Zend Certified Engineer. He has about four years of experience in the world of PHP. He has extensively worked on small and large scale social networking web applications developed in PHP and Zend Framework.

I'm grateful to my parents and Hasin Hayder (author at Packt Publishing). I would also like to thank my wife Jinat Jahan for her consistent support.

I would like to dedicate this book to my wife, Michelle

Table of Contents

Preface

As web developers we are always looking for ways to improve our systems and working practices. We have to move fast and handle ever-changing requirements from our managers, although this is what makes our work so exciting and challenging.

A very important tool that can meet today's fast-changing needs is the basic framework you use to build your application. This forms the basis of your application, and if you have a good framework then you should have fewer problems in the future.

A good example is Ruby on Rails, a very popular and successful framework. It has certainly gone a long way in popularizing the use of frameworks, especially in the PHP community, with a lot of PHP developers choosing to switch to Ruby. Why? Well Ruby on Rails will provide you with a lot of very good tools and I can see why people are drawn to it. But the PHP communities are never ones to sit around and since the release of PHP5 there has been a surge of new PHP5 frameworks released.

So with all these frameworks what's the best? Well, if you bought this book you have probably already chosen to use the Zend Framework. But I would say use whatever tool fits your project best. All the frameworks out there have good and bad points; it is up to you as a web developer to assess your needs and choose your tools.

Brief history and future developments

The Zend Framework was first announced at **ZendCon** in October 2005 as part of Zend's industry-wide PHP Collaboration Project. Its main aim was to provide a standardized way to build PHP applications and to assist in rapid application development using PHP.

The first production version was released in July 2007, and included many great features such as the MVC framework, database access, Lucene search engine, I18N support, authentication, authorization, and web service interfaces. The PHP community warmly welcomed this and the framework gained interest from many quarters.

Following on from version 1.0 the framework has grown rapidly, and has a large active community. Backed by a determined group of core contributors, the framework is in great shape and will continue to grow.

As of this writing, the current version is 1.5.3 and the core components are at a mature stable state. Future developments are promising to add many productivity features as well as improving on the already solid set of core features. One feature to note is the introduction of tooling components; these will provide new ways of managing projects and will also be able to integrate into some popular IDE's.

With their future plans and already excellent base, the Zend Framework is looking to be one of the major players in the PHP framework market.

What is it and why use it

Now that we know a bit about the Zend Framework, let's look at exactly what it can be used for.

The Zend Framework is a loosely-coupled collection of components; this means that you can use all of them or just one, enabling greater flexibility. For example, you may need to add OpenID support to one of your currently deployed applications. With Zend Framework, you can simply use the Zend_OpenID component without having to use the MVC functionality or any configuration files that are not concerned with OpenID. You could compare this type of modular design to PHP's PEAR library.

On the other side, Zend Framework is a fully functional MVC framework, meaning that it provides us with the tools to implement the Model View Controller design pattern. This design pattern is widely used in web development and provides a way for us to separate our applications business logic, flow of control, and display. The purpose of this is to make applications easier to maintain, and enables many developers to work on a project in isolation. This book is mainly focused on showing you how to use this functionality.

There are a few things that you should know about the Zend Framework. It is not a content management solution. It does not provide components like menu creators or user management areas. All that it provides are the tools for you to build these.

So we can use this framework as both an MVC framework or as a component library, but why would you choose to use it? Here are some of the main benefits that Zend Framework offers.

Licensing

Licensing is always a consideration when working with open source products. The Zend Frameworks license is based upon the new BSD license and also has a **Contributor License Agreement (CLA)** that all contributors sign before submitting code. This means that Zend Framework is safe for your business to use without worrying about the legal nightmares in the future.

Quality

From its initial conception, quality has been important to this framework. All code is thoroughly unit tested and has to meet at least 80 percent code coverage with 100 percent as the aim. This means you shouldn't get any nasty surprises down the line. Another important quality control is the proposal process. This process is very rigorous meaning that the Zend Framework is less likely to suffer from **bloat** in the future.

Simplicity

One of the important principles in the Zend Frameworks design is the 80/20 rule. This stipulates that each component should provide 80 percent of functionality that meets the majority of use-cases and the other 20 percent is left for your business specific requirements. By using this rule, Zend Framework provides a very simple way for developers to get on and implement their own requirements.

Flexibility

Zend Framework is very flexible. Whether you want to refactor an old application, create a new one, use a single component, or deviate from the common use-cases, Zend Framework provides many ways for you to extend and customize your application. This is achieved by its loosely-coupled design and its use of Object-Oriented practices.

Out-of-the-box features

There is a whole host of out-of-the-box features for you to choose from. These range from Google API support to input validation and filtering. Some of the most notable are:

- Model View Controller
- Authentication and Authorization
- Database Abstraction
- Session Management
- Search and Indexing
- Web Services
- Mail and Mime Support

There are plenty of others, far too many to list them all. Just having a look at the online reference guide shows you that Zend Framework is guaranteed to provide most of the tools you need. Also with a constant stream of new proposals coming out of the community you can be sure that it will stay ahead of the curve.

Community

All open source projects need a good community to survive. The Zend Framework community is active and more importantly, friendly. The mailing lists are always busy and people are very helpful to newcomers and seasoned users. Also the Zend staffers are very supportive and committed to the success of the project. I would suggest signing up to the mailing list to stay up-to-date with current developments, and the ongoing debates, which are always interesting.

What this book covers

Chapter 1: *A Basic MVC Application* gives a quick-start introduction about building a basic MVC application.

Chapter 2: *The Zend Framework MVC Architecture* gives a detailed look at all the MVC related Zend Framework components.

Chapter 3: *Storefront Basic Setup* helps in creating the foundation from which the Storefront will be created.

Chapter 4: *Storefront Models* provides a look at how Models are handled in the Zend Framework, their design, and related issues.

Chapter 5: *Implementing the Storefront Catalog* helps in creating the Storefront Catalog's Model, Controller, and Views.

Chapter 6: *Implementing the Storefront User Accounts* shows how to create the Storefront User Model, Controller, and Views.

Chapter 7: *Implementing the Shopping Cart* helps in creating the shopping cart Model, Controller, and Views.

Chapter 8: *Implementing the Administration Area* helps in creating functionality to administer the Storefront products.

Chapter 9: *Implementing Authentication and Access Control* explains how to secure the Storefront using Authentication and Access Control.

Chapter 10: *Storefront Roundup* explains how to use multiple modules and Services within your application.

Chapter 11: *Storefront Optimization* explains optimizing of the Storefront to improve application performance.

Chapter 12: *Testing with Storefront* explains the testing of the Storefront with Zend_Test and PHPUnit.

Appendix: *Installing Supporting Software* explains how to install various supporting software tools to help work with the Zend Framework on various platforms.

Who this book is for

This book is for PHP web developers who want to get started with Zend Framework. If you are already using this framework, you will learn how to use it in the best way and produce better applications.

Basic knowledge of Object Oriented design will be helpful.

Conventions

In this book, you will find a number of styles of text that distinguish between different kinds of information. Here are some examples of these styles, and an explanation of their meaning.

Code words in text are shown as follows: "In order to fetch an instance of the Front Controller, we use the `getInstance()` method."

A block of code is set as follows:

```
$front->setControllerDirectory(array(
    'default' => '/path/application/default',
    'product' => '/path/application/product'
));
```

When we wish to draw your attention to a particular part of a code block, the relevant lines or items are set in bold:

```
$route = new Zend_Controller_Router_Route_Hostname(
    ':username.domain.com',
    array(
            'controller' => 'account',
            'action' => 'index'
    ),
    array(
        // Match subdomain excluding www.
        'username' => '(?!.*www) [a-zA-Z-_0-9]+'
    )
);
```

Any command-line input or output is written as follows:

bin\zf.bat create project.

New terms and **important words** are shown in bold. Words that you see on the screen, in menus or dialog boxes for example, appear in the text like this: "A request is made and the **Request Object** is created."

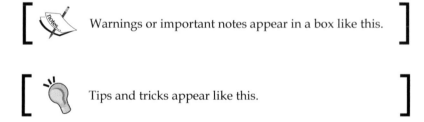

[Warnings or important notes appear in a box like this.]

[Tips and tricks appear like this.]

Reader feedback

Feedback from our readers is always welcome. Let us know what you think about this book—what you liked or may have disliked. Reader feedback is important for us to develop titles that you really get the most out of.

To send us general feedback, simply send an email to feedback@packtpub.com, and mention the book title via the subject of your message.

If there is a book that you need and would like to see us publish, please send us a note in the **SUGGEST A TITLE** form on www.packtpub.com or email suggest@packtpub.com.

If there is a topic that you have expertise in and you are interested in either writing or contributing to a book on, see our author guide on www.packtpub.com/authors.

Customer support

Now that you are the proud owner of a Packt book, we have a number of things to help you to get the most from your purchase.

Downloading the example code for the book

Visit http://www.packtpub.com/files/code/4220_Code.zip to directly download the example code.

The downloadable files contain instructions on how to use them.

Errata

Although we have taken every care to ensure the accuracy of our content, mistakes do happen. If you find a mistake in one of our books—maybe a mistake in the text or the code—we would be grateful if you would report this to us. By doing so, you can save other readers from frustration, and help us to improve subsequent versions of this book. If you find any errata, please report them by visiting http://www.packtpub.com/support, selecting your book, clicking on the **let us know** link, and entering the details of your errata. Once your errata are verified, your submission will be accepted and the errata added to any list of existing errata. Any existing errata can be viewed by selecting your title from http://www.packtpub.com/support.

Piracy

Piracy of copyright material on the Internet is an ongoing problem across all media. At Packt, we take the protection of our copyright and licenses very seriously. If you come across any illegal copies of our works, in any form, on the Internet, please provide us with the location address or web site name immediately so that we can pursue a remedy.

Please contact us at copyright@packtpub.com with a link to the suspected pirated material.

We appreciate your help in protecting our authors, and our ability to bring you valuable content.

Questions

You can contact us at questions@packtpub.com if you are having a problem with any aspect of the book, and we will do our best to address it.

1
Creating a Basic MVC Application

In this chapter, we will take our first steps into using the Zend Framework. This provides us with a very quick run-through of using the **Model-View-Controller (MVC)** components by creating a simple web page. We will look at the following aspects:

- What MVC is
- Setting up your environment
- Installing Zend Framework
- Creating a Project with `Zend_Tool`
- Bootstrapping and Configuration
- Creating Controllers
- Creating Views
- Handling Errors

By the end of this chapter, you should be comfortable with the general concepts and be ready to move on to creating more advanced functionalities.

Overview of MVC architecture

As we are going to be using MVC extensively throughout this book, it is important that you have an understanding of what MVC is and what its goals are.

Trygve Reenskaug first devised MVC in the late 1970s for Smalltalk. Since then, it has evolved and has many different implementations, and much debate surrounds them. Even with the great amount of debate surrounding MVC, it still retains its basic goal of separating user interface code into three separate areas. This basic concept is fairly easy to understand. However, the details of an MVC implementation can be very complex.

The three areas that **MVC** defines are **Model**, **View**, and **Controller**. These are responsible for domain logic, user interface, and control logic respectively. By separating application responsibilities in this way, we gain the following benefits:

- The addition, editing, and removal of interfaces is simple
- The ability to have multiple separate views of the same data
- Changes made to the logic control are easy
- Helps developers avoid repeating common code
- Helps developers to work together in segregation

There are, of course, disadvantages to MVC and situations where it should not be used. For example, the application we are about to create is very simple. Therefore, if it always stays this way, then there would be no point in using MVC, as the overhead created by the MVC implementation outweighs the benefit.

We will be looking at how the Zend Framework implements MVC in Chapter 2. For now, we will stick with this brief explanation of what MVC is and move on to creating our **Hello Zend** application. I hope this gives you an idea of the main aspects involved and the benefits you can get by using it.

Setting up the environment

First, we need to set up our environment and get a copy of the Zend Framework.

You can download the source package from `http://framework.zend.com/download`. For the purposes of the book, get version 1.8.0.

You may also wish to familiarize yourself with the projects Subversion repository. This is useful if you want to use any functionality that is still in development. Information on the Subversion layout can be found at http://framework.zend.com/wiki/display/ZFDEV/ Subversion+Standards.

The minimum PHP version to run the Zend Framework is **5.2.4**; Redhat users that are stuck at 5.1 should consider using Zend Server (http://www.zend.com/ products/server) to easily upgrade your PHP version.

For the examples in this book, you will also need a web server that has URL Rewrite support such as Apache (http://httpd.apache.org/).

Installation

Once we have downloaded the Zend Framework release package, we need to do some basic installation before we can start creating our application. First, create a new directory within your web server's document root, from which the application will be served. The examples in this chapter use the directory name of helloZend. Next, copy the library and bin directories from the release package into the newly created directory. The library directory contains all of the Zend Frameworks source files, and the bin directory contains the command line interface for the Zend Framework. The Zend Framework is now installed and ready for use!

Creating the project structure

We are now ready to start creating the directory structure for our project. In order to do this, we are going to use the command line interface provided by the Zend Framework. This interface uses the Zend_Tool component that provides a whole host of commands that makes it very easy to get up and running with the Zend Framework in just a few minutes.

In order to create the project structure, open up your command line and change into the hellozend directory, and then run the following command:

For Windows users:

```
bin\zf.bat create project
```

For Linux and Mac users:

```
bin/zf.sh create project
```

This command creates a Zend Framework project in the specified location. In our case, this is the current directory (.). We could specify another location for our project like this:

```
bin/zf.sh create project /my/other/path
```

When we run our create project command, `Zend_Tool` creates the basic application skeleton for us. The output of the command should look something like this:

`Zend_Tool` not only creates directories, but it also creates some basic elements that form a very basic MVC application for us. In order to see what it created, point your web server to the newly created `public` folder within our `hellozend` directory.

For Apache users, a basic virtual hosts setting for this would be something like:

```
Listen 8080
<VirtualHost *:8080>
    DocumentRoot /Users/keithpope/Sites/hellozend/public
</VirtualHost>
```

Once you have your web server configured, open your browser and browse to the `hellozend` site. In this case, it will be `http://localhost:8080/`. We should now see the Zend Framework start page, as shown in the following screenshot:

Wow, that was easy wasn't it! We are now ready to start looking at what `Zend_Tool` created and try out some of the basic Zend Framework features.

Application directory structure

When we create our project using `Zend_Tool`, it creates the basic directory structure for us. If we open our `hellozend` directory, we can see the folders that are shown in the following screenshot:

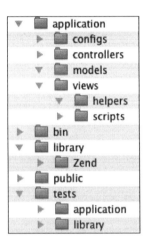

This structure has four main areas, **application**, **library**, **public**, and **tests**. These directories are probably common to most Zend Framework applications, though they may be named differently.

The `application` directory is responsible for holding our application-specific files such as `configs`, `models`, `controllers`, and `views`.

Inside the `application` directory, we have our main MVC folders—**controllers**, **models,** and **views**, which hold controller, model, and view files respectively. In other Zend Framework applications, you may also see modules, which are used to split controllers, models, and views into manageable groups. We will be using modules later in our storefront application.

The `library` directory is responsible for holding our supporting classes such as the Zend Framework components or our own components that do not come into the scope of a model.

Inside the `library` directory, we have the `Zend` directory that contains the Zend Framework source files.

The Zend directory

It is important to remember that you are not forced into placing the Zend directory in the library folder. For example, if you use the Zend Framework for multiple sites, then you can simply place it in a folder that is part of your PHP include path. By doing this, you will have access to the Zend Framework components in all PHP scripts.

The tests directory stores our tests for our application. We will be using this later when we use PHPUnit to test the Storefront.

The public directory is responsible for holding all of our publicly accessible assets such as images, CSS, and JavaScript.

Bootstrapping

Another aspect Zend_Tool took care of during installation is bootstrapping. This refers to the process of application initialization where we configure, and startup, the MVC process when someone requests a page. Zend_Tool did a lot for us here, so let's break it down and see exactly what it did.

The index file

Inside the public directory, Zend_Tool created the file index.php, which is the main entry point for all of the requests to our application. Inside this file we have the following code:

public/index.php

```php
<?php

// Define path to application directory
defined('APPLICATION_PATH')
    || define('APPLICATION_PATH', realpath(dirname(__FILE__) .
        '/../application'));

// Define application environment
defined('APPLICATION_ENV')
    || define('APPLICATION_ENV', (getenv('APPLICATION_ENV') ?
        getenv('APPLICATION_ENV') : 'production'));

// Ensure library/ is on include_path
set_include_path(implode(PATH_SEPARATOR, array(
    realpath(APPLICATION_PATH . '/../library'),
    get_include_path(),
)));
```

```
/** Zend_Application */
require_once 'Zend/Application.php';

// Create application, bootstrap, and run
$application = new Zend_Application(APPLICATION_ENV,
            APPLICATION_PATH . '/configs/application.ini');
$application->bootstrap()->run();
```

The index file is responsible for handling a user's request for a page of the application. All requests to the application are routed through the index file. If we look at what is happening within this file, then we see that the first code block defines the constant APPLICATION_PATH. This constant defines the path to the application directory. This is used throughout the application to access files stored within that directory.

Next, we set the APPLICATION_ENV constant. This is used by the application to change certain behaviors depending on how the application is being used. For example, we may want full error messages in a development environment. However, in a production environment, we may just want to log these messages and not display them to the user. Also, notice that this code block uses the getenv() PHP function that checks the system environment variables for the APPLICATION_ENV constant. This is one way of easily setting the environment for our applications. We will cover more on this later.

After our constants are set, we then configure PHP's include path for the Zend Framework to function. The library folder must be on the include path so that the component classes can be loaded.

After this, we initialize the application using Zend_Application. First, we include the Zend_Application file, and then create a new instance of this class. When instantiating Zend_Application, we pass the environment constant and the path of the configuration file to its constructor. We then call the bootstrap() method (which initializes the application) and the run() method (which starts the MVC process). We will look at Zend_Application in detail later.

As we mentioned before, all requests are routed through the index file. In order to make all requests do this, we need to configure Apache to rewrite all the requests to index.php. In order to do this, Zend_Tool has created a .htaccess file for us inside the public directory.

public/.htaccess

```
SetEnv APPLICATION_ENV development

RewriteEngine On
RewriteCond %{REQUEST_FILENAME} -s [OR]
RewriteCond %{REQUEST_FILENAME} -l [OR]
```

```
RewriteCond %{REQUEST_FILENAME} -d
RewriteRule ^.*$ - [NC,L]
RewriteRule ^.*$ index.php [NC,L]
```

The rewrite rule will route all requests to index.php, unless a file actually exists and if the file does exist, it will serve that file. This is because we can have images, CSS, and other assets accessible to the public. We also set the application APPLICATION_ENV environment variable using SetEnv, currently we are using development. If we were in another environment, then we would change that here.

The .htaccess is actually missing one important directive, that is to turn PHP short tags on. As we will be using short tags later in our Views, we can add this to our .htaccess.

```
php_value "short_open_tag" "on"
```

This can also be done in the php.ini. However, the .htaccess is better if you don't want short tags to be global.

Why route everything to index.php? In Zend Framework, we route all requests to index.php, as we are going to be utilizing Zend Framework's MVC architecture, the basis of which uses the **Front Controller** design pattern. This pattern is defined as:

> *The Front Controller consolidates all request handling by channeling requests through a single handler object. This object can carry out common behavior, which can be modified at runtime with decorators. The handler then dispatches to command objects for behavior particular to a request.*
>
> *Martin Fowler – Patterns of Enterprise Application Architecture*
> http://martinfowler.com/eaaCatalog/frontController.html

On its most basic level, the Front Controller in Zend Framework decides what controller/action to call when a request is made and stops us from the need to have multiple PHP files in the public directory like about.php.

Application configuration

Although Zend_Application is taking care of the bootstrapping for us, it requires some configuration. Zend_Tool again creates the basic configuration for us, which is stored in the configs directory.

application/configs/application.ini

```
[production]
phpSettings.display_startup_errors = 0
phpSettings.display_errors = 0
```

```
includePaths.library = APPLICATION_PATH "/../library"
bootstrap.path = APPLICATION_PATH "/Bootstrap.php"
bootstrap.class = "Bootstrap"
resources.frontController.controllerDirectory = APPLICATION_PATH
        "/controllers"

[staging : production]

[testing : production]
phpSettings.display_startup_errors = 1
phpSettings.display_errors = 1

[development : production]
phpSettings.display_startup_errors = 1
phpSettings.display_errors = 1
```

The default `config` file contains four sections that match the environment types that are available in our application. `Zend_Application` has many configuration options that we won't look at in detail yet. The three important ones for now are `boostrap.path`, `boostrap.class`, and `resources.frontController.controllerDirectory`. These tell `Zend_Application` where the main bootstrap file is located, tell `Zend_Application` the class name of the bootstrap class, and tell the Front Controller where its `controller` files are located respectively.

The bootstrap file

The final part of the bootstrapping process is the `Bootstrap` class. All Zend Framework applications that use `Zend_Application` must have at least one `Bootstrap` class. `Zend_Tool` must have created this for us, so let's look at what it did.

`application/Bootstrap.php`

```php
<?php
class Bootstrap extends Zend_Application_Bootstrap_Bootstrap
{}
```

We can see that the `Bootstrap` class is just an empty class that subclasses the `Zend_Application_Bootstrap_Bootstrap` class. Now, in most applications, this would not be the case, and the `Bootstrap` class would contain methods that initialize various parts of the application such as logging and so on.

We will come back to this later and add in some of our own initialization code. For now though, let's get on and look at some controllers.

Your first controller

At this point, we already have a fully working web page. However, to understand a bit more about what we have done, let's look at the controllers created by `Zend_Tool`. This controller is called an **Action Controller**, and `Zend_Tool` creates two controllers by default (`indexController.php` and `ErrorController.php`). These are located in the `application/controllers` directory. The Action Controller is concerned with our application's **control logic** and is part of the 3-tier separation that Model-View-Controller offers.

If we start by opening the `indexController.php` file, then we see the following:

application/controllers/indexController.php

```php
<?php
class IndexController extends Zend_Controller_Action
{
    public function init()
    {
        /* Initialize action controller here */
    }
    public function indexAction()
    {
        // action body
    }
}
```

The first thing to note about Action Controllers is their naming. Naming needs to take a consistent form so that the Front Controller can find the file and execute its Actions. In case of `IndexController`, we name the file as `IndexController.php`, which defines this as the index controller. Inside the file, we name the controller class `IndexController`, which matches the filename. The matching of the filename and class name is very important. If we don't do this, then it will cause the Front Controller to throw a *not found* exception.

Now, when we edit the index controller we are going to change the default controller so that we can test out some of the MVC features.

application/controllers/IndexController.php

```php
<?php
class IndexController extends Zend_Controller_Action
{
    public function init()
    {
        $this->_helper->viewRenderer->setNoRender();
```

```
    }

    public function indexAction()
    {
        $this->getResponse()
            ->appendBody('Hello from indexAction');
    }
}
```

Open your browser and browse to `http://127.0.0.1:8080/`.

You should now see the following screenshot in your browser:

Let's break this down and have a look at the Action Controller's functionality in more detail.

The Action Controller

Zend Framework provides the `Zend_Controller_Action` abstract class, which gives us the base functionality for our controllers. This includes view integration, data accessors, and utility methods.

Subclassing

In order to create a new controller, we have to subclass the `Zend_Controller_Action` while providing a concrete implementation for our controller. This can then be called by the Front Controllers dispatch process. We do this in our `IndexController`:

```
class IndexController extends Zend_Controller_Action
```

We could also create another abstract class that subclasses `Zend_Controller_Action` to create our own base action controller. This is useful if you have code that is common to all of your controllers. For example, if we needed to regularly access a logging object to add log messages for our controllers, then we could move the instantiation code into our own base controller. By doing this, we can remove repeated code in our controllers.

```
abstract class My_Controller_Action extends Zend_Controller_Action
{
    public $logger;
    public function getLog()
    {
        /* Returns a log instance */
    }
}
```

Once we have our own base controller, we can then use it to create our controllers.

```
class IndexController extends My_Controller_Action
{
...
```

We will now have access to the log instance in all of our controllers through the `getLog()` method. As you can see, Zend Framework provides a great deal of flexibility in the way we can work with our controllers. However, we should use the above controller sparingly, as we will have problems with inheritance down the line. A better approach for this would be to create an Action Helper. We will address these later.

Initialization

`Zend_Controller_Action` also provides us with an easy way to add controller initialization code through the `init()` method. This is called when the controller is instantiated by the Front Controller during the dispatch process. We can see this by looking at the constructor of `Zend_Controller_Action`.

`Zend_Controller_Action`

```
public function __construct(Zend_Controller_Request_Abstract
        $request, Zend_Controller_Response_Abstract $response, array
        $invokeArgs = array())
{
    $this->setRequest($request)
        ->setResponse($response)
        ->_setInvokeArgs($invokeArgs);
    $this->_helper = new Zend_Controller_Action_HelperBroker($this);
    $this->init();
}
```

We use this in our `IndexController` by overriding the `init()` method. It is important that we do not override the constructor, as this will cause errors later on if we forget to call the parent constructor. Therefore, we always use the `init()` for constructing time code.

application/controllers/IndexController.php

```
public function init()
{
    $this->_helper->viewRenderer->setNoRender();
}
```

The actions we perform in the `init()` method are controller wide, as `init()` is called every time the controller is instantiated. In `IndexController`, we are using the `viewRenderer` Action Helper to turn off automatic view rendering for all of the actions in our controller. We will look at Action Helpers in more detail shortly.

Actions

Some of the most important parts of our controllers are the actions they contain. Without actions, our controllers wouldn't do anything. In order to create an action, we add a new method that has `Action` appended to its name. The Front Controller will then automatically recognize them as actions. We can have as many actions as we like in our controllers, and we can also have other methods that are not actions. Non-action methods must not have `Action` appended to them. In our controller, you can see that we have the `init()` method, and that it does not have `Action`. This means that it is not publicly accessible.

If we look at `IndexController`, we have one `Action` method called `indexAction`. If we want to add another action, then we simply create a new method. So, if we wanted an action called `about`, then we would create a method called `aboutAction`.

`Zend_Tool` can create actions for us. In order to create a new action within a controller, we can run the following command:

For Windows users:

bin\zf.bat create action about index

For Linux and Mac users:

bin/zf.sh create action about index

This command will create a new action within the IndexController and a view script for this action. Once this is done, edit the IndexController and add the following to the aboutAction:

application/controllers/IndexController.php

```php
<?php
class IndexController extends Zend_Controller_Action

{
    public function init()
    {
        $this->_helper->viewRenderer->setNoRender();
    }

    public function indexAction()
    {
        $this->getResponse()
            ->appendBody('Hello from indexAction');
    }
    public function aboutAction()
    {
        $this->getResponse()
            ->appendBody('Hello from aboutAction');
    }

}
```

Easy, isn't it? Now, if we browse to http://127.0.0.1:8080/index/about, we should see the following screenshot:

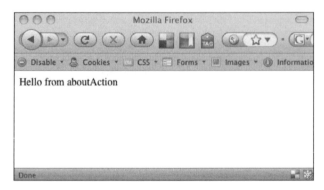

If we try deleting the `Action` from `aboutAction`, so that the method is now called `about`, and visit the above URL again you will see that an error saying that the action could not be found is displayed:

We can also add another method to handle undefined actions. This method is given below:

`application/controllers/IndexController.php`

```php
<?php
class IndexController extends Zend_Controller_Action
{
    public function init()
    {
        $this->_helper->viewRenderer->setNoRender();
    }



    public function indexAction()
    {
        $this->getResponse()
            ->appendBody('Hello from indexAction');
    }
    public function aboutAction()
    {
        $this->getResponse()
            ->appendBody('Hello from aboutAction');
```

```
    }

    public function __call( $method, $args )
    {
        if('Action' == substr($method, -6)) {
            $this->_forward('index');
        }
    }
}
```

Adding the PHP magic method `__call()`, will invoke this method when an undefined action is called. We can then check if it is an action call and then do something like display an error or call a different action. In our example, we use the `_forward()` utility method to call `indexAction`. By doing this, if we try to call an undefined action, we will get the `indexAction`.

The standard router

As we have mentioned before, Zend Framework uses a Front Controller that takes our request and processes it. An important part of this is the standard router. The router is responsible for taking a request and translating it to decide what module, controller, and action is being requested. The translation is based on predefined rules or **routes**. The standard router defines a default route, which we have already been using in our application. We will look more closely at routes and the dispatch process when we look at the Zend Framework's Architecture. For now, let's take a look at the default route.

The default route needs to determine the following elements from the request:

- Module
- Controller
- Action

In the Standard Router, this information is taken from the URI endpoint of the HTTP request. The endpoint is the part after the base URI. Therefore, the URI is broken down like this:

```
http://domain.com/moduleName/controllerName/actionName
```

As you can see, it's pretty straightforward. We simply give the names of the module, controller, and action that we want to call. You may be wondering where the module has come from, as it does not fit into our example. Zend Framework supports modules, which are used to group controller files into directories. This is so that we don't get directories full of more controllers than we can manage. Since our example does not use modules, our controllers are associated with the default module, imaginatively named `default`. For the default modules (and controllers), we are not required to enter their identifiers in the URI.

If we look at our `IndexController`, we can see that when we browse to `http://127.0.0.1:8080/index/about`, we are telling the Front Controller we want `IndexController` and `aboutAction`. You can also see that we have not set up a module, as the module part is not required.

In order to clarify a bit more, here is a table of the active routes in our application:

URI	Module / Controller / Action Called
`http://127.0.0.1:8080/`	Default / IndexController / indexAction
`http://127.0.0.1:8080/index`	Default / IndexController / indexAction
`http://127.0.0.1:8080/index/index`	Default / IndexController / indexAction
`http://127.0.0.1:8080/index/about`	Default / IndexController / aboutAction

In addition to being able to call the controller and action we want, we can also send extra data with the request through the URI. In order to send extra data or **user parameters**, we simply add them to the URI. For example, if we want to send a user parameter called `name` to the `aboutAction`, then we would create a URI like:

`http://127.0.0.1:8080/index/about/name/keith`

This would then create a new user parameter called `name` with the value of `keith`. The parameter would then be set in the request object and is available to our application. This behavior does not affect the standard HTTP GET, so you can still use GET in your URIs.

Therefore, this is valid, and you have access to all of the data passed here at:

`http://127.0.0.1:8080/index/about/name/keith?age=26&country=England`

Let's try some of this out on our `IndexController`. Edit the `indexAction` to this:

`application/controllers/IndexController.php`

```
public function indexAction()
{
    $name = $this->_getParam('name','guest');
    $this->getResponse()
        ->appendBody('hello ' . $name . ' from indexAction');
}
```

Now, browse to `http://127.0.0.1:8080/index/index/name/keith`, and you should now see **hello keith from indexAction** displayed in your browser as follows:

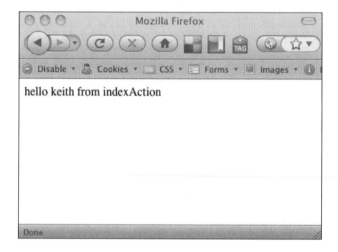

In `indexAction`, we use the accessor method `_getParam()` to retrieve our passed in username parameter value, and store it in `$name`. The `_getParam()` takes two arguments:

- the name of the parameter you want to retrieve
- default value if it is not set, which is optional

The data returned is retrieved from the **request object**. The request object is a value object that contains information about the request. When using `_getParam()`, it is important to note that the request object aggregates request data. This means that when we use `_getParam()`, the request object will look for data in user parameters GET and then POST. Therefore, the above example will still work if we send the name as a GET parameter. This behavior can be customized using the `setParamSources()` method of the request object.

Finally, we pass the $name into the response object's body so that it will be rendered at the end of the dispatch process. You may have noticed that we haven't escaped the data we are outputting. In a normal situation, we would have to escape the $name variable before outputting it to the browser to stop Cross Site Scripting attacks, this has been left out simply for brevity.

Utility methods

The Zend_Controller_Action abstract class provides utility methods that help us with some common tasks when using the MVC functionality.

_forward utility method

The _forward() utility method is used to call actions. This helps us to easily move from action to action if we need to.

```
_forward($action, $controller = null, $module = null,
         array $params = null)
```

Looking at the _forward definition, we can see that it takes up to four arguments, three of which are optional:

- $action (string required): The action to call.
- $controller (string optional): The controller the action is in.
- $module (string optional): The module the controller is in.
- $params (array optional): User parameters to send with the request.

If you only supply $action _forward(), then it will look for the action within the current controller. We can try this out by using our basic application.

We first need to create a new controller. We can do this by using Zend_Tool with the following command.

For Windows users:

bin\zf.bat create controller Contact

For Linux and Mac users:

bin/zf.sh create controller Contact

Running this command will create a new controller for us and create the related `View` directories for this controller. Once the controller is created, edit it so that it looks like the example that follows:

`application/controllers/ContactController.php`

```php
<?php
class ContactController extends Zend_Controller_Action
{
    public function init()
    {
        $this->_helper->viewRenderer->setNoRender();
    }
    public function indexAction()
    {
        $this->getResponse()
            ->appendBody(' You can contact me @ ' . $this
            ->_getParam( 'email', '' ) );

    }
}
```

Edit `IndexController` and add the following code:

`application/controllers/IndexController.php`

```php
    public function aboutAction()
    {
        $this->getResponse()
            ->appendBody('hello from aboutAction');
        $this->_forward( 'index', 'contact', null,
                        array( 'email' => 'me@example.org' ) );
    }
```

Now, if we browse to `http://127.0.0.1:8080/index/about`, then we should see the following screenshot:

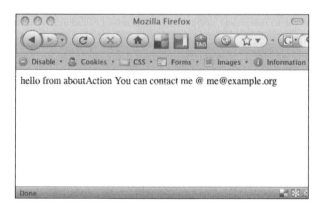

In `IndexController`, we have forwarded the request to our new controller's index action and passed with it a new user parameter called email. Then in `ContactController`, we have added some text and the new email user parameter to the response object. You should also notice that the URL does not change, and we are still in `/index/about`. This is important because when we forward, we forward internally, which means we are still using one request.

_redirect utility method

The `_redirect()` utility method is in a way the opposite to `_forward()`. Where `_forward()` calls an action within the same request, `_redirect()` performs an HTTP redirect creating a new request.

`redirect()` accepts the following arguments:

- `$url` (string required): The URL to redirect to
- `$options` (Array Optional)

And the `$options` can be:

- `exit` (Boolean): Whether to exit straight away, or not
- `prependBase` (Boolean): Prepend the base URL, or not
- `code` (String): The HTTP code to use

By default, `_redirect()` will do a `302` redirect.

Action Helpers

Action Helpers are used to provide extra functionality to Action Controllers, without the need to extend the abstract Action Controller. They are very useful when we need common functionality between controllers. We have already used one of the default Action Helpers in our own controllers to turn off view rendering.

application/controllers/IndexController.php

```
public function init()
{
    $this->_helper->viewRenderer->setNoRender();
}
```

During the initialization of `IndexController` and `ContactController`, we call the `viewRenderer` Action Helper and set the `noRender` flag on the view object. By doing this, we stop the default behavior of the `viewRenderer` from automatically rendering the view object for each action within our controller. If we did not do this for our examples, then we would get errors from the view object saying it could not find the view script. This is because we have not created any yet. The Action Controller Abstract contains the _helper property, which contains the Action Helper Broker. The broker is responsible for managing the registration and retrieval of helper objects. Therefore, we use $this->_helper to access our registered helpers. We can also use the getHelper() or getHelperCopy() methods, define our own helpers, and register them with the broker.

Zend Framework provides the following Action Helpers:

- ActionStack: Enables a **stack** of actions to be called
- AutoComplete: Ajax auto completion
- ContextSwitch: Switch response formats based on a context
- AjaxContext: Same as ContextSwitch, but for Ajax specifically
- FlashMessenger: Handles messages for the user between requests
- JSON: Easy JSON output
- Redirector: HTTP redirector
- ViewRenderer: View initialization and rendering

As you can see, there are many default Action Helpers defined. We will try and use many of these as we progress through the book. For now, let's move on and make our application actually output some HTML.

Your first view

Now that we have our basic application structure and our controllers working, let's look at views. Views obviously form the V part of MVC, and are responsible for the display. This display could be the user interface HTML, JSON output, and so on. By using views instead of writing directly to the response object like we have done so far in our examples, we achieve the MVC goal of separating view from control logic. Let's go ahead and create our first view.

View directories

When Zend_Tool created our project and as we added more Controllers and Actions to our application, various View-related folders and files were created. If we now look inside, we will see what Zend_Tool has created:

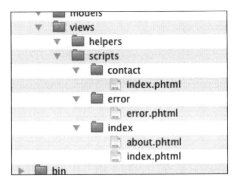

The first thing we see here is that we have a views folder within the application folder. This holds all of the Views, View Helpers, and View Filters for our application. Within the views folder, we have two directories helpers and scripts. These directories contain View and View Helpers respectively. We may also have a filters folder. However, Zend_Tool does not create this for us. Within the scripts folder, we have another three folders. Each folder relates to a controller name. So in our application—we have contact, error, and index that match the three controllers we have ContactController, ErrorController, and IndexController. All of these were created by Zend_Tool as we added the Controllers and Actions to our application.

Creating a view

As we have been using Zend_Tool, all of the Views have already been created for us. Therefore, we only need to edit what is already there to get our application working. Views in the Zend Framework are written in PHP and are known as **View Scripts**. All View Scripts have their files ending in .phtml. We can see that Zend_Tool has created all the .phtml files for us, and they are contained within their respective controller View Script folders.

So let's now edit the index controller's index view script and add in some of our own code. We can delete any code that is already in these files.

`application/views/scripts/index/index.phtml`

```
<html>
<head>
    <title>Hello Zend</title>
</head>
<body>
    <h1>Hello Zend</h1>
    <p>Hello from Zend Framework</p>
</body>
</html>
```

That's it! Our first view has been created. As you can see, it's just some very simple HTML. However, if we browse to `http://127.0.0.1:8080/`, we don't see this rendered. We need to refactor our controller to get things working.

`application/controllers/IndexController.php`

```
public function init()
{}

public function indexAction()
{
    $name = $this->_getParam('name', 'guest');
}
```

We first remove `$this->_helper->viewRenderer->setNoRender();` from the `init()` method. This tells the `viewRenderer` that we want its default behavior of automatically rendering the view scripts for us. Then, we remove `$this->getResponse()->appendBody('hello ' . $name . ' from indexAction');` from the `indexAction`. This is because the view will write to the response object for us.

If we now browse to `http://127.0.0.1:8080`, we should see the HTML rendered from our view script. When we visit our page, the `viewRenderer` Action Helper is automatically instantiating a view object and looking for our view script in `/application/views/scripts/index/` and then rendering it for us.

Of course, we can also pass data into the view. In order to do this, we simply set the data in the view object, which is stored in the Action Controllers $view property.

application/controllers/IndexController.php

```
public function indexAction()
{
    $this->view->name = $this->_getParam('name', 'guest');
}
```

application/views/scripts/index/index.phtml

```
<head>
    <title>Hello Zend</title>
</head>
<body>
    <h1>Hello Zend</h1>
    <p>Hello <?=$this->Escape($this->name);?> from Zend Framework</p>
</body>
```

In our IndexController, we assign the name user parameter into the view, and then in the view we echo it out. There are a couple of important things happening in the view. First, we are escaping the output using the Escape() view method. Second, we are using PHP short tags.

Escape() is used to safely output data in views. You should always make sure your data is escaped, unless you know that it has already been escaped. This will help prevent Cross Site Scripting attacks. By default, Escape() uses the htmlspecialchars() PHP function for escaping. You can customize this by using the setEscape() method of the view object. This accepts a callback function that will be used for escaping.

We are using PHP short tags, because it makes our view much easier to read and much more designer friendly. If you do not have short tags enabled, then you will need to enable them for the examples to work. There is also a special stream wrapper for views that will automatically convert short tags into long tags. However, you will take a performance hit when using it. I would only use this if you can't enable short tags. You can enable the stream wrapper using $view->setUseStreamWrapper(true); on the view.

Now, we have our view, which is rendering our user parameter. If we browse to http://127.0.0.1:8080/index/index/name/keith, then we should now see **Hello keith from the Zend Framework** displayed. We should note here that we have to use index/index/ to access the indexAction of the indexController. Using index/name/keith would not work, as the dispatcher would look for the nameAction in the indexController.

There is also another method of assigning variables to the view object using the `assign()` method. This can be helpful for assigning multiple values to the view. Let's have a little play with assigning some variables using `assign()`.

application/controllers/IndexController.php

```
public function indexAction()
{
    $date = new Zend_Date();

    $data = array(
        'hour' => $date->get(Zend_Date::HOUR),
        'min'  => $date->get(Zend_Date::MINUTE),
        'sec'  => $date->get(Zend_Date::SECOND)
    );

    $obj = new stdClass();
    $obj->day   = $date->get(Zend_Date::DAY);
    $obj->month = $date->get(Zend_Date::MONTH);
    $obj->year  = $date->get(Zend_Date::YEAR);

    $this->view->assign($data);
    $this->view->assign((array) $obj);
    $this->view->name = $this->_getParam('name', 'guest');
}
```

application/views/scripts/index/index.phtml

```
<html>
<head>
    <title>Hello Zend</title>
</head>
<body>
    <h1>Hello Zend</h1>
    <p>
        Hello <?=$this->Escape($this->name); ?> from Zend Framework
        @ <?=$this->Escape($this->hour); ?>:<?=$this->Escape($this-
            >min); ?>:<?=$this->Escape($this->sec); ?>
        on <?=$this->Escape($this->year); ?>/<?=$this->Escape($this-
            >month); ?>/<?=$this->Escape($this->day); ?>
    </p>
</body>
</html>
```

If we now browse to `http://127.0.0.1:8080/index/index/name/keith`, then we can see that the date and year is displayed after the hello message.

The first way in which we use `assign()` is to add values stored in an array using `$this->view->assign($data);`. This assigns the matched pair values to the view object, so `hour` gets assigned to the view with a value of the current hour, and so on.

In the second method, we use `assign()` to add the values of an object's public properties using `$this->view->assign((array) $obj);`. This will assign all of the public properties to the view, so `day` gets assigned to the view with a value of the current day, and so on. Note that we need to cast the object to an array for this to work, as the assign method only accepts both a string and a value or an array. It does not automatically convert objects for us.

View Helpers

View Helpers are an important tool in creating our view. Just as the Action Controller has Action Helpers, the view has View Helpers. These are helper classes that assist us in creating our view. Zend Framework packs a number of View Helpers, most of which are used for creating HTML elements. Let's look at an example of using a View Helper.

URL View Helper

One common task when creating web pages is creating links that point to other parts of your web site. To help with this, we have the URL View Helper. To use the URL Helper, we simply need to call it from within one of our view scripts.

`application/views/scripts/index/index.phtml`

```
<html>
<head>
    <title>Hello Zend</title>
</head>
<body>
    <h1>Hello Zend</h1>
    <p>
        Hello <?=$this->Escape($this->name); ?> from Zend Framework
        @ <?=$this->Escape($this->hour); ?>:<?=$this->Escape($this-
            >min); ?>:<?=$this->Escape($this->sec); ?>
        on <?=$this->Escape($this->year); ?>/<?=$this->Escape($this-
            >month); ?>/<?=$this->Escape($this->day); ?>
    </p>
    <p>
        <a href="<?=$this->url(array('controller' => 'contact',
            'name' => $this->name), null, true );?>">Contact Me!</a>
    </p>
</body>
</html>
```

All View Helpers are available through the view instance ($this). In order to invoke the URL Helper, we simply enter $this->url(). The URL Helper returns a string of the generated URL. We also have to provide some arguments to tell the helper where we want the link to point. If we do not provide any arguments, then the returned string will be the current URL. The URL Helper accepts the following arguments:

- $urlOptions (array optional): An associative array containing options for the router

- $name (string optional): The name of a route

- $reset (Boolean optional): Whether to reset the route or not

In our example, we supply $urlOptions to define the controller that we want to link (contact), and we also define a new user parameter (name). We do not supply a $name, as we don't have any routes setup in the router. The URL Helper uses the router to assemble the URL. This is partly why using the URL Helper is a good practice, as our links are then **router aware**. We will be using the router later, so don't worry about the fact that we haven't covered it yet. Finally, we set the reset flag to true so that any user parameters in the current request are not appended to the URL.

This will then produce a URL like /contact/index/name/guest if we browse to http://127.0.0.1:8080/ and will produce a URL like /contact/index/name/keith if we browse to http://127.0.0.1:8080/index/index/name/keith.

As you can see, using View Helpers is pretty straightforward. However, you may be wondering why you would use the URL Helper, as it adds a lot of code into the view. The reason we use the URL Helper is mainly for maintainability. If we change any of the routes later, then we won't need to update our code. You will see this in action when we start using custom routes later.

There are many more View Helpers available. These include the following:

- Action View: Calls an Action
- Partial: Renders another view in its own variable scope
- Placeholder: Persists content between Views
- Doctype: Returns the doctype
- HeadLink: Links CSS
- HeadMeta: Meta tags
- HeadScript: Script tags
- HeadStyle: Style tags

- `HeadTitle`: Document title
- `JSON`: Easy JSON output
- `Translate`: Language translation
- `InlineScript`: Inline script tag
- `HTML Object`: Flash
- `Various Form Element Helpers`: Creating forms

We have a wide range of View Helpers to choose from when creating our views. We will be using many of these as we progress and will create some of our own View Helpers.

View customization

There are many situations where we need to customize our view instance. We have briefly mentioned some of these customizations such as setting the escaping used by the view.

In order to show this, let's add some view customization to our `Bootstrap` class. Add the following method to the `Bootstrap` class:

`application/Bootstrap.php`

```
protected function _initViewSettings()
{
    $this->bootstrap('view');
    $view = $this->getResource('view');
    $view->doctype('XHTML1_STRICT');
}
```

Here, we have created a new bootstrap resource, which will be executed by `Zend_Application` during the bootstrap process. Inside the `_initViewSettings()` method, we first call the view resource (`$this->boostrap('view')`). This is a default resource provided by `Zend_Application` that initializes the view for us. Internally, the view resource creates a new view instance for us and registers a new `ViewRenderer` Action Helper to the Action Helper Broker. This allows us to then get the `Zend_View` instance from the resource and configure it.

We only apply one small configuration to our view instance. This is the `doctype` for `Zend_View` to use, and we set this to `XHTML1_STRICT`. This will now make `Zend_View` produce `XHTML1` compliant HTML. We can also use the `Doctype` view helper to add the doctype declaration to our pages. In order to do this, we simply edit any of our `.phtml` view scripts and add this at the top:

```
<?= $this->doctype() ?>
```

If we now browse to `http://127.0.0.1:8080` and view the HTML source, we see that we have the doctype definition added to our document.

Handling errors

Something that all applications need is error handling, and most important of all is displaying meaningful errors to users. So far, our application has no nice way to display errors to users, or to us for that matter. Zend Framework provides a default way of handling thrown exceptions through the `ErrorHandler` Front Controller plugin. This plugin is automatically registered and enabled by default. If you do not wish to use the `ErrorHandler`, then set the `noErrorHandler` parameter to `true` on the Front Controller or set `throwExceptions` to `true` on the Front Controller.

`Zend_Tool` has already created an `ErrorController` and error view for us. If we open the `ErrorController` and its view, then we see the following:

application/controllers/ErrorController.php

```php
<?php
class ErrorController extends Zend_Controller_Action
{

    public function errorAction()
    {
        $errors = $this->_getParam('error_handler');

        switch ($errors->type) {
          case Zend_Controller_Plugin_ErrorHandler::
              EXCEPTION_NO_CONTROLLER:
            case Zend_Controller_Plugin_ErrorHandler::
                EXCEPTION_NO_ACTION:

                // 404 error -- controller or action not found
                $this->getResponse()->setHttpResponseCode(404);
                $this->view->message = 'Page not found';
                break;
            default:
                // application error
                $this->getResponse()->setHttpResponseCode(500);
                $this->view->message = 'Application error';
                break;
        }

        $this->view->exception = $errors->exception;
        $this->view->request   = $errors->request;
    }
}
```

application/views/scripts/error/error.phtml

```
<!DOCTYPE html PUBLIC "-//W3C//DTD XHTML 1.0 Strict//EN";
    "http://www.w3.org/TR/xhtml1/DTD/xhtml1-strict.dtd>
<html xmlns="http://www.w3.org/1999/xhtml">
<head>
  <meta http-equiv="Content-Type" content="text/html; charset=utf-8"
/>
  <title>Zend Framework Default Application</title>
</head>
<body>
  <h1>An error occurred</h1>
  <h2><?= $this->message ?></h2>

  <? if ('development' == APPLICATION_ENV): ?>

  <h3>Exception information:</h3>
  <p>
      <b>Message:</b> <?= $this->exception->getMessage() ?>
  </p>

  <h3>Stack trace:</h3>
  <pre><?= $this->exception->getTraceAsString() ?>
  </pre>

  <h3>Request Parameters:</h3>
  <pre><? var_dump($this->request->getParams()) ?>
  </pre>
  <? endif ?>

</body>
</html>
```

In order to see this in action, we need to edit the .htaccess file and change the application environment to production. By default, we are in a development environment where the error controller is not used.

```
public/.htaccess
SetEnv APPLICATION_ENV production
```

Now, if we browse to a page that does not exist, we should see a 404 page, for example, http://127.0.0.1:8080/thisdoesnotexist.

Our ErrorController simply gets the ErrorHandler and then uses it to decide what type of error to display. At the moment, this is very simplistic. However, for most applications you will probably want to add a lot more into your ErrorController. For example, you could add logging through Zend_Log.

When an exception is thrown within one of our Action Controllers or from the Front Controller when it cannot find a Controller or Action, it will set the type of error. The type of error can be:

- EXCEPTION_NO_CONTROLLER
- EXCEPTION_NO_ACTION
- EXCEPTION_OTHER

These are set as class constants of the `Zend_Controller_Plugin_ErrorHandler` class. We also have access to the exception through the public exception property of the `ErrorHandler`. From this we can get the error message, stack trace, and so on.

It is important to note that the `ErrorHandler` handles only exceptions thrown from missing Action Controllers or internal application errors. It is not designed to catch errors from routing or other plugins.

Summary

In this chapter, we have looked at the basics of building a web application using the Zend Framework's MVC components. We have created a very simple application and have briefly looked at some of the core components and their various uses. Hopefully, you have an idea of what you can do with the Zend Framework and how flexible it really is. In the next chapter, we will look at the architecture and inner workings of the MVC components to help you understand just what exactly happens when a request is made, and show you the various ways in which you can customize and extend all of these features.

2
The Zend Framework MVC Architecture

So far, we have built a very simple web application. While doing this, we have skipped over a lot of the details surrounding what exactly is happening when we use the Zend Framework's MVC components. Understanding the objects and interactions of the MVC components are very important to us. Without it, we would never really be able to get the full benefit from the Zend Framework. The aim of this chapter is to take you through the main aspects of the Zend Frameworks MVC implementation and give you a good foundation in the conventions and language of the Zend Framework.

In this chapter, we will cover the following topics:

1. Zend framework MVC overview
2. The Front Controller
3. The router
4. The dispatcher
5. The Request object
6. The Response object

Zend framework MVC overview

Before we dive in and look at each MVC component, let's look at the general processes that happens when we make a request to a Zend Framework MVC application.

What is a request

A request can be a user sending an HTTP request from their browser, or any other type of request that accesses our application such as web service, socket, command line, and so on. A request contains information that is used by an application to produce a response. An example of this is when you request a web page from a web server. The web server takes the information provided in the URI and renders the page being requested. The response is the web page. A request is just the same in the Zend Framework. A user makes a request to the application, and the application produces the correct response.

Request handling

So how are requests handled in Zend Framework? We have already seen in Chapter 1, that the Front Controller handles requests and also produces a response. What we haven't looked at is what happens along the way to produce the response.

The request handling process is a bit like a factory production line. A customer makes a request, the manager tells the workers to create the product, and the product is delivered to the customer. This is illustrated below in the upcoming diagram. I have included some of the names of the main MVC components beside each element.

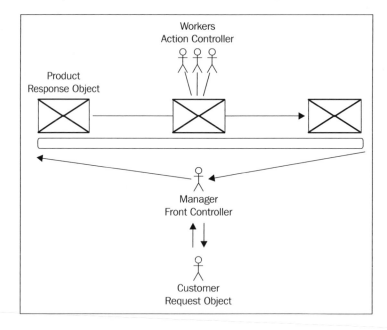

In our simplified example, the basic process is as follows:

1. The customer makes a request. This request is the **Request Object**.
2. The manager decides what should be done. This is the **Front Controller**.
3. The manager sends the product to the production line. This is the **Response Object**.
4. The workers add to the product to complete the request. These are the **Action Controller(s)**.
5. The workers give the finished product back to the manager, who in turn gives it to the customer.
6. The request has been fulfilled and everyone is happy.

We see that we now have a collection of objects that handle our request. We have already used these in Chapter 1 when we created our **HelloZend** application. We used the Request Object to retrieve variables passed into the request and to decide what Controller Action to call. We used Front Controller to handle our request, Response object to produce output when we had no views, and we used Controller Actions to create functionality.

Lets leave our simple example, and look at the process in a bit more detail.

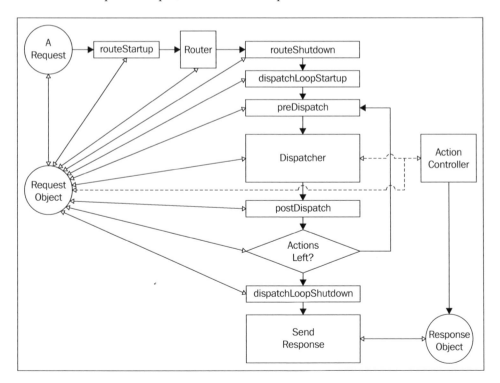

There is quite a bit going on here, but the main concept is still present. A request is made and a response returned. But what happened to the Front Controller? Well this is what happens inside the Front Controller, as you can see it does a lot of work for us! This process is usually called the dispatch process in the Zend Framework and happens when you call the Front Controllers `dispatch()` method. This can be a little confusing at first because we also have a dispatcher object, which is part of the dispatch process.

The process can be broken down like this:

1. A request is made and the **Request Object** is created.
2. The **routeStartup** event is fired.
3. The **Router** processes the request.
4. The **routeShutdown** event is fired.
5. The **dispatchLoopStartup** event is fired.
6. The dispatch loop is started.
7. The **preDispatch** event is fired.
8. The **Dispatcher** calls the **Action Controller**.
9. The **Action Controller** writes to the **Response Object**.
10. The **postDispatch** event is fired.
11. If there are actions left to call, then go to Step 7.
12. The **dispatchLoopShutdown** event is fired.
13. The **Response** is sent back.

It's not too far away from our example of the factory production line. The main bulk is taken up by events from which we can extend the dispatching process. The Front Controllers Plugin Broker handles the events. We have already used the `routeStartup` event to create our initialization plugin in Chapter 1. We also have some objects that we haven't seen before, that is, the **Router** and the **Dispatcher**. The **Router** is responsible for routing requests to the correct Action Controller (remember we used the Standard Router in Chapter 1). The **Dispatcher** is responsible for actually calling each Controller Action and is used inside the Dispatch Loop in the Front Controller.

Abstractness of MVC components

The abstractness of MVC components allows us to easily extend and change the MVC components to match our requirements. If we are using the MVC components to create web applications, we generally will never need to take advantage of this. However, this is an important part of the design of the Zend Framework's MVC components and is one of the reasons why the framework is so flexible.

This means that we can easily create our own versions of them, but why would we want to? There are some use cases where we may want to create our own custom functionality for one of the MVC components. For example, we may want to use a very specialized directory structure for our application. By subclassing the `Zend_Controller_Dispatcher_Abstract`, we could create a way to handle this requirement. There are, of course, other times when you may want to do this, but they are mainly advanced use cases. For the majority, the standard MVC components should suffice. I should also warn you that you should try and avoid doing this unless it is absolutely necessary. Always try to use Front Controller plugins, the Action Controller helpers, and so on, before resorting to extending the MVC components.

Now that we have a good overview of the MVC process, we can look at each MVC component in detail.

The Front Controller

The Front Controller is the main workhorse of the MVC components, as it instantiates objects, fires events, and sets up default behaviors. Its main purpose is to handle all the requests coming into the application.

Design

The Front Controller is a web presentation design pattern and is used by various MVC frameworks. When we refer to the Front Controller in Zend Framework, we actually refer to the `Zend_Controller_Front` class. This class implements the Front Controller design pattern.

Another point to note about the Front Controller's design is that it is **Singleton**. This means that it implements the Singleton design pattern. Singleton is used to manage object instantiation and usually limits the amount of objects that can be created to one. Therefore, this means that there can only ever be one instance of the Front Controller. It also means that we cannot directly instantiate the Front Controller, instead we must fetch one.

In order to fetch an instance of the Front Controller, we use the `getInstance()` method. You will remember that we did this in our bootstrap file earlier.

```
$front = Zend_Controller_Front::getInstance();
```

If we try to instantiate the class directly like this:

```
$front = new Zend_Controller_Front();
```

We will get an exception telling us that the Front Controllers construct is a protected method.

Defaults

As the Front Controller is responsible for instantiating various MVC components for us there are default behaviors created. The default behavior of the Front Controller is geared towards web applications, which means that many of the objects instantiated by the Front Controller are specialized for an HTTP environment. Let's look at some of the defaults that the Front Controller uses. The following table shows the default objects used by the Front Controller.

Type	Abstract class	Concrete class used
Request	Zend_Controller_Request_Abstract	Zend_Controller_Request_Http
Response	Zend_Controller_Response_Abstract	Zend_Controller_Response_Http
Router	Zend_Controller_Router_Abstract	Zend_Controller_Router_Rewrite
Dispatcher	Zend_Controller_Dispatcher_Abstract	Zend_Controller_Dispatcher_Standard
Plugin Broker *	Zend_Controller_Plugin_Abstract	Zend_Controller_Plugin_Broker

*Plugin Broker is not customizable

This table shows us the type of object created, the abstract class that the concrete is based upon, and the concrete class actually used by the Front Controller. The plugin broker is a bit special as it is the same no matter the environment, so it would be the same in HTTP as it would in CLI. I have included it only as it is instantiated by default. All of the other classes can be replaced with your own concrete implementation. This is one of the reasons I like the Zend Framework so much; it enables you to customize it in every way possible.

There are default Front Controller plugins available. The following table shows the default plugins and whether they are registered by default or not:

Name	Stack index	Registered by default?
Zend_Controller_Plugin_ErrorHandler	100	Yes
Zend_Controller_Plugin_ActionStack	n/a	No

The only Front Controller plugin currently registered by default is the ErrorHandler. This is used if an error occurs to forward it to the ErrorController. We have used this in our Hello Zend application earlier. We can disable this by setting the noErrorHandler invoke parameter through setParam().The Stack Index is important, since the higher it is, the later it will be called. This can be very useful to know when you are creating your own plugins.

The Front Controller also registers the ViewRenderer Action Helper with the Action Helper Broker by default. You can disable this by setting the noViewRenderer invocation parameter.

Using the Front Controller

Now that we know a bit more about the Front Controller, let's look at how we can customize its behavior.

Invocation parameters

Invocation parameters can be used to store data inside the Front Controller. This data is then passed into the Action Controller, Router, and Dispatcher. For example, say we needed to pass an object created during the bootstrap to the Controller Action, we could do the following:

In bootstrap:

```
$obj = new MyClass();
$front->setParam('myObj',$obj);
```

We can then retrieve this from one of our controllers using the getInvokeArg() method:

```
$myObj = $this->getInvokeArg('myObj');
```

Invocation parameters serve as an easy way to have common objects or variables passed to your MVC components.

The Front Controller has the following methods for handling invocation parameters:

- `setParam(String $name, Mixed $value)`: Set an invocation parameter
- `setParams(Array $params)`: Set multiple invocation parameters
- `getParam(String $name)`: Retrieve an invocation parameter
- `getParams()`: Retrieve all invocation parameters
- `clearParams(String|Array|Null $name)`: Clear a single or multiple or all invocation parameters

Options

As well as invocation parameters, the Front Controller has some options that affect its default behavior. The main methods are:

- `throwExceptions(Boolean $flag)`: Whether exceptions thrown during the **Dispatch Loop** should be thrown or captured in the Response object.
- `setBaseUrl(String $base)`: Sets the base URL used to determine the path information of the request. Path information is used to route the request to the correct Action Controller. This is useful if we are running our application from a sub-directory. For example, if we have our application inside the `/myapp` folder, then we would use `setBaseUrl('/myapp');`. Remember not to use the full URL like `http://domain/myapp` as this will cause errors.
- `returnResponse(Boolean $flag)`: By default, the Front Controller will render the Response object once the dispatch loop has ended. If we set `returnResponse()` to `true`, then the `dispatch()` method will return the Response object instead of rendering it.
- `setDefaultControllerName(String $controller)`: The default controller name is `Index`. You can change this by using `setDefaultControllerName()`.
- `setDefaultAction(String $action)`: The default action name is `Index`, you can change this using `setDefaultAction()`.

Modules, controllers, and actions

A major part of the Front Controllers responsibility is to help with the configuration of modules, controllers, and actions. In order to work correctly, the Front Controller needs to know where we have placed our controllers and how they are organized.

In our Hello Zend application, we used the most basic directory structure available in the Zend Framework.

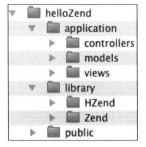

Using this structure, all of our controllers, models, and views are held in one folder. However, this can become hard to manage and does not promote code reuse. In order to overcome this, we can use modules. Modules simply enable us to group controllers, models, and views into manageable units.

The two most common directory structures when using modules are as follows:

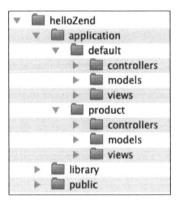

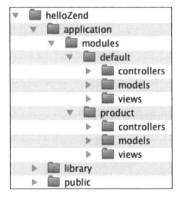

As you can see they are almost identical, but the second layout uses a **modules** directory. The main reason for this is the way we tell the Front Controller about our modules. It is also important to mention that you are not forced to used any of these directory layouts. They are all customizable, however, these probably serve 99 percent of use cases.

If we consider our first layout, to enable this using the Front Controller, we can either use the `setControllerDirectory()` or `addControllerDirectory()` methods. So for our first layout we could do:

```
$front->setControllerDirectory(array(
    'default' => '/path/application/default',
    'product' => '/path/application/product'
));
```

Or:

```
$front->addControllerDirectory('/path/application/product', 'product');
```

These two methods are really the same. The only real difference is that `setControllerDirectory()` accepts an array of modules and `addControllerDirectory()` adds one module at a time. Remember that we **must** specify a default module, which can be done either by passing the default array key using `setControllerDirectory` or by not specifying the module name using `addControllerDirectory()`.

Our second layout is only slightly different, and all modules are held within a **modules** directory. We can also add lots of modules using the `addModuleDirectory()` method very quickly. So for our second layout we can use:

```
$front->addModuleDirectory('/path/application/modules');
```

This method is by far the easiest way to add many modules in your application. It also means you don't have to reconfigure when you add new modules.

When we use modules, our Action Controllers that reside in non-default modules need to follow a different naming convention to prevent namespace clashes. Therefore, in our example, all Action Controllers within the product module would need to be prepended with Product namespace. For example, the details Action Controller of the products modules would be named `Product_DetailsController`. This is **not** required for default (global) module Action Controllers. For example, the details Action Controller of the default module would be named `DetailsController`. However, you can change this behavior by setting the `prefixDefaultModule` parameter in the Front Controller. You do this first by entering `$front->setParam(' prefixDefaultModule ', true);`. After this, your default module Action Controllers would need to be prefixed with `Default_`.

All of the examples that we have looked at so far use the default configuration. However, the Front Controller provides us with a variety of methods to help customize this. Let's have a look at some of these methods:

- `setDefaultModule(String $module)`: Changes the module name from default to something else. In our example, if we need to change the default directory name to say `core`, then we would use `$front->setDefaultModule('core');`. This means that rather than having something like `http://domain/default/index`, we would have `http://doamin/core/index`.

- `setModuleControllerDirectoryName(String $name)`: Sets the name of the controllers directory. In our example, we could use `$front->setModuleControllerDirectoryName('c');` to enable us to use the directory name of `c` rather than controllers.

- `setDefaultControllerName(String $name)`: Sets the default controller name. By default, this is index. If we change the default controller name when we send a request that does not specify the controller, then the new default name will be used. For example, if we change the default index name to base (`setDefaultControllerName('base')`), and browse to `http://domain/`, then the controller that will be called will be `BaseController`.

- `setDefaultAction(String $name)`: This works exactly like `setDefaultControllerName` but changes the default action name instead. For example, if we change the default action name to base (`setDefaultAction('base')`), and browse to `http://domain/index`, then this will call `IndexController` and the `baseAction`.

MVC component customization

For most scenarios, the default MVC components serve us well, but what if we need to customize part of the MVC architecture? The Front Controller provides us with methods to easily add in our own MVC components and replace the default ones. Let's take a look at how to do this by replacing all of the default MVC components with our own.

```
$front = Zend_Controller_Front::getInstance();

$myRequest    = new MyRequest();
$myResponse   = new MyResponse();
$myRouter     = new MyRouter();
$myDispatcher = new MyDispatcher();

$front->setRequest($myRequest);
$front->setResponse($myResponse);
$front->setRouter($myRouter);
$front->setDispatcher($myDispatcher);
```

In our example, we have replaced all the MVC components with our own implementations. In order to do this, we can subclass each of the MVC component's abstract classes or one of the concrete implementations to create our own MVC components. We can then easily set them using their corresponding setter methods. In most cases, you would probably only need to customize one or two of the MVC components, if any at all.

Plugins

Front Controller plugins act as an easy way for us to extend the dispatch process. If we look at our earlier diagram, then we can see that there are six extension points in the dispatch process:

- routeStartup
- routeShutdown
- dispatchLoopStartup
- preDispatch
- postDispatch
- dispatchLoopShutdown

We have already used the routeStartup hook when we created our Initialization Plugin back in Chapter 1. From the diagram, we can see that **routeStartup** is the earliest hook we can extend from, and we chose it because we can apply any setting we need before the routing and dispatch process starts.

As long as there is an order in which the hooks are called, we have the stackIndex. The stackIndex is present and so we have control over the order in which plugins are called when more than one is registered to the same hook. The stackIndex is stored in ascending order, so lower the stackIndex, the sooner it is called. We have a good example for this within the Front Controller. By default, the Front Controller registers the ErrorHandler plugin and this is placed at 100. This is so that the ErrorHandler is called last.

In order to create a Front Controller plugin, we simply need to subclass the Zend_Controller_Plugin_Abstract class, and then it is a case of implementing a concrete method of the hook you want to use. Remember that a single plugin can hook into one or more extension points. Once we have a plugin, we can register it using the Front Controller. Let's look at the plugin related methods of the Front Controller:

- registerPlugin(Zend_Controller_Plugin_Abstract $plugin, Optional Int $stackIndex) ;: Registers a plugin with the plugin broker.

- `unregisterPlugin(Zend_Controller_Plugin_Abstract|string $plugin);`: Unregisters a plugin from the plugin broker. If you supply a string, then it will unregister all plugins of that class name.

- `getPlugin(String $class);`: Gets a registered plugin of the given class name. This either returns `false` if none are found, a single plugin class if one is found, or an array of plugins if more than one is found.

- `getPlugins();`: Gets all registered plugins.

- `hasPlugin(String $class);`: Checks if a plugin is already registered.

There are, of course, many uses for Front Controller plugins. You should consider using them when you need to affect the application as a whole such as initialization. If you need to affect a subset of your application, such as a module, then you would be better to use an Action Helper. Front Controller plugins are typically used for tasks such as application initialization, access control, caching, and more. The main thing to remember is to choose your hook carefully. Different things are happening throughout the dispatch process and you need to be aware of what you can affect at each stage.

We will be using a lot of Front Controller plugins in our storefront application. They can be a little confusing at first, but as you become more familiar with the dispatch process, you will find that they become a valuable tool in your MVC toolkit. I would also suggest looking at the source code of the Front Controller, especially the dispatch method, to see what is happening at each hook.

The Front Controller provides us with a centralized place from which we can control our MVC components. We have looked at the major ideas and functions of the Front Controller and you should now have a good idea of what processes are involved. However, we have not looked at every method available in the Front Controller. This is because including all of them would just repeat the online reference manual. Therefore, I suggest that you have a look through the reference manual and remember that all the setters we have looked at usually have a corresponding getter. Another good thing to help you learn would be to play with the various settings and try to really familiarize yourself with the Front Controller.

The router

The router is responsible for translating the request and deciding what module, controller, and action, is being requested. It also provides us with a way to apply custom routing schemas to our application, which makes it one of the most useful MVC components.

Design

As routing in an application can be very specialized, it stands to reason that the designs of the router components are very abstract. This enables us, as developers, to easily create our own heavily specialized routing schemas. However, the default routing components should serve most requirements. Remember, this is the place to start if you have non-standard routing needs.

The router actually has two parts, the router and the route. The router is responsible for managing and running the route chain, and a route is responsible for actually matching the request against the predefined rule of the route. This means that we have one router to many routes.

The routing components are based from two main interfaces, `Zend_Controller_Router_Interface` and `Zend_Controller_Router_Route_Interface`. The two abstract classes `Zend_Controller_Router_Abstract` and `Zend_Controller_Router_Route_Abstract` implement these interfaces and provide us with our base functionality. If we need to create our own router, or route at the very least, then we need to implement the corresponding interfaces or subclass the abstract classes.

The router is located at the start of the dispatch process, and route calculation happens only **once**. Routes are calculated before any controller actions are dispatched (see the *Dispatcher* section for details). Once routes are calculated, the Router will apply the routing information to the Request object. This information will be what module, controller, and action call plus any extra user parameters. The Dispatcher then uses this information to dispatch the correct action.

The router also has two Front Controller Plugin hooks associated with it, `routeStartup` and `routeShutdown`. These are called before and after routes are calculated respectively.

Defaults

By default, the router used is the `Zend_Controller_Router_Rewrite` router, which is an HTTP based router. This means that it expects the request to be an HTTP request and that the request object used is `Zend_Controller_Request_Http` (or subclass of).

The default route used is the `Zend_Controller_Router_Route_Module`, which gives us the standard route that we looked at in Chapter 1. This route is stored using the default index in the routers route chain array.

Using the router

Using the router can either be complex or simple depending on our needs. Obviously, if we have a very complex set of routing needs, then it will create a complex route setup. However, using the router is very simple. You generally create a router to manage your routes, then you add routes to it, and then you're done.

The route types available to us are as follows:

- `Zend_Controller_Router_Route`
- `Zend_Controller_Router_Route_Static`
- `Zend_Controller_Router_Route_Regex`
- `Zend_Controller_Router_Route_Hostname`
- `Zend_Controller_Router_Route_Chain`
- `Default Routes`

The most basic route we can use is the `Zend_Controller_Router_Route`, which is the general-purpose route and provides easy use but less fine-grained control. For more fine-grained control, we can use the `Zend_Controller_Router_Route_Regex` route. This gives us the full power of PHP's regex library. The other routes are slightly more specialized, and we will look at all the route types in just a second. First, let's look at the Router and how we interact with it. The router we use throughout this section is the `Zend_Controller_Router_Rewrite` router, which is the default router.

Before we can add any routes, we need to first get an instance of a router class. In order to do this, we can either create a new router using `new`, or we can get the default router from the Front Controller.

```
$router = new Zend_Controller_Router_Rewrite();
```

or

```
$router = $front->getRouter();
```

Once we have the router, we can then add some routes as follows:

```
$router->addRoute('myRoute',$route);
$router->addRoute('myRoute1',$route);
. . .
```

We also have the option to add routes from a `Zend_Config_Ini` or `Zend_Config_Xml` object like:

```
$config = new Zend_Config_Ini('/path/to/config.ini', 'production');
$router->addConfig($config, 'routes');
```

When adding routes, beware of the order in which you add them. Routes are matched in reverse order in relation to the order they are registered. This means that you should put most generic at the top and least at the bottom.

The router also provides us with various other methods to get and set information contained within it. Some important ones to note are as follows:

- `addDefaultRoutes()` and `removeDefaultRoutes()`: These add or remove the default routes. By default, the router will add the default routes.

- `assemble()`: It is used to help with the creation of URI's based upon a given route. This is very useful if you need to create links to your routes. This method is used by the URL View Helper to produce its links, which we looked at in Chapter 1.

- `getCurrentRoute()` and `getCurrentRouteName()`: If we ever need to get the route or route name that was matched from another part of our application, then we can use `getCurrentRoute()` and `getCurrentRouteName()`.

- `getRoute()`, `getRoutes()`, `hasRoute()`, and `removeRoute()`: These are used to manage our routes.

All router setup can either occur within your bootstrap or, better still, within your initialization plugin. Now that we have an idea of how to set up the router, let's look at the route types and how we use them.

Zend_Controller_Router_Route

The standard route `Router_Route` actually provides a very powerful way to route requests and is very easy to use. In order to create a new `Router_Route`, we simply need to instantiate it and then add it to the Router.

```
$router = new Zend_Controller_Router_Rewrite();

$route = new Zend_Controller_Router_Route(
    'product/:ident',
    array(
        'controller' => 'products',
        'action'     => 'view'
    )
);
$router->addRoute('product', $route);
```

In our example, we are trying to match URL's that point to a single product, something like `http://domain.com/product/chocolate-bar`. In order to do this, we have passed in two arguments to the `Zend_Controller_Router_Route` constructor. The first argument is the path to match and the second is the Action Controller to route to. The `Router_Route` constructor also takes a third argument for regex matches, which we will look at in a second.

The path uses a special markup to tell the route how to match each segment of the path. This markup has two markers, as shown below, to help us create our route:

- :

- *

Colon (`:`) is used to specify that the segment contains a variable that we want to pass into our Action Controller as a parameter. The parameter it creates will have the name of the preceding text to the colon. In our product example, this would be `ident`, so `http://domain.com/product/chocolate-bar` would create a parameter called `ident` that contains the text `chocolate-bar`. We could then access this in our Action Controller by using `$this->_getParam('ident');`. We can also set default values for our route variables by adding them to the second arguments array. For example, if we wanted to default `ident` to unknown, then we would create out route like:

```
$route = new Zend_Controller_Router_Route(
    'product/:ident',
    array(
        'controller' => 'products',
        'action'     => 'view',
        'ident'      => 'unknown'
    )
);
```

Asterisk (`*`) is used as a wildcard and means that all URL segments after it will be stored as wildcard data. In our example, if we had the path `/product/:ident/*` and the URL `http://domain.com/product/chocolate-bar/test/value1/another/value2`, then it would work just like above, but all the segments past `chocolate-bar` would be made into parameters. So this would give us the following results:

- `ident = chocolate-bar`

- `test = value1`

- `another = value2`

This behavior is just like the standard route in which it creates parameters from **pairs** of segments. Remember that they have to be pairs in order to be made into parameters, so /test/value1/ would **not** set another parameter.

Like our markers, we have the static parts of the route. These are the parts that are simply matched in order to satisfy the route. In our example, the static part is product.

As you can see, Router_Route provides us with great flexibility to our routing. However, there is more like regex matches. Regex matching enables us to put extra restraints on the way the route is matched by using regular expressions. The regex matching uses PHP's **preg** engine.

In our product example, we are getting the ident (identity) of the product the user wishes to view. This is then used to search the database and get the correct product. However, if we were given the requirement that the system can accept product ID numbers as well as product ident strings, then we can use routes to achieve this.

Consider the following two routes:

```
$router = new Zend_Controller_Router_Rewrite();
$route = new Zend_Controller_Router_Route(
    'product/:ident',
    array(
        'controller' => 'products',
        'action'     => 'view'
    ),
    array(
        // match only alpha, numbers and _-
        'ident' => '[a-zA-Z-_0-9]+'
    )
);

$router->addRoute('productident', $route);

$route = new Zend_Controller_Router_Route(
    'product/:id',
    array(
        'controller' => 'products',
        'action'     => 'view'
    ),
    array(
        // match only digits
        'id' => '\d+'
    )
);

$router->addRoute('productid', $route);
```

In order to achieve our requirement, we create two routes. The first route is the same as our earlier example except that we have added a regex requirement to match ident of `[a-zA-Z-_0-9]+;`. This requirement is that the ident must be alphanumeric. Our second route tries to match an ID number of a product. We have used `\d+` to match only digits.

With these routes added to the router, if we now browse to `http://domain.com/product/12` the `id` parameter is set and if we browse to `http://domain.com/product/chocolate-bar` the `ident` parameter is set.

When using regular expression matches, remember that the route will add `^` and `$` to the front and end of your regex pattern. Also, the delimiter that the route uses is #. Therefore, if you are matching the # character, then you must escape it. These rules also apply to the `Router_Route_Regex` route type.

Zend_Controller_Router_Route_Static

If we do not need to have any variables matched, then instead of using the `Router_Route` we can use the `Router_Route_Static`. This route matches a static URL, and to create a static route we just need to instantiate it like before:

```
$route = new Zend_Controller_Router_Route_Static(
    'products/rss',
    array(
        'controller' => 'feed',
        'action' => 'rss'
    )
);
$router->addRoute('rss', $route);
```

As you can see, `Router_Route_Static` route is just a very basic version of the `Router_Route`. In our example, `http://domain.com/products/rss` now maps to the `feed` controller and the `rss` action.

Zend_Controller_Router_Route_Regex

The routes we have looked at so far do a very good job of basic routing. However, they have their limitations. This is where the `Router_Route_Regex` comes in. This route gives us the full power of PHP's **preg** library, but this makes writing routes more complex. Even though they are a little more complex to use, I still use them for most of my routing as they are slightly faster than `Router_Route`.

To start, let's convert our product example to use `Router_Route_Regex`:

```
$route = new Zend_Controller_Router_Route_Regex(
    'product/([a-zA-Z-_0-9]+)',
    array(
        'controller' => 'products',
        'action'     => 'view'
    )
);
$router->addRoute('product', $route);
```

You can see that we have now moved our regex pattern into the path. This route should now match an alphanumeric ident for us just like in our example. However, how is the ident parameter created? Well, if we use this route the parameter set will be 1 (one). Therefore, to access it in a controller we would enter `$this->_getParam(1);`. Ok, so that's ugly, we can't be bothered to remember numbers! To get around this problem, we need to provide a variable to match mappings. This is done in the third argument as shown below:

```
$route = new Zend_Controller_Router_Route_Regex(
    'product/([a-zA-Z-_0-9]+)',
    array(
        'controller' => 'products',
        'action'     => 'view'
    ),
    array(
        1 => 'ident'
    )
);
$router->addRoute('product', $route);
```

Here, we have simply mapped 1 (one) to the `ident` string. When this route is now matched it will set the ident parameter for us. If you are not very familiar with regular expressions, then the numbering of the matches comes from the capturing groups of the expression. Capturing groups are marked out by parentheses, so to capture more than one variable you simply need to enclose each one in parentheses. If you have no idea about capturing groups, I would suggest reading about them before using the regex route.

Another side effect of using the regex route is that other Zend Framework components such as the URL View Helper can't translate the regex pattern back to a URL. To get around this, we can provide a reverse rewrite for our route. This rewrite works just like `sprintf()`.

To add the rewrite, we add the following as the fourth argument:

```
$route = new Zend_Controller_Router_Route_Regex(
    'product/([a-zA-Z]+)/([a-zA-Z-_0-9]+)',
    array(
        'controller' => 'products',
        'action'     => 'view'
    ),
    array(
        1 => 'category'
        2 => 'ident'
    ),
    'product/%s/%s'
);
$router->addRoute('product', $route);
```

Now that we have added the reverse rewrite, our route can now be easily linked. If you look at the route above, we have actually added in a category parameter to capture. We then give the reverse rewrite product/%s/%s, so the route can inject the parameters for us. Remember to read the sprintf() documentation if you have not used it before.

As this is a fairly complex set of functionality, let's finish it off with another example.

Imagine that we have been busy refactoring our old storefront application so that it uses the Zend Framework. We have decided that we want our products to have nice search engine friendly URLs. However, the products have already been indexed, and our managers don't want to lose these valuable links. To achieve this, we decide to use the power of the router.

Our old URL's have this format:

http://storefront/products.php/category/{categoryID}/product/{productID}

And our new URL's will have this format:

http://storefront/product/{categoryName}/{productID}-{productIdent}.html

So to start, we want to redirect the requests for the old URL's to the new ones. We do this by using the route:

```
$route = new Zend_Controller_Router_Route_Regex(
    'products.php/category/(\d+)/product/(\d+)',
    array(
        'controller' => 'products',
```

```
                'action'        => 'old'
        ),
        array(
                1 => 'categoryID',
                2 => 'productID'
        )
);
```

This route will now match the old URLs and extract the category and product IDs from them. Since the route maps to the old action of the products controller to redirect, we could do something like:

```
public function oldAction()
{
    $catID = $this->_getParam( 'categoryID' );
    $productID = $this->_getParam( 'productID' );

    // model finds the product ident and category names
    //....
    $ident = 'coolproduct';
    $catName = 'coolstuff';

    $this->_redirect( '/product/' . $catName . '/' . $productID . '-'
                        . $ident . '.html',
        array( 'code' => 301 )
    );
}
```

The old action now takes the matched parameters from the route and uses them to redirect the user to the new URL using a 301 redirect. I have left the database calls out for brevity. Also, remember that we should not add request variables directly to a redirect as it may compromise security. We have done this with the productID in our example.

Now that we have our old URLs mapping to the new ones, let's create the route for our new URLs.

```
$route = new Zend_Controller_Router_Route_Regex(
    'product/([a-zA-Z-_0-9]+)/(\d+)-([a-zA-Z-_0-9]+).html',
    array(
        'controller' => 'products',
        'action'     => 'view'
    ),
    array(
        1 => 'categoryIdent',
        2 => 'productID',
```

```
            3 => 'productIdent'
        ),
        'product/%s/%d-%s.html'
    );
```

This route will match our new URLs. The regex contains three capturing groups for category name, product ID, and product ident. We are assigning these to the `categoryIdent`, `productID`, and `productIdent` parameters respectively. Also, we provide a reverse rewrite string so that we can link to this route. The format of this string uses the `sprintf()` syntax so our string says `product/{string}/{digit}-{string}.html` and parameters are added left to right.

Having mapped our old and new URLs successfully, we can now carry on with looking at the other route types. The `Router_Route_Regex` is a very powerful route, but does require a good knowledge of regular expressions to get the full benefit from using it. I would suggest having a good play with this route, as I am sure you will find it more than useful.

Zend_Controller_Router_Route_Hostname

`Router_Route_Hostname` unsurprisingly handles hostname routing. A common use case for this is matching usernames that are in the sub domain segment of the hostname. For instance, if we have our public facing web site on www.domain.com and our registered users have account URL like user1.domain.com, then we can use the `Router_Route_Hostname` route to rewrite the requests to the account controller.

```
$route = new Zend_Controller_Router_Route_Hostname(
    ':username.domain.com',
    array(
            'controller' => 'account',
            'action' => 'index'
    ),
    array(
        // Match subdomain excluding www.
        'username' => '(?!.*www)[a-zA-Z-_0-9]+'
    )
);
$router->addRoute('account', $route);
```

As you can see, `Router_Route_Hostname` works in much the same way as `Router_Route`. We can get parameters, set defaults, and use regex matches. The regular expression we use here is important as we ignore the www sub domain by adding `(?!.*www)`. If we do not do this, then all requests would go to the account controller. We can also expand this to ignore multiple subdomains by using `(?!.*www|blog)`, which would ignore www and blog subdomains.

If we run this route, then it will not give us exactly what we want. In its current form, all requests that contain a username are routed to the index action of the account controller. This would be OK if we did not have multiple account actions, but this is very unlikely. To get around this, we need to chain our route, which brings us nicely onto our next route `Router_Route_Chain`.

Zend_Controller_Router_Route_Chain

The router manages a chain of routes that it runs and tries to match. Internally, this chain is a simple PHP array. When the routers `route()` method is called, this array is looped over and each route tries to get a successful match. But what if we need to do further routing/matching after a route has been matched? This is where `Router_Route_Chain` comes in. By using the chain route, we can easily stack routes together. This can be a little confusing as we can have lots of routes connected to other routes. The diagram below shows an example of a routing chain, which utilizes route chaining:

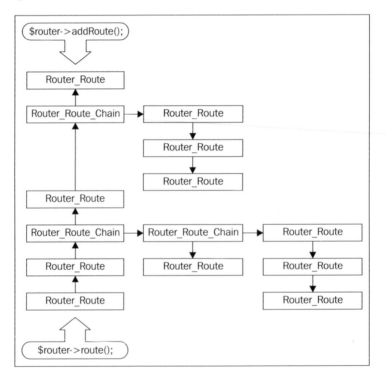

The diagram shows how routes are added in a downward direction and then called in reverse order. Also, we can see that the `Router_Route_Chain` routes contain more routes that do further matching for us. Route chains are called in the order they are chained together, unlike the root chain in the router.

This is all a bit abstract at the moment, so let's go back to our hostname example and fix the problem we had with the route by only going to one controller action.

```
$actionRoute = new Zend_Controller_Router_Route(
    ':action/*',
    array(
        'action' => 'index'
    )
);


$route = new Zend_Controller_Router_Route_Hostname(
    ':username.domain.com',
    array(
            'controller' => 'account',
            'action' => 'index'
    ),
    array(
        'username' => '(?!.*www)[a-zA-Z-_0-9]+'
    )
);
$router->addRoute('account', $route->chain($actionRoute));
```

We had the problem earlier where if one of our users visits user1.domain.com or user1.domain.com/profile, then they would be routed to the same action. This was not at all useful. By adding a route chain, we can now route the user to the correct actions. So what is happening?

- user1.domain.com is matched using the account route
- The action parameter is then matched and extracted using the action route
- The user is routed to the correct action

To add a route chain, we do not instantiate a Zend_Controller_Router_Route_ Hostname object like we do with the other routes. Instead, we use the chain() method of the route we want to chain from.

Zend_Config

When we have a lot of routes, managing them can become tricky. To help with this, we can load multiple routes using the routers addConfig() method. This method allows us to add routes contained in a Zend_Config instance. Zend_Config can consume either XML or ini files. Choose whichever format you are most familiar with.

Let's convert some of our example routes into an `ini` file:

```
[production]

routes.rss.type = "Zend_Controller_Router_Route_Static"
routes.rss.route = "products/rss"
routes.rss.defaults.controller = feed
routes.rss.defaults.action = rss

routes.oldproducts.type = "Zend_Controller_Router_Route_Regex"
routes.oldproducts.route = "products.php/category/(\d+)/product/(\d+)"
routes.oldproducts.defaults.controller = products
routes.oldproducts.defaults.action = old
routes.oldproducts.map.categoryID = 1
routes.oldproducts.map.productID = 2

routes.product.type = "Zend_Controller_Router_Route_Regex"
routes.product.route = "product/([a-zA-Z-_0-9]+)/(\d+)-([a-zA-Z-_0-
9]+).html"
routes.product.defaults.controller = products
routes.product.defaults.action = view
routes.product.map.categoryIdent = 1
routes.product.map.productID = 2
routes.product.map.productIdent = 3
routes.product.reverse = "product/%s/%d-%s.html"

routes.user.route = "user/profile/:username/*"
routes.user.defaults.controller = user
routes.user.defaults.action = profile
routes.user.defaults.username = "Unknown"
routes.user.reqs.username = "([a-zA-Z-_0-9]+)"
```

Once we have created the `ini` file, we can then load it into the router.

```
$config = new Zend_Config_Ini('config.ini', 'production');
$router = new Zend_Controller_Router_Rewrite();
$router->addConfig($config, 'routes');
```

This will now load all of our routes into the control for us. Adding routes this way is very convenient. However, beware of an overhead while loading and parsing the `ini` file. If we have large numbers of routes, then it would be best to cache the `ini` file once `Zend_Config` has parsed it. This is easily done using `Zend_Cache`.

Another slight drawback is that you cannot currently add chains using this method, though you probably would never have large amounts of chains anyway.

The router performs a very important function in our applications and I hope this has shown you its power and inspired you into ways you can use it for yourself. We have looked at all the major aspects involved in routing from managing routes to fulfilling complex functional requirements using routes. Once again, I would suggest playing with some routes on your own to really get a good grasp of what can be achieved.

The Dispatcher

The Dispatcher is responsible for actually calling our Action Controllers. By its nature, the Dispatcher is more of an internal component of the MVC components and the Front Controller handles most interaction with it. However, there are some important processes involved that are helpful to understand.

Design

As the Dispatcher is an internal component, its design is fairly straightforward. Its main responsibility is to dispatch the correct Action Controllers action. This means that it has to first load the Action Controller classes, instantiate them, and then call the action. As it has to do all the loading and calling of Action Controllers, the Dispatcher holds all the settings or rules that govern the naming of MVC components. These settings include things like the default module, controller, and action names.

The Dispatcher, like the other MVC components, does provide an interface and abstract class that we can use to create our own or extend the Dispatcher. These are `Zend_Controller_Dispatcher_Interface` and `Zend_Controller_Dispatcher_Abstract`.

Request dispatching

It is important to understand how requests are dispatched. This process is known as request dispatching. When the Dispatcher dispatches a request, it extracts the module, controller, and action names from the request object and then calls the specified Controller Action. All dispatching happens during the Front Controllers dispatch loop. Therefore, we have three components involved in the actual dispatching of a request. They are the Front Controller, the Request Object, and the Dispatcher.

Let's take a look at the steps involved:

1. Front Controller starts the dispatch loop.

2. Front Controller calls Dispatcher.

3. Dispatcher receives the Request object.

4. Dispatcher tries to get the Action Controller name from the Request object.

5. Dispatcher tries to load the Action Controller.

6. Dispatcher tries to instantiate the Action Controller.

7. Dispatcher tries to get the action name from the Request object.

8. Request flag dispatched set to `true`.

9. Dispatcher tries to dispatch the Action Controller's action.

10. Front Controller checks the Request objects dispatched flag. If it is not `true`, then it starts the loop again.

The Request object's dispatched flag is very important and controls when the dispatch loop stops. It also enables us to change or add actions to be called. To demonstrate, let's have a look at some examples using the dispatched flag.

The most basic example is that of the `_forward()` method in `Zend_Controller_Action`. We looked at this in Chapter 1, and it enables us to forward the request to another action from within an action that is being called. For this example, we have two modules named default and product. Both these modules contain an `IndexController`.

Default modules IndexController

```
class IndexController extends Zend_Controller_Action
{
    public function indexAction()
    {
        $this->_forward('index', 'index', 'product');
    }
}
```

Product modules IndexController

```
class Product_IndexController extends Zend_Controller_Action
{
    public function indexAction()
    {}
}
```

So now if we request the default modules index controller's index action, it will forward the request to the product modules index controller's index action. But what is happening? When the request comes in, the _forward() call sets the module, controller, and action names in the request object to product, index, and index respectively. It also sets the dispatched flag to false, which means that the Front Controller will restart its loop and the Dispatcher will dispatch the new request.

Just to clarify, here is an example of forwarding a request without using the _forward() method.

```
class IndexController extends Zend_Controller_Action
{
    public function indexAction()
    {
        $request = $this->getRequest();

        $request->setModuleName('product')
                ->setControllerName('index')
                ->setActionName('index')
                ->setDispatched(false);
    }
}
```

The example above does exactly the same as the previous example using _forward(), but we directly augment the request instead.

Using the Dispatcher

Now that we know how request-dispatching works, let's look at some of the ways in which we can interact with the Dispatcher. Nearly all the interactions with the Dispatcher are to affect its default behaviors. If we look at some of its main setters, then we notice that we have already seen most of these in the Front Controller:

setDefaultAction (string $action)

setDefaultControllerName (string $controller)

setDefaultModule (string $module)

So when we use these methods on the Front Controller, they simply proxy to their corresponding Dispatcher method. With this in mind, we won't worry about recapping over what these methods actually do. However, there is one method that is important to look at. This method is setParam().

There are situations where we want to pass an object or variable to all of our Action Controllers so that we can access them globally. Normally, we can do this through the Front Controller like this:

```
$front->setParam('myGlobal','globalvar');
```

However, there is a special situation that can catch us out. This is if we are trying to set parameters after the Front Controllers `dispatch()` method is called. So this could be within a Front Controller plugin, Action Helper, and so on. A good example of this is our Initialization plugin. If we need to set a Dispatcher parameter, then we need to directly interact with it.

Inside a Front Controller Plugin we add the following code:

```
public function routeStartup(Zend_Controller_Request_Abstract
                             $request)
{
    $front = Zend_Controller_Front::getInstance();
    $dispatcher = $front->getDispatcher();

    $dispatcher->setParam('myGlobal', 'glboalvar');
}
```

Now, from our direct interaction with the Dispatcher, our global parameter is successfully set. Technically, the reason why using `$front->setParam()` does not work is because when `$front->dispatch()` is called the parameters are passed into the Dispatcher from the Front Controller before the `routeStartup` event is fired (and before any subsequent events). Therefore, any Front Controller parameters set after this point are not set in the Dispatcher and Action Controllers.

The Dispatcher and the dispatching process is an important part of the Zend Frameworks MVC implementation and allows great control over how dispatching occurs in our application. Now let's move on and look at the Request object.

The Request object

We have already used the Request object quite a bit. It provides us with a way of encapsulating a request in a way that our MVC components can understand and interact with. Without it, our application would ultimately do anything.

Design

Requests come in many ways and the design of the Request object reflects this. All Request objects are based upon the `Zend_Controller_Request_Abstract`. This abstract class provides us with the base functionality that our other MVC components need to operate. This base functionality includes setting module, controller, and action names that are to be dispatched. It also includes setting request parameters and setting the dispatch status.

The Request objects design being abstract means that we can easily create our own request types by subclassing the abstract class, and it also means that the Zend Framework is not locked into any one environment. So, we can use the Zend Frameworks MVC components in an HTTP, CLI, or any specialized environment we like.

Defaults

The default Request object used by the Zend Framework is `Zend_Controller_Request_Http`, which is registered to the Front Controller by default. The HTTP Request object is designed for the HTTP environment, and therefore contains extra properties such as `$_GET` and `$_POST` data. We also have the following Request objects available to us:

- `Zend_Controller_Request_Simple`
- `Zend_Controller_Request_Apache404`

The `Simple` Request object is a very basic request type and mainly provides the same functionality as the abstract class. This request type can be used for CLI MVC operation.

The `Apache404` Request object is actually an extension of the HTTP Request object and provides HTTP functionality for two edge use cases where Apache 404 handler is used instead of mod_rewrite or where the PT flag is used in rewrite rules.

Using the Request object

The Request object is accessible through the `getRequest()` method, which is available in the Front Controller and the Action Controller. The Request object is either automatically instantiated by the Front Controller, or set by the developer.

To get the Request object from the Front Controller, we can use the `getRequest()` method:

```
$front = Zend_Controller_Front::getInstance();
$request = $front->getRequest();
```

If we need to use a custom Request object, we can set it by using the `setRequest()` method.

```
$front = Zend_Controller_Front::getInstance();

$myRequest = new My_Controller_Request_Custom();
$request = $front->setRequest($myRequest);
```

 If we need to set a Request object, then we need to set it on, or before, the `routeStartup` stage of the dispatch.

Once we have the Request object, most likely we will need to get or set some information to it. To do this, the Request object provides us with various getters and setters. Some of the most important of these are mentioned as follows:

- `getModuleName()` and `setModuleName()`
- `getControllerName()` and `setControllerName()`
- `getActionName()` and `setActionName()`
- `isDispatched()` and `setDispatched()`

All of these methods get or set information used by the Dispatcher to determine what should be dispatched. We have already looked at this when we used these methods to forward a request from inside a controller action in the Dispatcher section. These methods are very important as they give us control over the dispatching of Action Controllers.

The Request object provides us with a way to store request information through its parameters. The methods for accessing parameters are as follows:

- `getParam()` and `setParam()`
- `getParams()` and `setParams()`
- `getUserParams()` and `getUserParam()`

These methods enable us to store information about the environment or request. There is an important difference here between user parameters and environment parameters. User parameters are set directly on the Request object, meaning that they are set using `setParam()` or `setParams()`. Other parameters are set from the environment and are usually automatically created by the request.

This becomes very important when dealing with the HTTP Request object. An HTTP request contains a lot of extra information such as post and query data. To keep things tidy, the HTTP Request object separates these environment parameters from the other Request object parameters. Therefore, when we use getUserParam() or getUserParams(), we are only getting parameters that have been set directly on the Request object such as by the router or ourselves. When we use getParam() or getParams(), we are getting parameters from the entire pool of user parameters and environment parameters. We will look at this behavior further when we look at the HTTP Request specific methods.

The HTTP Request object

As the HTTP Request object is used by default, and is the most commonly used request type, it is important to be aware of the HTTP specific functionality it provides.

When we access data using the HTTP Request object, we have many options and can access either environment data such as $_GET and $_POST or user parameters such as the data sent from the routers matches. There are rules that govern the access data that we need to be aware of. The main rule is that when accessing data through getParam(), getParams(), or the magic getter (__get) functionality, the data returned is an aggregate of all the data the Request contains. This means that the Request object holds a stack of data that it queries in a specific order to return the requested data. Therefore, we need to be careful when using these for where the data is coming from. There are, of course, ways to get data from each specific data type, which we will look at in a second.

First, let's look at accessing data using the magic getter functionality. If you are not aware of how getters and setters work in PHP5, please check the manual before reading this section.

When we access data using the magic getter functionality, the Request object searches data in the order mentioned below:

- User parameters
- $_GET
- $_POST
- $_COOKIE
- $_SERVER
- $_ENV

As you can see, this is a large stack of information that is queried and we need to be aware of the order when we use this functionality so that we get the correct data returned.

The other way of accessing data is using `getParam()` and `getParams()` methods. These work in a similar manner as the magic getter, but they query from a smaller stack of data types. Also, this behavior is customizable by us and so it is a lot more flexible than the magic getter. By default, the stack of data and the order these methods use is as follows:

- User parameters
- `$_GET`
- `$_POST`

To customize this, we can set the sources using the `setParamSources()` method. Using this, we can only take away from, or add to, the existing stack. We cannot remove User parameters. This means we cannot add things like `$_SERVER` or change the order in which they are queried.

To change the parameter sources, simply pass in an array containing the keys like:

```
$request->setParamSources(array('_GET'));
```

This would then make `getParam()` and `getParams()` query user parameters and then `$_GET`.

Obviously, there are times when we must be certain where the data is coming from. For this, the Request object provides various getters for each data type mentioned as follows:

- `getQuery()`: `$_GET`
- `getPost()`: `$_POST`
- `getCookie()`: `$_COOKIE`
- `getServer()`: `$_SERVER`
- `getENV()`: `$_ENV`
- `getRawBody()`: `php://input` (RAW post data)
- `getHeader()`: Gets a HTTP header

With all these methods and the exception of `getRawBody()` and `getHeader()`, we simply pass in the variable name that we want to retrieve. We can also pass in a second argument that specifies a default value if the variable is not found. By default, they will return null if the variable is not found.

Other than data accessors, the HTTP Request object provides us with many convenient methods that are mainly for checking the environment.

The environmental checking methods provided are as follows:

- `isDelete ()`: Is the HTTP Request method a DELETE?
- `isFlashRequest ()`: Is the user agent Shockwave Flash?
- `isGet ()`: Is the HTTP Request method a GET?
- `isHead ()`: Is the HTTP Request method a HEAD?
- `isOptions ()`: Is the HTTP Request method an OPTIONS?
- `isPost ()`: Is the HTTP Request method a POST?
- `isPut ()`: Is the HTTP Request method a PUT?
- `isSecure ()`: Is the request over HTTPs?
- `isXmlHttpRequest ()`: Does the X_REQUESTED_WITH header equal `XMLHttpRequest`?

The environmental checking methods are very useful for quickly checking the request containing certain types of information. All of them return Boolean values. Most of these also have getter methods associated with them, which they used to do the checking.

The Request object, and the HTTP Request object, both have many methods to help us access information about the request. We have not covered all of the methods available, but have covered the core functionality, which we need to use the Request objects. I would strongly advise you to look over the API reference or check the source code if you want to know the available method.

The Response object

We are down to the final component, and the final part of the dispatch process. The Response object is the counterpart of the Request object. It acts as a container for all the data that is needed to successfully response to a request.

Design

Just like requests, responses come in many ways. All Response objects are based upon the `Zend_Controller_Response_Abstract`. This provides the base functionality we require to form a Response to a request. The Response is available to us throughout the dispatch process and we add to it during dispatching. It can contain headers, exceptions, and other data such as the HTML that is used to respond to a request.

Another similarity to the Request object is that the Response is context sensitive, meaning that we can have different response types for different environments. Again, this means that the MVC components can be used in CLI, HTTP, or any specialized environment. We can easily create our own response types by subclassing the abstract class and implementing our own requirements.

Defaults

By default, the Zend Framework uses the HTTP Response object `Zend_Controller_Response_Http`. The HTTP Response object, like the HTTP Request object, is for use in an HTTP environment. With the HTTP Response object, we also have the CLI response object `Zend_Controller_Response_Cli` available to us. This can be used in a command line environment.

Using the Response object

The Response object handles three types of data. They are exceptions, headers, and response body. The response body is anything we want to return to the request (For example: The user requesting the web page) be it HTML, text, XML, binary image data, and so on.

The response body is segmented to allow easy management of the response body and control over the order in which this appears. To set response body, we can use the `setBody()` method.

```
$response = new Zend_Controller_Response_Http();
$response->setBody('<h1>Default Body</h1>');
```

When we do this, the response will write the data we provided to the default segment of the Response object, and usually this is from a View. It will also overwrite any data currently stored in the default segment and remove all other named segments.

This gives us a response body like:

```
array(
    'default' => '<h1>Default Body</h1>'
);
```

When using `setBody()`, if we pass in a second argument, then we can specify a named segment to add the data to.

```
$response = new Zend_Controller_Response_Http();
$response->setBody('<h1>Default Body</h1>');
$response->setBody('<p>More body</p>', 'test');
```

This gives us a response body like:

```
array(
    'default' => '<h1>Default Body</h1>',
    'test' => '<p>More body</p>'
);
```

As we can see, this segment is appended to the response body array. If we send the response, then it will produce:

```
<h1>Default Body</h1><p>More body</p>
```

Obviously, we need more control over how the response is ordered than just being able to add to it. The Response object provides the following methods to allow this:

- append (string $name, string $content)
- appendBody (string $content, null|string $name = null)
- prepend (string $name, string $content)
- insert (string $name, string $content, string $parent = null, boolean $before = false)

Both append() and prepend() create new segments by either appending or prepending them to the response body array. The appendBody() method will actually append data to a segment, and insert() allows us to create segments at specific points in the response body.

Consider the following example:

```
$response = new Zend_Controller_Response_Http();
$response->setBody('<h1>Default Body</h1>');
$response->setBody('<p>More body</p>', 'test');
$response->appendBody('<p>append to test segment</p>','test');
$response->prepend('header','<html><body>');
$response->append('footer','</body></html>');
$response->insert('extra','<h2>Extra body</h2>','default', false);
$response->insert('more', '<p>Before footer</p>', 'footer', true);
```

This example would produce a response body array of:

```
array(
    'header'  => '<html><body>',
    'default' => '<h1>Default Body</h1>',
    'extra'   => '<h2>Extra body</h2>',
    'test' => '<p>More body</p><p>append to test segment</p>',
    'more'    => '<p>Before footer</p>',
    'footer'  => '</body></html>',
);
```

We can see that the Response object gives us great control over where body segments are placed and what data is contained within them. In the example, we are able to organize the segments event, though they are added in a different order to the way we want them to appear. This type of segment organization could happen anywhere during the dispatching process.

We can also manage headers using the Response object. There are many getters and setters available to manipulate headers. The main ones are setHeader(), setRawHeaders(), and setResponseCode(). When using the Zend Framework, we should only use the Response object to send headers, but should never send headers manually.

Here is an example of setting headers in an Action Controller:

```
public function indexAction()
{
    $response = $this->getResponse();
    if ($response->canSendHeaders()) {
        $response->setHeader('Content-Type', 'text/html');
        $response->setRawHeader('HTTP/1.1 404 Not Found');
    }
}
```

In our example, we first check if the headers have already been sent, and then we add two headers to the response. The first header uses setHeader(), which takes a pair of arguments, header key, and header value. We also force it to overwrite the current Content-Type header. The second uses setRawHeader(), which takes only one argument, the header string. The Response object's header API also provides methods for cleaning and retrieving header values such as cleanHeaders() and getHeaders().

Finally, we have exceptions. The Response object provides accessors to various exceptions that are thrown during the dispatching process. It also acts as a good place for us to store our own application exceptions.

We can set register exceptions with the response using the setException() method.

An Action Controller

```
public function indexAction()
{
    try{
        // model throws an exception...
        throw new My_Model_Exception('Model error', 500);
    }catch(My_Model_Exception $e){
        $this->getResponse()
            ->setException($e);
    }
}
```

Here we first throw an exception that gives the error `Model error` and sets the exception code to `500`. We then catch this and set the thrown exception in the response. This is then stored so it can be used later. In this case, if we had an ErrorController setup like in our Hello Zend application, then we could access the exception in that controller to display to the user. It also helps as we can use the exception more than once so that logging can be separated.

Let's look at how we can retrieve our example exception:

```
$response = $this->getResponse();

// get by code

if ($response->hasExceptionOfCode(500)){
    $errors = $response->getExceptionByCode(500);
}

// get by Message

if ($response->hasExceptionOfMessage('Model error')){
    $errors = $response->getExceptionByMessage('Model error');
}

// get by type

if ($response->hasExceptionOfType('My_Model_Exception')){

    $errors = $response->getExceptionByType('My_Model_Exception');
}

// get all exceptions

if ($response->isException()){
    $errors = $response->getExceptions();
}
```

Here we are using the getter's corresponding "has" methods to first check if the exception exists. Then, we are retrieving the actual exceptions. Remember that all of the exception getters can return more exception. We will look at the best ways to handle exceptions when we build our Storefront application.

The Response object provides us with a great way to manage complex output, and it helps us handle body content, headers, and exceptions. We will look at more ways in which we can use the Response object throughout this book.

Summary

Ok, take a deep breath, we did it! I know it was a long one and I am sure your head might be spinning, but trust me, it's worth it. In this chapter, we have looked at how the Zend Framework handles requests using the dispatch process. It is very important that we understand this as it forms the basis of the MVC architecture and a good understanding will help us solve problems, as well as inform us about the ways in which we can customize MVC architecture for our own requirements.

We also looked at each of the individual MVC components that make the dispatch process work. This included the Front Controller, Router, Dispatcher, Request object, and the Response object. For each of these components, we looked at how they were constructed, the design patterns they use, and the common ways in which we can use them. Again, it is very important to understand the workings of these components so that we can get the most out of them.

We have now covered all the major MVC components and looked at how they work together. With this knowledge, we can now get the most out of the Zend Framework. Obviously, there is a lot to take in from this chapter, but we will be recapping and building on the principles we have learned here throughout the rest of the book. So with the theory out of the way, we can now start to design and build our storefront application.

3
Storefront Basic Setup

It is time to start building our main application, the Storefront. Over the rest of the book, we will be looking at the process of building a "real life" application. To begin with, we will create a simple Storefront, and then will start to refactor and add more functionality. This chapter lays the foundations of our Storefront application from which we will build in all the functionality that we require. This includes:

- Storefront requirements
- Basic application structure
- Bootstrapping with `Zend_Application`
- Global layouts
- Application build
- Installing the Storefront database
- Application configuration
- Logging and debugging

By the end of the chapter, we will be ready to dive in deeper and start creating the Storefront components.

Getting started

Before we start, we will need some extra software other than the Zend Framework. As we are going to be building a "real life" application, we thought it right to use some real world tools. These are mainly testing and build tools. This will also help us understand some of the principles behind the Zend Framework, as these tools are used to develop the framework's code-base.

Software requirements

To follow the examples, we will need the following software installed:

- PHP PEAR
- PHPUnit (http://phpunit.de)
- XDebug (http://www.xdebug.org)
- Apache Ant (http://ant.apache.org)

For installation instructions, please see the Appendix, *Installing Supporting Software*. Once we have these installed, we can quickly set up and test our examples.

Coding standards

All the examples in this book follow the Zend Framework's coding standards. These standards can be found at http://framework.zend.com/manual/en/ coding-standard.html. Please take time to familiarize yourself with the coding standards; also feel free to submit errata if I break them myself.

As we are going to be building an example application that uses the Zend Framework, there will be times when we have to use non-Zend Framework code. This code is mainly to deal with the **Model** of the MVC triad.

The Storefront requirements

So we have been approached by a venture capitalist that wants to pay us a load of cash to create a Storefront, great easy money, right? Before we start, we need to know what this Storefront thing is going to do. We decide that we will begin by creating a basic set of functionality and from there slowly build upon our base. So what's the minimum set of requirements for a Storefront?

- To provide a catalog of products
- To provide a user interface to the catalog
- To provide a way of categorizing products in the catalog
- To provide a shopping cart
- To provide a way to add, edit, and delete products from the catalog
- To provide user accounts

These requirements form the basis of our Storefront application. Obviously, we have left out a few requirements that would be there in real life, as we do not want to get too bogged down in writing the model classes, the most notable exclusion being a way to order products. Hopefully this will not matter so much, as by the end of the book you should be able to easily add it yourself.

The Storefront overview

The Storefront application will hopefully serve as a good example for you to understand the Zend Frameworks MVC components. There are of course many ways that one can skin the proverbial cat. However, we will try to cover all of the decisions that were involved in the creation of the Storefront.

The core tasks we need to perform pan out to something like this:

- Create the basic structure
- Create our own library to deal with the model
- Implement our model
- Implement the application

Seems pretty simple written in a list like this, but we have a lot of work to do before we get a fully working application, and many problems to consider and overcome. In this chapter, we will be covering the first item on this list, which will provide a base to build upon later.

Basic structure and setup

Lets start by looking at the first task on our list, creating the basic structure. This process is very much like in the Hello Zend application. We first create the directories and then bootstrap and initialize the application.

The directory structure

For the Storefront, we will not be using `Zend_Tool` to create our project as the 1.8 release does not support modules. We are also going to use a slightly customized layout. Therefore, create a directory structure that matches the one below:

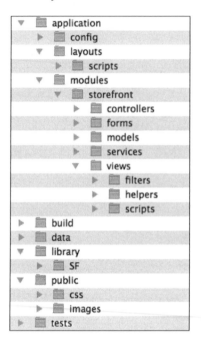

As you can see, this structure has many more folders than our `Hello Zend` application, but basically we still have three main folders `application`, `library`, and `public`. Let's have a look at the new folders and what we will be using them for:

- `application/config`: This is used to store our configuration files. `Zend_Config` will go here for its data.

- `application/layouts/*`: This is used to store our global layout scripts. These will contain HTML and placeholders that `Zend_Layout` will use.

- `application/modules`: This stores our modules. These help us to separate our controllers into groups. For now, we have just one module storefront. This will be our default module. Inside our storefront module folder, we have folders for `controllers`, `models`, and `views`, just like in the `Hello Zend` application. However, we have also added two new folders `forms` and `services`. `forms` will contain `Zend_Form` classes and `services` will contain service classes that do not naturally fit into our models.

- `build`: This is not really a Zend Framework recommended folder, but we will be using this to store our Ant build files to help automate some tasks.

- `data`: This stores any data that our application creates such as cache data.

- `tests`: This is used for our unit tests.

Bootstrapping with Zend_Application

Previously in the `Hello Zend` application, we used a Front Controller plug-in to initialize our application, but for the Storefront we are going to use the new `Zend_Application` component. `Zend_Application` encapsulates the application initialization process, making the process much easier and more consistent. It works in much the same way as our Front Controller plugin. However, it also provides useful things like resource auto-loading.

Zend_Application basics

Before we carry on with the bootstrapping process, let's take a minute to look at how `Zend_Application` handles bootstrapping. For any application, there are always many settings that need to be applied to various components. Previously, we used an initialization plugin to move all this setup code into one manageable place. `Zend_Application` replaces this method and provides a standardized way for us to bootstrap our application.

The `Zend_Application` bootstrap process is constructed around the idea of bootstrap resources. Each resource is responsible for a certain aspect of the bootstrap process. For example, you may have the `db` resource, which will configure the application's database adapter. We define all bootstrap resources. Therefore, we need to create all the resources required to fully configure our application. There are two ways to define bootstrap resources. They are by using a bootstrap class and by creating a bootstrap resource plugin.

The bootstrap class contains a set of methods that are used to bootstrap the various application components, and each method can be seen as a bootstrap resource.

A bootstrap resource plugin is like one method in the bootstrap class, and will be used to perform one aspect of the bootstrap process. `Zend_Application` also comes with some standard bootstrap resources plugins that perform common bootstrap operations such as Front Controller or database configuration.

Now that we know the basic principles behind `Zend_Application`, let's continue and start to bootstrap the Storefront. We will need to create all the bootstrap resources that the Storefront requires.

Bootstrapping the storefront

To start, we need to first create the .htaccess file that routes requests to the Zend Framework. You can copy this from the Hello Zend application.

```
public/.htaccess
php_value "short_open_tag" "on"

RewriteEngine On

RewriteCond %{REQUEST_FILENAME} -s [OR]
RewriteCond %{REQUEST_FILENAME} -l [OR]
RewriteCond %{REQUEST_FILENAME} -d
RewriteRule ^.*$ - [NC,L]
RewriteRule ^.*$ /index.php [NC,L]
```

Next we need to create the index.php file to which requests are routed, and that includes the application.php, which will initialize our application. The index.php used here is different to the one Zend_Tool creates and only contains one line of code.

```
public/index.php
<?php
require '../application/application.php';
```

We then create our application.php file. We are going to do this slightly differently than in Hello Zend. The main difference is that we are going to use Apache Ant to set the environment variable for us.

```
application/application.php.dist
<?php
$paths = array(
    get_include_path(),
    '../library',
);
set_include_path(implode(PATH_SEPARATOR, $paths));

defined('APPLICATION_PATH')
    or define('APPLICATION_PATH', realpath(dirname(__FILE__) . '/../
application'));
defined('APPLICATION_ENV')
    or define('APPLICATION_ENV', '@ENVIRONMENT@');

require_once 'Zend/Application.php';

$application = new Zend_Application(
    APPLICATION_ENV,
    APPLICATION_PATH.'/config/store.ini'
);
$application->bootstrap();
$application->run();
```

We can see that this file is very different to what we used in `Hello Zend`. The first major difference is that we have used a `.dist` file extension. The reason for this is that we are going to use Apache Ant to copy the `.dist` file to `application/application.php` and replace the `@ENVIRONMENT@` placeholder with the environment we are using (development or production). We do not have to use Apache Ant when creating a Zend Framework based application. This is simply a preference of mine as I use Ant for many other tasks when managing a project.

Looking at the code within `application.php.dist`, we first set up the include path. This time we are using an array to specify the include paths and then using implode to create the path string for `set_include_path()`. Setting the include path this way makes it much easier to add more paths later, for example, if we wanted to use components in the incubator.

Next, we create two global constants, `APPLICATION_PATH` and `APPLICATION_ENV`. These define the path to the application directory and the application environment respectively. We make sure that these have not already been set using the `defined()` function. If they have not, then we assign the values. The value for `APPLICATION_PATH` is created using the `realpath()` function. This will give us the full path to the application directory. The value for `APPLICATION_ENV` is where we use our `@ENVIRONMENT@` placeholder. This will be replaced by Ant when we run a build and the `application.php` file is created. The application environment can be production, development, or test. These are not Zend Framework specific, and you can have as many different environments as required.

After configuring our global settings, we first include the `Zend_Application` component. This will be the only requirement that we will need, as `Zend_Application` will set up the autoloader for us. Next, we instantiate a new `Zend_Application` instance, and we pass two parameters to this construct, `APPLICATION_ENV` and `APPLICATION_PATH`. The `'/config/store.ini'` define the application's environment and the path to the configuration file respectively. The application's environment will be made accessible to all bootstrap components. This means that when we write our file, we can easily apply settings based on the environment. The configuration file contains the settings for `Zend_Application`. This includes things like autoloader namespaces and where our bootstrap file is located. We do not have to use a configuration file here, and we could also pass in an array containing the settings of `Zend_Application`.

With `Zend_Application` configured, we then call the `bootstrap()` method. This will execute all the bootstrap resources that are registered to `Zend_Application`. We can also choose to only bootstrap a certain resource by passing its name to the `bootstrap()` method. For example, if we only wanted to set up the database, then we could do `bootstrap('db')`. This would call only the `db` resource. The main use for this functionality is during testing. Once the application is bootstrapped, we call the `run()` method, which will start up the application. In our case, this is to start the MVC dispatch process.

Zend_Application configuration

In our `application.php.dist` file, we have opted to use `Zend_Config` to define the options we send to the `Zend_Application` instance. All options for the application will be stored within the `store.ini` in the `config` directory.

application/config/store.ini

```
[bootstrap]
Autoloadernamespaces[] = "Zend_"
Autoloadernamespaces[] = "SF_"

phpsettings.display_errors = 0
phpsettings.error_reporting = 8191
phpsettings.date.timezone = "Europe/London"

bootstrap.path = APPLICATION_PATH"/bootstrap/Bootstrap.php"

resources.frontcontroller.moduledirectory = APPLICATION_PATH"/modules"
resources.frontcontroller.defaultmodule = "storefront"
resources.frontcontroller.params.prefixDefaultModule = true
resources.frontcontroller.throwerrors = false

resources.view = ""
resources.layout.layoutPath = APPLICATION_PATH "/layouts/scripts"
resources.layout.layout = "main"

[production : bootstrap]

[development : production]
phpsettings.display_errors = 1
resources.frontcontroller.throwerrors = true

[test : production]
```

`Zend_Config` provides us with an easy way to centrally configure our application by placing our config directives in either an `INI` or `XML` file. It also allows us to separate our `config` into sections, which can inherit from each other. This means that we can have different settings for different environments. Therefore, if we are developing our application, then we can have development specific directives and another set of directives in production.

For our application, we have decided to use an INI file. Even though using an XML file works in just the same way, choose whichever file type you prefer. The INI file has four sections. These are defined using square brackets and are bootstrap, production, development, and test. Zend_Application will automatically load the correct section from the config file based on the application environment. For example, if we are in a test environment, then Zend_Application will load the test section.

To avoid duplicating directives for each environment, we are using inheritance functionality of Zend_Config. By using a colon in the section name followed by another sections name, we can inherit that section's directives. For example, the production section inherits from the bootstrap section ([production: bootstrap]), meaning that production contains exactly the same directives as the bootstrap section.

Configuration options

Our configuration file contains a lot of directives. All of these will be used by Zend_Application to configure our application.

Autoloader namespaces

Our first set of directives is autoloadernamespaces:

```
autoloadernamespaces[] = "Zend_"
autoloadernamespaces[] = "SF_"
```

Zend_Application uses the Zend_Loader_Autoloader component to handle the automatic loading of library files. This component is a replacement for registerAutoload() functionality of Zend_Loader. The Zend_Loader_Autoloader provides a simple way of managing PHP's SPL Autoloader. By using this component, we can easily add multiple autoloaders to our application. We will also use Zend_Loader_Autoloader during the bootstrap process to enable autoloading of our application resources such as Models and Forms.

The Zend_Loader_Autoloader works by registering itself to the SPL Autoloader and then acts as a stack that we can add and remove autoloaders from. When we add our autoloadernamespaces to Zend_Application, we are doing the equivalent of:

```
$autoloader = Zend_Loader_Autoloader::getInstance();
$autoloader->registerNamespace('Zend_');
$autoloader->registerNamespace('SF_');
```

Here we are adding our two autoloader namespaces, Zend_ and SF_. Both use the standard autoloader callback—array('Zend_Loader', 'loadClass') or Zend_Loader::loadClass. This callback will be used to load classes that match the namespace.

The namespace is therefore very important and we must be careful in the way we use it. First off all, the namespace is used to match the class name passed to the `Zend_Loader_Autoloader` component by the SPL Autoloader, so if we do `Zend_Log();`, then the autoloader will match the `Zend_` part of the class name and use the autoloader connected to that namespace. We can already see the potential problems that we will have if we define our namespaces badly. For example, Zend Framework has an extra library, which has the class naming convention of `ZendX_Class_Name`. If we were to add the namespace `Zend` without the underscore, then the autoloader would not be able to differentiate between the main Zend components and the ZendX components.

PHP settings

Our second set of directives contains our PHP settings. These are the settings that we would usually set through the `ini_set()` function.

```
phpsettings.display_errors = 0
phpsettings.error_reporting = 8191
phpsettings.date.timezone = "Europe/London"
```

Here we specify that the `display_errors` setting should be off, `error_reporting` should be `E_ALL|E_STRICT`, and that the `timezone` is `Europe/London`.

The error reporting setting here has to be an integer, as the `E_ALL|E_STRICT` that we would usually use will not work because it does a bitwise `Or(|)` on the two constants to create the `8191` value, and the `ini` can not run PHP functions. An easy way to find the integer of the error reporting level you want is to simply echo it out (for example `echo E_ALL|E_STRICT`).

The date time zone is also another very important setting, and you should not use a Zend Framework based application without this set.

Bootstrap class path

Next we have the bootstrap class path directive:

```
bootstrap.path = APPLICATION_PATH"/bootstrap/Bootstrap.php"
```

To bootstrap our application, we are going to use a bootstrap class. In order to do this, we need to tell `Zend_Application` where it is. Here, we simply use the `APPLICATION_PATH` constant we set earlier to create the full path to the bootstrap file. This will give us a path similar to `/home/keith/storefront/application/bootstrap/Bootstrap.php`. Notice that we are able to use PHP constants inside our `.ini` file.

Bootstrap resource plugins

Next, we configure our bootstrap resource plugins. These are bootstrap resources that have their own separate class away from the main bootstrap class. Currently, we are using Zend_Application_Resource_Frontcontroller, Zend_Application_Resource_View, and Zend_Application_Resource_Layout. These are default resource plugins that are shipped with Zend_Application.

```
resources.frontcontroller.moduledirectory =
        APPLICATION_PATH"/modules"
resources.frontcontroller.defaultmodule = "storefront"
resources.frontcontroller.params.prefixDefaultModule = true
resources.frontcontroller.throwerrors = false

resources.view = ""
resources.layout.layoutPath = APPLICATION_PATH "/layouts/scripts"
resources.layout.layout = "main"
```

To add a bootstrap resource plugin to Zend_Application, we define it within the resources directive, followed by the resource name and its parameters (if there are any). For example, if we were using the db bootstrap resource, then we would use resources.db.

For the frontcontroller resource, we first define the moduledirectory parameter. Previously in Hello Zend we did not use modules so we simply set the controller directory path. For the storefront, we are going to use a module called storefront as our default module. To achieve this, we set the module directory path to APPLICATION_PATH"/modules". This directory will contain a set of directories that contain one module each; currently we only have one module storefront. By using the moduledirectory setting, the Front Controller will automatically set the controller directory for each of our modules.

The default module for an application will be called default. However, as we do not have a module called default in the modules directory, we need to change the default module name. We do this by using the defaultmodule parameter of the frontcontroller resource and setting the value to "storefront". This will make the storefront module our default module.

As we have changed the default module to storefront, we also add the Front Controller parameter, prefixDefaultModule, which will tell the Dispatcher to prefix the Action Controller class names with Storefront_. We do this so that our modules controllers are namespaced correctly.

Our final frontcontroller resource parameter is throwerrors. This will set the Front Controllers throwExceptions() flag for us. By default, we set it to false as we want exceptions to be handled by the ErrorController.

Next, we initialize the View part of our application using the view resource plugin. The first parameter we use is `resources.view = ""`. This part simply tells `Zend_Application` to create a new `Zend_View` instance for us that we can use later. Once we have our View instance ready, we can start using the View related plugins. In this case, we configure our application to use a layout. This layout will be used to provide the general interface for the Storefront. To use a layout, we first tell our application where our script files are located using `resources.layout.layoutPath = APPLICATION_PATH "/layouts/scripts"`. Our global view scripts will be stored in this directory. Our final piece of configuration is to define which layout script should be used. In this case, we use `resources.layout.layout = "main"`, which will use the `main.phtml` script.

Using the view and layout resource plugins, as shown here, is equivalent to using this code:

```
// get the view instance
$viewRenderer = Zend_Controller_Action_HelperBroker::getStaticHelper('
viewRenderer');
$viewRenderer->init();

// init the layouts
Zend_Layout::startMvc(array(
        'layout' => 'main',
        'layoutPath' => APPLICATION_PATH . '/layouts/scripts'
    )
);
```

Using an array

So far we have defined all of our settings using the `store.ini` file. However, this can be a little confusing as it is hard to see what `Zend_Application` accepts in its options array. Given below is the exact configuration we created in `store.ini` but this time passed to `Zend_Application` using an array:

```
$application = new Zend_Application(
    APPLICATION_ENV,
    array(
        'autoloadernamespaces' => array('Zend_', 'SF_'),
        'phpsettings' => array(
            'display_errors' => false,
            'error_reporting' => E_ALL|E_STRICT,
            'date.timezone' => 'Europe/London'
        ),
        'bootstrap' =>
            APPLICATION_PATH . '/bootstrap/Bootstrap.php',
```

```
    'resources' => array(
        'frontcontroller' => array(
            'moduledirectory' =>
                APPLICATION_PATH . '/modules',
            'defaultmodule' => 'storefront',
            'throwerrors' =>false,
            'params' => array(
                'prefixDefaultModule ',true
            ),
        'view' => '',
        'layout' => array(
            'layoutPath' => APPLICATION_PATH .
                '/layouts/scripts',
            'layout' => 'main'
            ),
        ),
    ),
    )
);
```

Note that by using an array we would lose the ability to easily reconfigure the application on a per-environment basis.

Environment specific configuration

The final aspect of our configuration file is how we specify environment specific directives. So far we have defined our entire configuration within the [bootstrap] section of the store.ini. This section forms the basis of our application configuration and is inherited by each environment specific section. Therefore, to apply environment specific configuration, we simply need to override the [bootstrap] sections directive with the environment specific value.

```
[production : bootstrap]

[development : bootstrap]
phpsettings.display_errors = 1
resources.frontcontroller.throwerrors = true

[test : bootstrap]
```

Here are our three environment sections, each extending the [boostrap] section. For the [production] and [test] sections we have no specialization. For the [development] section, we redefine the phpsettings.display_errors and resources.frontcontroller.throwerrors directives. This will then turn on errors and throw the Front Controller exception when we are in a development environment.

The bootstrap class

To complete our basic bootstrapping, we need to create the bootstrap class for `Zend_Application`.

`application/bootstrap/Bootstrap.php`

```
class Bootstrap extends Zend_Application_Bootstrap_Bootstrap
{
    public $frontController;

    protected function _initLocale()
    {}

    protected function _initViewSettings()
    {}
}
```

To create a bootstrap class for `Zend_Application`, we must subclass the `Zend_Application_Bootstrap_Bootstrap` class. This class contains all the base functionality required for our bootstrap class. We call the class `Bootstrap`. This is the default name that `Zend_Application` will look for when loading the bootstrap file.

> We can also use a different name if required by using Zend_Application's bootstrap class configuration directive. To do this in our configuration file, we would use:
>
> ```
> bootstrap.path = APPLICATION_PATH"/bootstrap/
>                         Bootstrap.php"
> bootstrap.class = "MyBootstrapClass"
> ```

The Bootstrap class contains two methods, `_initLocale()` and `_initViewSettings()`, which will be called during the bootstrap process.

Bootstrap resource execution order

The order in which our Bootstrap Resources are executed is very important to us. For example, some parts of the bootstrap may depend on others, meaning we need to be able to control what is executed and when.

To handle dependencies between bootstrap resources, we use the `bootstrap()` method. By using this method, we can call any bootstrap resource registered to `Zend_Application`. For example, if `view` resource (`_initViewSettings()`) require that the `frontcontroller` resource be executed before it runs, we could add `$this->bootstrap('frontcontroller');` inside the `_initViewSettings()` method's body. By doing this, we would make sure that the `frontcontroller` was ready before we configured our view. `Zend_Application` will also make sure that resources are only ever called once. Therefore, we do not have to worry about multiple executions of bootstrap resources.

`Zend_Application` also has a "natural" order in which bootstrap resources are executed. First the resources within the bootstrap class are executed and then the registered bootstrap plugins are executed. All execution of both class resources and plugin resources are executed in **FIFO (first in first out)** order. Therefore, currently our bootstrap execution stack will be:

- Locale class resource — `initLocale()`
- ViewSettings class resource — `_initViewSettings();`
- Front Controller plugin resource
- View plugin resource
- Layout plugin resource

Bootstrap abstract class

The `Zend_Application_Bootstrap_BootstrapAbstract` class provides many methods that can help us with our bootstrapping process. Following are the main ones we should know about:

- `bootstrap($resource = null)`: Calls the bootstrap resource(s)
- `$resource null|array|string`: Calls All | Multiple | single resource(s)
- `getApplication()`: Gets the `Zend_Application` instance
- `getEnvironment()`: Gets the application environment
- `getOption($key)`: Get an option that was passed to `Zend_Application` `$key` string
- `getOptions()`: Get all options passed to `Zend_Application`
- `hasOption($key)`: Check if an option exists `$key` string
- `getClassResources()`: Get an array of the Class Resource method names
- `getPluginResources()`: Get an array of Plugin Resources
- `getPluginResource($resource)`: Get a single Plugin Resource instance `$resource` string — The Resource name
- `hasPluginResource($resource)`: Check if a Plugin Resource is registered `$resource` string — The Resource name

Custom options

We can use custom options when instantiating `Zend_Application`. This means that we can pass in our own options that our resources can use through the options related methods.

Accessing Plugin Resource properties

If a Plugin Resource has data we need to access, then we can access it by getting the Resource Plugin instance using the `getPluginResource()` method, and then access its public properties.

Creating the bootstrap resources

So far we have only created a basic skeleton for our Bootstrap class. Let's add the functionality to our three Bootstrap class resources now.

Locale initialization

The `Locale` resource configures the applications locale. This is always a good practice when creating an application as many Zend Framework components are locale aware. To set the locale, we simply create a new `Zend_Locale` instance and set it in the registry using the string `Zend_Locale`. This will then be accessible by all the locale aware components.

application/bootstrap/Bootstrap.php

```
protected function _initLocale()
{
    $locale = new Zend_Locale('en_GB');
    Zend_Registry::set('Zend_Locale', $locale);
}
```

View initialization

Next, we need to configure our View. Here we need to apply all our global view settings to `Zend_View`.

application/bootstrap/Bootstrap.php

```
protected function _initViewSettings()
{
    $this->bootstrap('view');

    $this->_view = $this->getResource('view');

    // set encoding and doctype
    $this->_view->setEncoding('UTF-8');
```

```
$this->_view->doctype('XHTML1_STRICT');
// set the content type and language
$this->_view
    ->headMeta()
    ->appendHttpEquiv(
        'Content-Type', 'text/html; charset=UTF-8'
    );
$this->_view
    ->headMeta()
    ->appendHttpEquiv('Content-Language', 'en-US');

// set css links
$this->_view
    ->headStyle()
    ->setStyle('@import "/css/access.css";');
$this->_view
    ->headLink()
    ->appendStylesheet('/css/reset.css');
$this->_view
    ->headLink()
    ->appendStylesheet('/css/main.css');
$this->_view
    ->headLink()
    ->appendStylesheet('/css/form.css');

// setting the site in the title
$this->_view->headTitle('Storefront');

// setting a separator string for segments:
$this->_view->headTitle()->setSeparator(' - ');
}
```

We are doing a lot here, so let's break this down further and look at each step involved.

Instantiating Zend_View

To apply any settings to the view, we first need to retrieve an instance of Zend_View. We do this by calling the view resource plugin using $this->bootstrap('view'). Remember, we need to do this, as when this method is called, the view plugin resource will not have been called. Therefore, we need to call it within our class resource before we can use the view. After we have called the view plugin resource, we can then retrieve the Zend_View instance from it using $this->getResource('view'). Once we have this, we can carry on and configure the view.

Doctype and encoding

One very important setting is the doctype and encoding, which is essential for a web application.

```
// set encoding and doctype
$this->_view->setEncoding('UTF-8');
$this->_view->doctype('XHTML1_STRICT');
```

We need to set the encoding and doctype so that the View and its related helpers know what to encode text as and what type of HTML standard they should output. We do this by using the `setEncoding()` and `doctype()` methods, respectively.

Adding metadata

Next, we need to set the various metadata that our view scripts will use.

```
// set the content type and language
$this->_view
    ->headMeta()
    ->appendHttpEquiv(
        'Content-Type', 'text/html; charset=UTF-8'
    );

$this->_view
    ->headMeta()
    ->appendHttpEquiv('Content-Language', 'en-US'
    );
```

This will then be used globally in our layout scripts (more on layouts in a minute). To add these, we use the corresponding View Helpers.

To add metadata, we use the `headMeta()` helper. In our example we add two meta items, one for the `content-type` and `charset` and other for the `content-language`. This will produce the following HTML.

```
<meta http-equiv="Content-Type" content="text/html; charset=UTF-8" />
<meta http-equiv="Content-Language" content="en-US" />
```

Both of these are special `http-equiv` meta tags, and therefore we use the `appendHttpEquiv()` method. If we were adding something like standard metadata, we use the `appendName()` method instead. For example, to add keywords we use:

```
$this->_view->headMeta()->appendName('keywords', 'my keys');
```

The `appendName()` produces a named meta tag like `<meta name="" content="" />`, which is what we would use mostly when adding metadata.

Adding CSS stylesheets

Next we need to add our stylesheets. We use two different helpers here,
headStyle() and headLink().

```
$this->_view
    ->headStyle()
    ->setStyle('@import "/css/access.css";');

$this->_view
    ->headLink()
    ->appendStylesheet('/css/reset.css');
```

For most stylesheets, it is best to use the headLink helper. However, in our case, we
need to include access.css using the @import method. This simply makes sure that
some screen readers do not include the file. This will produce the following HTML:

```
<style type="text/css" media="screen">
<!--
@import "/css/access.css";
-->
</style>

<link href="/css/reset.css" media="screen" rel="stylesheet"
    type="text/css" />

<link href="/css/main.css" media="screen" rel="stylesheet"
    type="text/css" />

<link href="/css/form.css" media="screen" rel="stylesheet"
    type="text/css" />
```

As we can see, the headStyle helper produces an inline <style> tag, whereas the
headLink helper produces a head <link> tag.

Setting the document title

We are going to need a title for our document; we can set this using the headTitle()
View Helper.

```
$this->_view->headTitle('Storefront');

$this->_view->headTitle()->setSeparator(' - ');
```

Here we are simply setting the default title to Storefront and then setting the
separator to ' - '. Later, we can add to this title using headTitle('Product1',
'PREPEND') or headTitle('Product1', 'APPEND'), which will then either
prepend or append onto our default title.

All of the view helpers we have used here are actually a concrete implementation of the placeholder view helper. Most of them also provide methods to allow you to append, prepend, unset, and manage the order of the items contained within them. I would suggest checking the latest documentation for more details on how to use each of these helpers.

Bootstrapping complete

With our final resource created, our bootstrapping is complete. As we can see, `Zend_Application` provides us with a great way to easily manage even the most complex of configurations. We will be coming back to the bootstrap on a regular basis as we progress through the book, so don't worry if you can't take it all in now, we will have plenty of practice later on.

The basic layout

With all the bootstrapping done, we are now nearly ready to fire up our application. However, first we need to create the layout view scripts and a controller to handle our request. To start, let's create our layout scripts that will form the basis of the storefront.

`application/layouts/scripts/main.phtml`

```
<?= $this->doctype() ?>

<html xmlns="http://www.w3.org/1999/xhtml" lang="en" xml:lang="en">
<head>
    <?= $this->headMeta(); ?>

    <?= $this->headTitle(); ?>

    <?= $this->headStyle(); ?>

    <?= $this->headLink(); ?>

    <?= $this->headScript(); ?>
</head>
<body>
    <h1 class="noDisplay"><?= $this->
        placeholder('Zend_View_Helper_HeadTitle');?></h1>

    <div id="headwrap" class="clearfix">

        <div class="right">
            <?= $this->render('_topnav.phtml') ?>
        </div>

        <div id="logo" class="left">
            <img src="/images/layout/logo.png" alt=
                    "Shop till you drop..." />
        </div>
```

```
        </div>

        <div id="contentWrap" class="clearfix">
            <div class="left categorylist">
                Category list
            </div>
            <div class="content left">
                <?= $this->layout()->content ?>
            </div>
        </div>

        <div id="footer" class="clearfix">
            <div class="left">
                <span class="rss"><a href="/rss" title="products feed">
                                RSS 2.0</a></span>
            </div>
            <div class="right">
                &#169; 2008 Keith Pope
            </div>
        </div>
    </body>
</html>
```

Again, we have a lot going on here, so let's look at the important stuff that is happening within our view script.

First, we render the output of the main View helpers, `doctype()`, `headMeta()`, `headTitle()`, `headStyle()`, `headLink()`, and `headScript()`. The helpers will output their contents, which we set earlier in the Bootstrap class.

For the document title, we also want to have a `<h1>` tag that contains the title and which is hidden for the visual display (we do this simply out of good practice). However, we have a problem. The `headTitle` helper produces a `<title>` tag. Therefore, we cannot use it within the `<h1>`. To get around this, we simply access the `headTitle` helper's data directly through the placeholder view helper. We can do this as most of the helpers use the placeholder internally to store their data.

Next, we render the top navigation menu. This contains the links to the main Storefront areas. We have used another view script here so our main layout is easier to read and maintain. To render the top navigation script, we use:

```
<?= $this->render('_topnav.phtml') ?>
```

By using the `render()` method of `Zend_View`, we can render as many additional subviews as we like. The `_topnav.phtml` script should be located in the same folder as the `main.phtml` script. This is included in the example files, and remember to copy it over.

When we use render like this, it is important to remember that the subview
(_topnav.phtml) will have the same variable scope as the script from which they
are called. Therefore, we must be careful of variable clashes. If you want to be sure
that this does not happen, you can use the partial helper, which will render a view
script within its own scope. There is one downside to the partial helper though. It
has to clone a lot of objects to get the view into its own scope, meaning that there
is a performance hit when using it, so use partial() carefully.

Our final piece of PHP in the view script renders the output from our controllers
within the template.

```
<?= $this->layout()->content ?>
```

Here we are using the layout view helper to render the default response segment
contained in the Zend_Controller_Response_Http instance. If you remember
from the previous chapters, the Action Controllers render their views into the
HTTP Response object. This means that the output from our actions will be
rendered within our template. Of course, we can also render other response
segments that are contained within the Response object.

A little task for you

Now that we have our layouts, we need to create some controllers and views to
actually use all this. However, rather than recapping on what we have already
covered, I will leave it up to you to create these.

To get the application working, you will need to create:

- IndexController.php with an indexAction
- ErrorController.php with an errorAction
- Two View scripts for each Controllers Action (index.phtml and
  error.phtml)

These are included with the example files for this chapter if you need them.
However, it is worth giving it a go.

Building the Storefront

We are ready to fire up our application. To do this, we will use Apache Ant to
write our bootstrap file for us. This step is not really related to the Zend Framework
as such, but hopefully you will find it a useful insight into how you can manage
your applications.

The files for the build are held in the build folder inside the root directory of the application. You can find these in the downloadable example files. Copy them over if you haven't already done so. Inside the build folder we have two files, `ant.properties` and `build.xml`. These hold settings for the build and build commands, respectively. Ant's build files work just like shell scripts. You can run many commands and automate most of your applications setup requirements.

To build our application from the command line, move into the build folder and then execute the following command:

`ant`

This will start the build with the default properties stored in the `ant.properties` file. You should see something similar to the following screenshot:

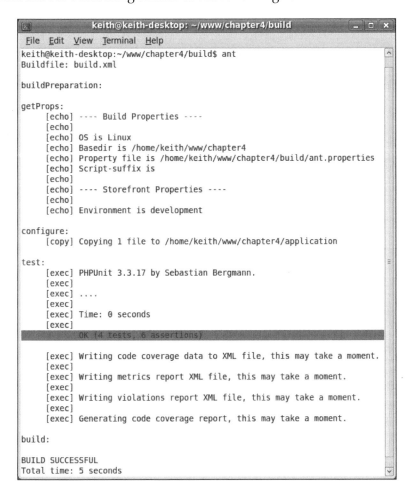

We have a successful build and `bootstrap.php` has been created for us. The environment used is the default development. We can now change this easily by editing the `ant.properties` file and then re-running the build. Also, for quick builds using a different environment, we can send the environment variable through the command line using the following command:

```
ant -Denvironment=production
```

Now that we have a successful build, we can see our new creation. To do this, simply point your web server to the public directory and fire up your web browser. You should get something like the one shown in the following screenshot:

The Storefront database

With the basic storefront now running, we still have a little more work to do before we are ready to carry on.

We will need to create the database that will store all of our product and customer information. For this, we are going to use MySQL® as it is the most common database server in the LAMP/WAMP stack. If you do not have MySQL® installed, please install it now.

Database installation

Database installation should be straightforward. We first need to create a schema for our tables to live in and then simply import the tables and data from the example files. You can call the schema whatever you like but in the examples here, we are going to use `storefront`. Once you have the database schema ready, you can import the tables using the two SQL scripts that are located within `src/sql`. To import the tables from the command line, change into the `src/sql` directory and run the following commands substituting your database username, password, and database name as appropriate.

```
mysql -umyUser -pmyPass storefront < structure.sql
mysql -umyUser -pmyPass storefront < data.sql
```

The Storefront database is very simple and currently contains only four tables. They are `product`, `productImage`, `category`, and `user`, which form the basis of our catalog.

Product table

The product table holds all of our product information and is the main table we will be using.

Field	Type	Null	Key	Default	Extra
productId	int(10) unsigned	No	PRI	NULL	Auto_ increment
categoryId	int(10) unsigned	No	MUL	NULL	
ident	varchar(100)	No	UNI	NULL	
name	varchar(64)	No		NULL	
description	Text	No		NULL	
shortDescription	varchar(200)	No		NULL	
price	decimal(10,2)	No		NULL	
discountPercent	int(3)	No		NULL	
taxable	enum('Yes','No')	No		Yes	
deliveryMethod	enum('Mail','Download')	No		Mail	
stockStatus	enum('InStock','PreOrder', 'Discontinued','Unavailable')	No		InStock	

Each product has a `categoryId`. This is the category to which the product is linked, and this means products have a one-to-one relationship with their category. This is somewhat unusual for a storefront application, as you would normally allow products to be in multiple categories. We have gone with a simpler approach so as not to over complicate the implementation later on. We also have an `ident` field, which is used to uniquely identify a product using a human friendly string, and also to create search engine friendly URLs. The final thing to note is that the price is stored as a decimal. Storing monetary value as decimals can be problematic because of rounding inaccuracies. Generally, it is best to store such values as integers and convert them to decimal when required. Again, we use decimal storage to simplify the implementation.

ProductImage table

The productImage table holds our products image information. This is so that we can have images for each product.

Field	Type	Null	Key	Default	Extra
imageId	int(10) unsigned	No	PRI	NULL	Auto_ increment
productId	int(10) unsigned	No	MUL	NULL	
thumbnail	varchar(200)	No		NULL	
full	varchar(200)	No		NULL	
isDefault	enum('Yes','No')	No		No	

Each product can have multiple images and will have one default image. The table stores the filenames of the thumbnail and full size image files.

Category table

The category table holds our category information, which is used to categorize our products.

Field	Type	Null	Key	Default	Extra
categoryId	int(10) unsigned	No	PRI	NULL	Auto_ increment
name	varchar(200)	No		NULL	
parentId	int(10) unsigned	No		NULL	
ident	varchar(200)	No	UNI	NULL	

Each category has a `parentId`. This is used to create a hierarchical structure where categories contain other categories. Categories that have a `parentId` of `0` form the top level category tier. All non top tier categories `parentId` field values will contain the `categoryId` of their parent category. The category table also has an `ident` field like the product table, which will be used again to create search engine friendly URLs.

The user table

The user table holds our user information. This is used to define our customers and administrators.

Field	Type	Null	Key	Default	Extra
userId	int(10) unsigned	No	PRI	NULL	Auto_increment
title	varchar(10)	No		NULL	
firstname	varchar(128)	No		NULL	
lastname	varchar(128)	No		NULL	
email	varchar(128)	No	UNI	NULL	
passwd	char(40)	No		NULL	
salt	char(32)	No		NULL	
role	varchar(100)	No		customer	

Each user will require a password so that they can log in to the storefront. For security, we will hash the `passwd` and `salt` fields using the sha1 and md5 algorithms respectively.

Introducing Zend_Db

Now that our database is installed, our application will need a way of accessing it. To do this, we are going to use `Zend_Db`. `Zend_Db` among other things provides a way to easily connect and interact with the various brands of RDBMS. I suspect that you may have already used similar things in the past such as ADODB or the PEAR DB library.

To use `Zend_Db`, we need to configure it. This is done by using one of the RDBMS specific adapters provided.

```
$db = Zend_Db::factory('Pdo_Mysql', array(
    'host'     => '127.0.0.1',
    'username' => 'root',
    'password' => 'root',
    'dbname'   => 'storefront'
));
```

In the example above, we use the `Zend_Db::factory()` method to configure our database connection. The first parameter specifies the adapter to use. In our case, this is the `Pdo_Mysql` adapter. Our second parameter is an array containing the actual details for this connection. This is used to connect, authenticate, and select the schema (`dbname`). You can find a full list of options for each adapter in the online reference manual.

To use the `Pdo_Mysql` adapter, you must have the **PDO (PHP Data Objects)** MySQL PHP extension installed. If you have trouble installing this extension, then you can choose to use the `mysqli` extension instead by specifying the adapter as `mysqli` in the factory method.

Adding Zend_Db to the Storefront

At this point, we can now add the database connection settings to our configuration file.

`application/config/store.ini`

```
[bootstrap]

resources.db.adapter = "PDO_MYSQL"
resources.db.isdefaulttableadapter = true
resources.db.params.dbname = "storefront"
resources.db.params.username = "root"
resources.db.params.password = "root"
resources.db.params.hostname = "localhost"
resources.db.params.charset = "UTF8"
```

To configure our database connection, we use the db bootstrap plugin resource. This resource is a standard resource that is shipped with `Zend_Application`.

The options we pass to the db resource are the same as in our previous example. We set the `adapter` to `Pdo_MYsql`, dbname to `storefront`, username to `root`, password to `root`, and hostname to `localhost`. Remember, you will need to change these options to reflect your own database connection details.

The other additional settings are `isdefaulttableadapter` and `driver_options`. The `isdefaulttableadapter` tells the db resource to set this adapter as the adapter that all the `Zend_Db_Table` instances should use.

Logging and debugging

As we develop our application, we are going to need a good way to debug and find errors. Zend Framework provides some very useful tools for this in the form of the `Zend_Debug` and `Zend_Log` components.

Zend_Debug

`Zend_Debug` is a very simple component that provides a quick way to dump variables to screen for ad-hoc debugging.

Here is an example usage of dumping the `$_SERVER` PHP global array:

```
Zend_Debug::dump($_SERVER, 'SERVER VARS', true);
```

This command will dump out the `$_SERVER` array with the label SERVER VARS prepended to the output, and the output will be echoed.

Zend_Log

`Zend_Debug` is very good for ad hoc debugging. However, for more permanent debugging, we can use `Zend_Log`. `Zend_Log` has some great features, one of my favorites being the Firefox Firebug stream writer that enables us to log to the Firebug console!

Basic `Zend_Log` usage is very simple. We just need to instantiate it and then pass in one of the provided log stream writers.

```
$log = new Zend_Log(
    new Zend_Log_Writer_Stream('php://output')
);
```

In our example, we are using the `Zend_Log_Writer_Stream` that logs to a PHP stream, in this case `php://output` (writes to screen). This is a very basic example, and `Zend_Log` has much more functionality such as multiple loggers and the ability to define your own events and log levels. For the full breakdown of features, consult the reference manual, which covers all of `Zend_Log` functionality.

Adding Zend_Log to the Storefront

We are going to need some permanent logging for the Storefront, so let's add `Zend_Log` into our `Bootstrap` class and make it available to the whole application.

Add the following to the `bootstrap` class:

application/bootstrap/Bootstrap.php

```
    protected function _initLogging()
    {
        $this->bootstrap('frontController');
        $logger = new Zend_Log();

        $writer = 'production' == $this->getEnvironment() ?
```

```
            new Zend_Log_Writer_Stream(APPLICATION_PATH
                .'/../data/logs/app.log') :
            new Zend_Log_Writer_Firebug();
        $logger->addWriter($writer);

        if ('production' == $this->getEnvironment()) {
            $filter = new Zend_Log_Filter_Priority(
                    Zend_Log::CRIT
            );
            $logger->addFilter($filter);
        }

        $this->_logger = $logger;
        Zend_Registry::set('log', $logger);
    }
```

The Logging bootstrap resource uses quite a bit of Zend_Log functionality. However, it is mixed in with some logic that sets up logging for the different application environments, so let's break it down a little. Note that the Logging resource depends on the frontContoller resource. Therefore, we call $this->bootstrap('frontController') at the start of the _initLogging() method.

```
$logger = new Zend_Log();

$writer = 'production' == $this->getEnvironment() ?
    new Zend_Log_Writer_Stream(APPLICATION_PATH
        .'/../data/logs/app.log'):
    new Zend_Log_Writer_Firebug();
$logger->addWriter($writer);
```

This section first creates a new Zend_Log instance so that we can add our configuration to it. Next, we create our writer. We use a different writer depending on the environment. If the environment is "production", then we will use a file to log, which will be stored inside the data/logs directory and will be called app.log. If we are not in the "production" environment, we use the Firebug writer. This will write log messages to the Firebug console. Finally, we add the writer to Zend_Log.

To use the Firebug writer, we need to be using the Firefox web browser and two Firefox add-ons, Firebug and FirePHP. You can get Firefox from http://www.mozilla.com and the add-ons are available from https://addons.mozilla.org. If you do not wish to do this, then change the code so that the writer simply uses a file instead.

```
if ('production' == $this->getEnvironment()) {
    $filter = new Zend_Log_Filter_Priority(
            Zend_Log::CRIT
    );
    $logger->addFilter($filter);
}
```

In this section, we add a filter to the `Zend_Log` instance if we are in a production environment, which filters out all log calls below the critical level. `Zend_Log` supports a number of log levels, as mentioned in the following table:

Log level	Class constant	Integer value	Description
Emergency	Zend_Log::EMERG	0	System is unusable
Alert	Zend_Log::ALERT	1	Action must be taken
Critical	Zend_Log::CRIT	2	Critical condition
Error	Zend_Log::ERR	3	Error condition
Warning	Zend_Log::WARN	4	Warning condition
Notice	Zend_Log::Notice	5	Normal but significant condition
Information	Zend_Log::INFO	6	Information message
Debug	Zend_Log::DEBUG	7	Debug message

Log levels are used when we write to a log. For example, to write a debug message, we would use:

```
$logger->log('Debug message', Zend_Log::DEBUG);
```

Or:

```
$logger ->debug('debug message');
```

Adding a filter when we are in the production environment, means that we will not have any unnecessary log message filling up the log. This also means that we can permanently leave development log messages in our code and not worry about removing them when releasing our software.

```
$this->_logger = $logger;
Zend_Registry::set('log', $logger);
```

Our final section of code simply assigns the logger to the protected `$_logger` class property and adds a reference to the logger into the Registry so that we can access it throughout the application.

Using the logger

Now that our logger is configured, we can start using it. To get us started, let's log the Bootstrap process. To do this, add the following to the bootstrap.

```
protected function _initLocale()
{
    $this->_logger->info('Bootstrap ' . __METHOD__);
...
```

```
protected function _initView()
{
    $this->_logger->info('Bootstrap ' . __METHOD__);

...
```

To see this working, run a build and make the environment "development". Once the build has completed, open Firefox and browse to the Storefront.

If you have not installed the Firebug and FirePHP add-ons for Firefox, then install them now and allow your local site in the FirePHP options. You should now be able to open the Firebug console and should see our new log messages. The following screenshot shows the output:

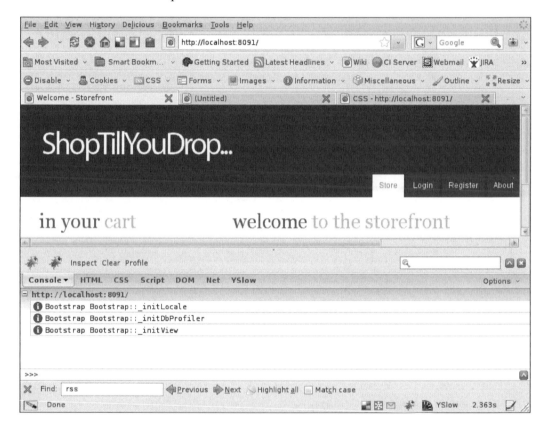

As we can see when each of the resources is called, they log this to Firebug for us. With the logger writing to the Firebug console like this, we can easily debug our application using the logger from within Firefox.

Database profiling with Zend_Log

There is another great feature we can use to help debug our application using Zend_Log. This is to couple it with the Zend_Db profiling functionality. To do this, we need to add a new bootstrap resource to the Bootstrap class.

application/bootstrap/Bootstrap.php

```
protected function _initDbProfiler()
{
    $this->_logger->info('Bootstrap ' . __METHOD__);

    if ('production' !== $this->getEnvironment()) {
        $this->bootstrap('db');
        $profiler = new Zend_Db_Profiler_Firebug(
            'All DB Queries'
        );
        $profiler->setEnabled(true);
        $this->getPluginResource('db')
            ->getDbAdapter()
            ->setProfiler($profiler);
    }
}
```

The profiler setup is simple. We first check to make sure that we are not in a production environment and then we call the db resource. We need the db resource to be executed before we can add the profiler to the database adapter.

To configure the profile, we create a new Zend_Db_Profiler_Firebug instance and pass in the label 'All DB Queries' to its constructor. Once the profiler is instantiated, we enable it by using the setEnabled() method. We then need to add the profiler to the database adapter. To do this, we need to get the database adapter from the db resource using getPluginResource('db')->getDbAdapter(). This will return the adapter instance, and we can then set the profiler on the adapter using its setProfiler() method.

All database queries are now logged for us to the Firebug console. Obviously, we have no database queries at the moment so you can't see it working yet, but we will have some soon, so keep an eye on the Firebug console.

Summary

We now have the basic skeleton of the Storefront completed. From here we can start to add the rest of the functionality required.

In this chapter, we have covered:

- Application directory structure
- Bootstrapping with `Zend_Application`
- Creating and using bootstrap resources
- Using `Zend_Config` with `Zend_Application`
- Configuring modules, views, locale, logging, layouts, and profilers
- Installing the storefront database and its structure
- Building our application using Apache Ant

The most important aspect of this chapter is `Zend_Application`. It provides the basic building blocks for configuring and maintaining our application. It is highly extensible and deals with the many issues of application bootstrapping for us. We will be coming back to `Zend_Application` quite regularly as we add more functionality to the Storefront that needs to be configured.

With all this done, we can now start creating the rest of the Storefronts components. In the next chapter, we will look at how we can implement the Model part of the MVC triad.

4
Storefront Models

Before we continue with building the Storefront, we need to cover the Model part of the MVC triad. The Model represents the business logic within our application. This contains the most complex part of any application and requires careful thought before we dive in and start creating it. There are also some Zend Framework specific problems that we need to overcome before we can use our models.

We will look at the following topics in this chapter:

- Models in the Zend Framework
- Model design strategy
- The Storefront Model implementation
- Loading Models and Resources
- The SF Library

Models in the Zend Framework

You may be expecting Zend Framework to provide you with a Model. However, it does not. The reason for this is that the Model represents your business logic and as such it would be very hard to make a generic implementation of a model as they are specialized for a certain business task. So a model that consumes a SOAP based web service would be very different from a model that calculates your tax returns. Therefore, a generic implementation of a model would cause more problems than it solves.

The good news is that the Zend Framework provides us with plenty of tools to help create our models. However, we must be aware of some design rules and strategies that models can use helpfully. MVC has been around for a fairly long time now and a lot of the problems that we face have already been solved, and design patterns have been created for these designs. Obviously, we will still need to make our own implementations of some of these patterns and make sure that they work effectively within the Zend Frameworks MVC environment.

Model design

How we approach the design of our Model is very important. Over the next few sections we will try to cover some of the rules, ideas, and strategies that can help us create our Model.

The application stack

Where do I put my code? This is one of the most asked questions that I see when people talk about Model design and MVC in general. People ask this for good reason too, as the way our layers (Model-View-Controller) interact with each other has far reaching implications when it comes to testing and maintaining a code base. If we do not manage the dependencies with our layers properly, then we could end up undoing the advantages that MVC offers. The image below shows how dependencies flow through our application stack:

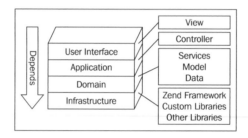

Here we can see the application stack with dependencies going in a downward direction from the highest layer. The dependency chain goes **User Interface**, **Application**, **Domain** and finally **Infrastructure**. The rule we try to follow here is that **dependencies should only ever go in a downward direction**. For example, a Model in the Domain **should not** depend on a View in the User Interface but a View **can** depend on a Model. This rule is quite simple but can greatly help with consistency and also helps when deciding which layer your code should reside in. Now, like everything in life, there are times when we may need to break this rule either for simplicity or performance. However, I would suggest that you try to adhere to it as much as possible, and if you do break it, then make sure you document it and tell your team!

In our stack, we also have two new concepts that we have not mentioned before, namely, the **Domain** and **Infrastructure** layers. The Domain is a general term used to describe the business logic within an application. The reason we do not simply call this layer Model is that we can also have Services and other business related components within this layer. The Infrastructure layer simply describes any components that form the basic infrastructure of the application such as the Zend Framework or our own class libraries.

Fat Model Skinny Controller

Along with our original question of where we should put our code, there are also many questions about whether code should reside in either the Controller layer or the Domain layer. This is where the concept of the **Fat Model Skinny Controller** comes in. The idea here is that we should try to push as much logic as possible into our Domain layer. By doing this, we hope to achieve the following goals:

- Reduce code duplication
- Enhance readability
- Enhance maintainability
- Enhance separation of concerns

Fat Controller

Obviously this is easier said than done. Let's go through a brief example to illustrate this point.

Product Controller

```
class ProductController extends Zend_Controller_Action
{
    public function listAction()
    {
        $model = new productModel();

        $select = $model->select();
        $select->from(array('p' => 'product'))
                ->where('categoryId', $this->_getParam('catId'));

        $this->view->products = $model->fetchAll($select);
    }
}
```

Product Model

```
class ProductModel extends Zend_Db_Table_Abstract
{
    protected $_name     = 'product';
    protected $_primary  = 'productId';
}
```

The Controller here is considered to be fat as it is doing work that could be performed by the Model. You can also see that our Model is very skinny and is simply utilizing `Zend_Db_Table` for its functionality. For a lot of people (myself included), when starting out with MVC, the Controller often ends up fat, as it seems right to use the Model and Controller in this way. However, there are distinct disadvantages to this technique, which are mentioned as follows:

- **Code reuse is hard**: If another controller needs the product list, then we would potentially have to **copy-and-paste** this code into that controller. We could also call the list Action from the other Controller. However, there is a performance hit by doing this and none when accessing a Model.

- **Controller readability is bad**: A developer looking at the Controller for the first time would need to parse a lot of code lines to gather any meaning from the operation.

- **Maintainability can be problematic**: As we add more functionality to the Controller, the maintenance cost will rise as we would have a lot of lines in one Controller.

Fat Model

Let's take our Fat Controller and refactor it to use a Fat Model instead.

Product Controller

```
class ProductController extends Zend_Controller_Action
{
    public function listAction()
    {
        $model = new ProductModel();

        $this->view->products = $model->getProductsByCategoryId(
            $this->_getParam('catId')
        );
    }
}
```

Product Model

```
class ProductModel extends Zend_Db_Table_Abstract
{
    protected $_name    = 'product';
    protected $_primary = 'productId';

    public function getProductsByCategoryId($id)
    {
```

```
        $select = $this->select();
        $select->from(array('p' => 'product'))
                ->where('categoryId', $id);

        return $this->fetchAll($select);
    }
}
```

We have now moved our functionality into the Model by creating a new public method called `getProductsByCategoryId()`, and moved the query code from the Controller into this method.

By doing this we gain the following:

- **Code reuse is enhanced**: Now we can easily reuse this code anywhere in our application through the Model.

- **Readability is enhanced**: A developer reading this Controller has fewer lines of code to parse through, and the naming of the Model method speaks a lot more about the intent of the operation. It is now easy to see that we are getting a list of products filtered by the `categoryId`. Naming Model methods in this way is very useful when creating Models. The more they explain the operation the better. A long verbose method name that speaks to the developer is much better than a short one that does not.

- **Maintainability is easier**: Our Controller is now much easier to maintain with fewer lines of code and a lot less logic contained in it. Also, if our Model gets too big and hard to maintain, then it is easier to split a Model into smaller Models than to split a Controller.

As you can see from, a simple refactoring of the code we gain a lot. Obviously this is a fairly simple example, and in the real world these improvements can be harder to spot. If you find yourself wondering where your code should reside, then I would first look at the dependencies in the application stack and then start considering things like code reuse. Another good rule of thumb is that your Model should be able to work independently from the Controller and View layers. By doing this, you automatically get a cleaner separation of concerns, and it helps to identify what should be included in the Model.

Model design strategies

So far we have looked at the interaction between the various MVC layers, but we must also be aware of the various design strategies available to use when actually implementing our Model/Domain. Now, as a Domain is specialized for a certain business task, before we start, let me define the context from which this discussion will be based. As this is a book about the Zend Framework and more importantly the web based MVC components that it provides, the context for our Domain discussion is a typical web based scenario, this being a dynamic web site that uses a database to store data. Therefore, as a Model handles data and logic, we are also interested in what components the Zend Framework provides that can be used as data sources for our Models, such as Zend_Db, Zend_Feed, and Zend_Session.

For our examples, we are going to use Zend_Db_Table as the data source for our Models. This use-case is by far the most common so it is logically fit. Obviously the data source can be anything we want (even other libraries) but for the purpose of this discussion we will focus on the relationship between our Models and the Zend_Db_Table components.

Generally, we have three options available when implementing the data source for a Model. These are:

- Direct inheritance of the data source
- Has-a relationship (composition)
- A Domain Model

Obviously these are not the only options we have, but I think they mark the milestones you get as you try to abstract the data source from your Model.

Direct inheritance

Direct inheritance is probably the most common Model implementation you will see. For example, if we had a Customer Model, then we would directly extend from the data source gateway class. Don't worry too much about the code here, as it's just an example. We will be covering Zend_Db_Table later on.

Example of direct inheritance

```
class Customer extends Zend_Db_Table_Abstract
{
    protected $_name = 'customer';
    protected $_primary = 'customerId';

    // Domain logic here..
}
```

In our example, the Customer Model directly extends from `Zend_Db_Table_Abstract` and utilizes the functionality provided by it. We would then use our Model in the following way:

```
$customer = new Customer();
$customerWithId1 = $customer->find(1);
```

When we do this, the Customer Model would return a `Zend_Db_Table_Row` object containing the row data from the matched row of the customer table.

Advantages:

- Simple and easy to implement

Disadvantages:

- Hard to test without a database connection
- Breaks the **Object Oriented(OO)** inheritance principle — A customer is not a database
- Tight-coupling with `Zend_Db_Table`

This type of Model was popularized by Ruby On Rails but really suffers from some major drawbacks:

- You cannot test your Model without requiring a database. This requirement can become a problem if you have a large project as your unit tests will get slower over time. This will make developers reluctant to run them regularly and defeat the idea of having unit tests at all.
- This Model type breaks the OO inheritance principle. This problem's severity depends on how closely you wish to follow OO practices, but it is worth considering.

There are some good points to this Model as well, mainly that its implementation is very simple and quick. It means that it is great for quickly prototyping a system, and once the prototyping is done, it should not be too hard to port the functionality in a more maintainable Model design.

Has-a relationship (composition)

If we want to negate some of the problems caused by inheritance, then the natural solution is to use composition over inheritance or a has-a relationship. If we go back to our Customer Model and refactor it to use a has-a relationship, then the Model will look something like this:

Example of composition

```
class Customer
{
    protected $_customerTable;

    public function getTable()
    {
        if (null === $this->_customerTable) {
            $this->_customerTable = new CustomerTable();
        }

        return $this->_customerTable;
    }

    public function getCustomerById($id)
    {
        return $this->getTable()->find($id);
    }
}
```

Here we have a simplified version of a Model using a has-a relationship with its data source. During the refactoring process we have added getTable() to the table and a method to find a customer by their unique ID field (getCustomerById()). Using the Model is similar to the direct inheritance method.

```
$customer = new Customer();
$customerWithId1 = $customer->getCustomerById(1);
```

The data returned here again would be a Zend_Db_Table_Row object. However, we can change this behavior by using the $_rowClass property of Zend_Db_Table and have it return a row class of our own.

Using a custom row class in Zend_Db_Table

```
class CustomerTable extends Zend_Db_Table_Abstract
{
    protected $_name = 'customer';
    protected $_primary = 'customerId';
    protected $_rowClass = 'CustomerTableRow';
}

class CustomerTableRow extends Zend_Db_Table_Row_Abstract
{}
```

Here we specify the row class we want `Zend_Db_Table` to use using the `$_rowClass` property. Now, when `Zend_Db_Table` populates its rows, it will use the `CustomerTableRow` class. This then enables us to put row level functionality into the row classes, meaning we can have **smart** objects rather than just **dumb** data containers.

Advantages:

- Does not break the OO inheritance principle
- Abstracts database from Model
- Easier to test without the need for a database

Disadvantages:

- More complex to implement
- More files to manage

This type of Model is slightly more complex to implement but has some real advantages over the direct inheritance route. The main reason I like this method is that you are able to test your Models without needing a database, making your unit tests easy to run regularly. Also if we ever need to replace our data source with say a web service, then we can now easily swap it out. All the advantages here really come from following the OO principle of composition. We do have to work a little to get everything working, but once you have the infrastructure you're good to go. I would use this type of Model for medium to large projects. From this we have a lot of scope to increase the abstraction and scale the project.

Domain Model

Domain Model is actually an enterprise level design pattern. It is concerned solely with the Domain layer of an application and is highly abstracted from the rest of the layers in the application, and this high level of abstraction creates a loosely-coupled domain layer. The high level of abstraction from its other layers allows a Domain Model to be highly specialized and creates an arena where highly complex business rules and tasks can be modeled without the worry of interference from things like database access. Usually, this design pattern is used alongside the Domain Driven Design methodology, which is used to create a rich cohesive Domain layer.

Domain Modeling and the Domain Model are very big subjects, and for that reason we will not look at any hard examples here. The real reason for even mentioning it is that it hopefully shows us how far we can take the abstraction of our layers, as everything we have covered in this section is really concerned with separating the duties of our application layers.

Advantages:

- Can handle very complex business logic
- Scalable
- Maintainable
- Highly abstracted
- Handles requirement changes easily

Disadvantages

- Complex implementation
- Overkill for most projects
- Getting it right is hard

Implementing a Domain Model is not for the faint-hearted. It requires some serious infrastructure to really achieve the level of abstraction required to protect the Domain from outside forces. However by using it, we can fully harness the power of the OO design and create applications that are maintainable, scalable, and that can handle the most complex business rules.

Further reading

This brings our Model design discussion to an end. I have probably not done the subject the justice it deserves, especially when it comes to the Domain Model, but I hope it has got your interest and showed you in a limited way the possibilities available while designing your Domain. To me this is really the heart of a programmer's job and greatly interesting. With this in mind, I could not finish this section without giving some further reading suggestions.

Here are a couple of the books that I have found useful:

- Fowler, M. (November 15, 2002). *Patterns Of Enterprise Application Architecture*. Addison-Wesley Professional. 978-0321127426.

- Evans, E. (August 30, 2003). Domain-Driven Design: *Tackling Complexity in the Heart of Software*. Addison-Wesley Professional. 978-0321125217.

- You may also want to look at the `Zend_Entity` and `Zend_Db_Mapper` proposals by Benjamin Eberlei that are on the Zend Framework Wiki (`http://framework.zend.com/wiki/pages/viewpage.action?pageId=9437243`). This proposal outlines an implementation of the Data Mapper design pattern and can be used to create a Domain Model. We can also see some of the complexities involved in creating the infrastructure to support a Domain Model.

Storefront Models

Now that we have a general idea of the ways in which we can handle our Models, let's look at how the Storefront deals with its Models. Here are the basic requirements for our Models:

- Unit testing should be possible without the need for a database
- Models should be able to use multiple data sources
- Data sources should be loosely-coupled with Models

For our first requirement, we will need to make sure that we can replace our data sources with stub classes or mock objects so that we can return canned responses for data. For our second requirement, we will use a has-a relationship with our data sources. This way our Models can use more than one data source easily. Our final requirement will help us greatly with unit testing. We will try to create a high level of abstraction using interfaces and abstract classes.

Okay, with our general requirements outlined for our Models, let's break this down further and look at some of the objects involved and their relationships.

Model Resources

First we will introduce the concept of Model Resources. We will use the term Model Resource to generically describe data sources. Models will use Model Resources to access data. The following image illustrates this relationship:

Here we can see that our Model has a one-to-many relationship with Model Resource. Therefore, our Models will contain and have access to multiple Model Resources. By using Model Resources, we go a step further to satisfying our requirement that Models should be able to use multiple data sources.

Managing Model Resources

For our Models to use Model Resources effectively and to create a loosely coupled architecture that is simple to test, we need to create some infrastructure to handle the instantiation of our Model Resources.

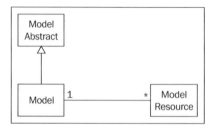

Our Models will now subclass the abstract Model class that will contain the functionality for them to be able to instantiate Model Resources in a consistent manner. We do not need to worry about class file loading here, as we will be using the `Zend_Loader_Autoloader` component which will take care of that for us. This is covered further in the *Loading Models and Resources* section of this chapter.

Model Resource data sources

So far we have looked at the relationship between Models and their Model Resources. Now it's time to introduce the data source. The following image shows the Model-to-Model Resource relationship with the addition of the data source:

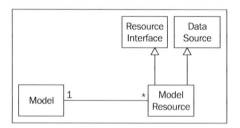

We have two new elements, namely, the **Resource Interface** and the **Data Source**. The **Model Resource** will typically extend from its Data Source. The Data Source could be `Zend_Db_Table`, `Zend_Feed`, though it can also simply use a Data Source using a has-a relationship. This is where our Model Resources get their Data Source specific functionality from. However, we also need to protect our Model from Data Source specific functionality. If we do not, then testing will become difficult. To achieve this, we use an interface. By adding the Resource Interface, the Model then has a clean contract for accessing its Model Resource. As long as we only use this contract to access our Model Resource, we can easily test the Model.

Model Resource Items

Model Resources will need to return data. What they return is important to us. To deal with this, we need to define some more objects and relationships. The following image shows the Model Resources relationship and its returned data:

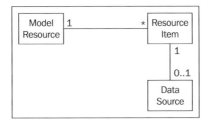

Here we can see that the **Model Resource** has a one-to-many relationship with **Resource Item**. So we can say that Model Resources will always contain many items. We could also describe the **Model Resource** as acting like a gateway to our Resource Items and that all Resource Items must pass through this gateway.

Resource Items may also have a data source. This is generally the case when we are using `Zend_Db_Table` as the Model Resource data source, where the Model Resource will then represent the table and the Resource Item will represent the table row.

Resource Item business logic

Resource Items may also need to contain business logic. The reason for this is that if we get a Resource Item back from our Model, then we will probably want it to do something, or else all the Resource Item objects within our system will just be data containers. The following image shows how we can deal with this new requirement.

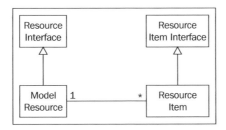

Just like the Model uses the Resource Interface as a contract to access the Model Resource, the Model Resource will now use the Resource Item Interface as a contract to access the Resource Item.

Let's now review what we have so far. The figure below puts all the aspects that we have discussed together:

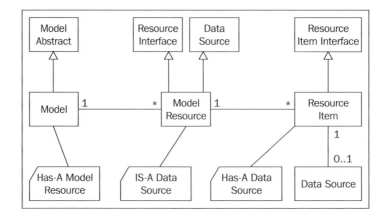

Going back to our original requirements for our Models, let's see how we satisfied them:

- **Unit testing should be possible without the need for a database:** This is achieved by the use of the Model abstract and by using interfaces to maintain strict contracts that the Model and Resource classes adhere to.

- **Models shall be able to use multiple data sources:** This is achieved by using a has-a relationship between Model and Model Resource, meaning that we can have more than one Model Resource per Model.

- **Data sources should be loosely-coupled with Models:** This is achieved by abstracting our data source from our Model as much as possible. Again this is mainly from the use of interfaces and using the has-a relationship.

I have obviously taken some time to come up with this design. However, no design is perfect, and as the Zend Framework progresses you may find that some of the ideas I have used can be replaced with Zend Framework components. I would suggest joining the Zend Frameworks mailing list to keep up with the latest updates. Also remember that this design may not be correct for your own application. Remember, to question the design, and be prepared to change or use a different approach. As always, you need to choose the correct tool for the job.

Loading Models and Resources

When we come to use our Models, we are going to need some way to load the class files. To help with this, we can use the `Zend_Loader_Autoloader` and `Zend_Loader_Autoloader_Resource` components. We have already used `Zend_Loader_Autoloader` during bootstrapping to enable autoloading of the `Zend` and `SF` library classes, and `Zend_Loader_Autoloader_Resource` builds upon the basic autoloading functionality to provide easy loading of application resources.

Zend_Loader_Autoloader_Resource

To load our application resources, we are going to use the resource autoloader. It is important to note that the word resource used here is not connected to our Model Resources. This component was created after the Storefront Model implementation was designed and unfortunately shares the name. A resource in this case is any class we wish to have autoloaded that is not in our library, and this includes Models, Model Resources, Forms, Services, or anything else we wish to load.

Resource Autoloading

To use the Resource Autoloader, we need to specify a basepath, namespace, and a set of resources that the autoloader will load. These terms are explained as follows:

- The **basepath** is the path from which all resources will be loaded
- The **namespace** is the prefix for all resource classes
- A **resource** is a subset of the namespace. Resources have a path and namespace of their own, which is used to autoload classes within the basepath

After looking at the Storefront's directory structure, let's have a look at an example of autoloading resources:

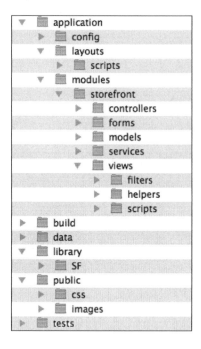

If we want to autoload resources within the storefront directory, then we first create a new Zend_Loader_Autoloader_Resource instance while defining the basepath and namespace for this set of autoloaders:

```
$loader = new Zend_Loader_Autoloader_Resource(array(
        'namespace' => 'Storefront',
        'basePath'  => '/path/to/modules/storefront',
));
```

This will add a new Zend_Loader_Autoloader_Resource instance into the autoloader namespace of Storefront for us, making our autoloader match classes that are prefixed with Storefront_ and that are located within the modules/storefront.

Next we need to define some resources to autoload. We can define resources one at a time or together.

```
$loader->addResourceType('model', 'models','Model');

$loader->addResourceTypes(array(
    'form' => array(
        'path'      => 'forms',
        'namespace' => 'Form',
```

```
    ),
    'service' => array(
        'path'      => 'services',
        'namespace' => 'Service',
    ),
));
```

With our resources added to the autoloader, they will now be autoloaded for us when required. The resources we have defined will load the following class types:

- `Storefront_Model_ModelName`
- `Storefront_Form_FormName`
- `Storefront_Service_ServiceName`

With the resource autoloader configured, we can then load our classes using the `Zend_Loader_Autoloader_Resource` or by simply instantiating the class.

```
// using instantiation
$form = new Storefront_Form_MyForm();

// using the load
$form = $loader->load('MyForm', 'form');

// using the resource getter (proxies to load)
$form = $loader->getForm('MyForm');
```

There are many other methods provided by the Resource Autoloader for getting, setting, defaulting, clearing, and checking the resources managed by it. Check the reference manual for a full list.

The Resource Autoloader is a valuable tool that we will use to load all of our application resources. In Chapter 5, we will be configuring the Resource Autoloader to load our module resources.

The SF Library

To implement our design, we need to create some infrastructure components. We create these in the SF Library. The SF library is located within the `library/SF` directory and its classes are configured to autoload during bootstrapping. A brief explanation of what each class is used for is given below. However, we will cover these in more detail as we use them.

- `SF_Exception`: The `SF_Exception` class is a general exception class used to throw general application errors. It subclasses the main PHP Exception class.
- `SF_Model_Interface`: The `SF_Model_Interface` class defines the basic functionality found in all of our Models. This interface is implemented by the `SF_Model_Abstract` class and all other Model classes.

- **SF_Model_Abstract**: The SF_Model_Abstract class provides the base functionality for all Models. It provides methods for getting Model Resources, Forms, and initializing Model classes. It implements the SF_Model_Interface class so that we can easily identify Models by their type.

- **SF_Model_Exception**: The SF_Model_Exception class is a specialized exception for models. This class subclasses the SF_Exception class.

- **SF_Model_Resource_Interface**: The SF_Model_Resource_Interface class is an empty interface implemented by Model Resources and is used to identify classes as Model Resources.

- **SF_Model_Resource_Db_Interface**: The SF_Model_Resource_Db_Interface class defines the extended functionality that Model Resources contain if they use Zend_Db_Table as their data source.

- **SF_Model_Resource_Db_Table_Abstract**: The SF_Model_Resource_Db_Table_Abstract class is used when a Model Resources data source is Zend_Db_Table. This class provides functionality for saving rows that our Model Resources commonly share.

- **SF_Model_Resource_Db_Table_Row_Abstract**: The SF_Model_Resource_Db_Table_Row_Abstract class is used to compose Zend_Db_Table_Row objects returned by Zend_Db_Table. This implements our has-a relationship between the Model Resource Item and its data source (Zend_Db_Table_Row).

Summary

In the first part of this chapter, we looked at the application stack and its dependencies, introduced the concept of the Fat Model Skinny Controller, and discussed the issues around Model design and how we can abstract them from their data sources. In the second part, we looked at the Storefront Model design, how to handle class loading, and took a brief tour of the SF Library. I hope this has inspired you to think about your Model/Domain and the way in which it is designed. With all design discussions there are always a lot of opinions and a vast number of ways to achieve our goals. Remember that there is really no right or wrong way, and you need to decide what is right for your project. Over the next few chapters, we will create the components that make up the Storefront. Yes, it's time to start coding at last.

5
Implementing the Catalog

It is finally time to start using some of what we have learned over the first part of the book. So far, we have created the basic structure of our storefront and looked at how we might implement our Models. Over the next chapter, we will focus on implementing the catalog. The catalog will contain our categories and products. To achieve our goals, we will need to use various Zend Framework components and some of our own components that form the SF library.

We will be covering the following areas:

- Creating the Catalog Model and Resources
- Loading Resources
- Creating the Catalog Controllers
- Creating the Catalog Views

By the end of this chapter, we will have a working catalog that a user will be able to browse and view the product information stored in the database. So, get your favorite editor ready and let's start coding.

Getting started

For this chapter, we will be building upon our basic storefront that we created in Chapter 3. Therefore, you will need to have this ready so that we can add to it. Additionally, you will need to download the example files for this chapter as they contain some assets that you will need. Also, make sure that you have set up your web server to point to the Chapter 3 storefront's public folder. We will need this to run our application as we build it.

The example files for this chapter contain the complete catalog implementation. As we progress through this chapter, you can either follow along by copying the code from the book, or copy the code segments from the example files. How you approach this is really up to you as we all learn in different ways. Do whatever you feel is most comfortable.

Creating the Catalog Model and Resources

To get started, we need to import some files and folders from the downloaded Chapter 5 example files. These mainly contain the SF library and some other bits and pieces like exception classes.

Please copy the following directories and files from the Chapter 5 example files download package into `library/SF` of the Chapter 3 application:

- `library/SF/Model`
- `library/Exception`
- `library/Exception.php`

We will explain how all these classes work as we build our Model. They are mainly used to abstract the Model from the database.

Catalog model skeleton

Let's define the functionality we want to get from our Catalog model. We know that the Catalog will contain both categories and products. So the basic functions we want are:

- To get categories from the database by parent ID or ident string
- To get products from the database by ID or ident string
- To get products from the database by category
- To get category parents and children

From this, we can create our basic Model skeleton. Now let's add the following to the storefront:

```
application/modules/storefront/models/Catalog.php

    class Storefront_Model_Catalog extends SF_Model_Abstract
    {
        public function getCategoriesByParentId($parentID)
```

```
        {}

        public function getCategoryByIdent($ident)
        {}

        public function getProductById($id)
        {}

        public function getProductByIdent($ident)
        {}

        public function getProductsByCategory($category, $paged=false,
                $order=null, $deep=true)
        {}

        public function getCategoryChildrenIds($categoryId,
                $recursive = false)
        {}

        public function getParentCategories($category)
        {}
    }
```

Usually, when creating our Model, we would not have this amount of detail because we would create each method in the way that we require them. In the same way, we create our unit tests. However, here we already know the detail as the development has already been done.

Naming conventions

The first important point to cover with our Model is the class naming. The way we name the class must be consistent so that the autoloader can find and load them. The convention we have used tries to namespace our Model classes. This is important as we are using a modular application structure and we do not want any namespace clashes further down the line.

The general structure for our Model class names is:

`ModuleName_Model_ModelName`

This is why our Model is called `Storefront_Model_Catalog`, which then clearly conveys that this class is part of the Storefront Module and is a Model.

This way of naming our application resources will also be used when we start to add things like forms, model resources, and service classes. Therefore, a form class in the Storefront Module would be `Storefront_Form_MyForm`. We will cover this later when we add our forms and services. However, from this example, we can see the advantages of a clear naming convention for our resources.

Catalog methods

The next aspect of our Catalog Model is its methods. These will provide our functionality and will contain all of our business logic. Currently, they are empty, but we will change this shortly. For now, let's look at what each method does.

Method	Description
getCategoriesByParentId()	Gets a list of categories based on their parent ID.
getCategoryByIdent()	Gets a single category based on its ident string.
getProductById()	Gets a single product based on its ID.
getProductByIdent()	Gets a single product based on its ident string.
getProductsByCategory()	Gets a list of products that are contained within the given category.
getCategoryChildrenIds()	Gets a list of children category IDs of a given category.
getParentCategories()	Gets a list of parent categories for a given category.

The table above describes the basic functionality for each of our Catalog Models methods. You will notice that the method names are slightly more verbose than you may be used to. This is an attempt to provide a **Fluent Interface** to our Model. The idea of Fluent Interfaces was first coined by Martin Fowler and Eric Evans. Its purpose is to form a Domain Specific Language, or Ubiquitous Language, that conveys the functionality of a method or class in a clear way. This makes our code much easier to read and ascertain its function.

Our Model does not actually use what you would typically see in Fluent Interface examples. The typical examples use method chaining to achieve fluidity like PHPUnit's object mocking interface:

```
$mockObj = $this->getMock('Customer');
$mockObj->expects($this->once())
        ->method('createNewCustomer')
        ->will($this->returnValue(true));
```

Here we can see that by using method chaining, PHPUnit provides a Fluent Interface to specify a mock object's operation. However, even without method chaining, we can still get some of the advantage from the idea of Fluent Interfaces by providing the details in our method naming. The general rules that have been followed when creating our method names are as follows:

- The method name should describe its function (get, set, save, and so on)
- The method name should describe its return type
- The method name should describe its possible parameter types

By following these rules, we go some way to providing at least a more readable and clear interface to our business logic.

Catalog Model Resources

With the basic outline for our Model complete, lets move on and look at Model Resources. If we go back to Chapter 4, we remember that our Models will use Model Resources to access various data sources. In case of the Catalog Model, this is the storefront database. To provide access to the database tables that hold our data, we are going to use `Zend_Db_Table`. `Zend_Db_Table` uses the **Table Data Gateway** pattern to provide an interface to all rows in a database table. The Table Data Gateway pattern is defined as:

> **Table data gateway**
>
> An object that acts as a Gateway to a database table. One instance handles all the rows in the table.
>
> Martin Fowler — Patterns of Enterprise Application Architecture
> `http://www.martinfowler.com/eaaCatalog/tableDataGateway.html`

Therefore, one table instance will handle access to all rows in our database tables. For the Catalog Model, the tables we will be accessing are product, category, and productImage. This means that we will need to create three Model Resource classes (one for each table). For now, let's create the basic skeletons for each of our Model Resources.

 You will need to create the `resources` directory within `application/modules/storefront/models` where resources will be stored.

`application/modules/storefront/models/resources/Product.php`

```
class Storefront_Resource_Product extends SF_Model_Resource_Db_Table_
Abstract
{
    protected $_name    = 'product';
    protected $_primary = 'productId';
}
```

`application/modules/storefront/models/resources/ProductImage.php`

```
class Storefront_Resource_ProductImage extends
SF_Model_Resource_Db_Table_Abstract
{
    protected $_name = 'productImage';
    protected $_primary = 'imageId';
```

```
        protected $_referenceMap = array(
            'Image' => array(
                'columns' => 'productId',
                'refTableClass' => 'Storefront_Resource_Product',
                'refColumns' => 'productId',
            )
        );
    }
```

application/modules/storefront/models/resources/Category.php

```
    class Storefront_Resource_Category extends
    SF_Model_Resource_Db_Table_Abstract
    {
        protected $_name = 'category';
        protected $_primary = 'categoryId';

        protected $_referenceMap = array(
            'SubCategory' => array(
                'columns' => 'parentId',
                'refTableClass' => 'Storefront_Resource_Category',
                'refColumns' => 'categoryId',
            )
        );
    }
```

Here, we see that all the resource classes are constructed in a very similar way. This is because they are using the functionality provided by the Zend_Db_Table_Abstract of which the SF_Model_Resource_Db_Table_Abstract is a subclass. The SF_Model_Resource_Db_Table_Abstract contains some functionality that we will use later when saving data to the database. For now though, we are only going to be querying the database, not writing to it.

Zend_Db_Table

Let's look at how Zend_Db_Table works to get an idea of what is happening in our new Model Resource classes. We will only cover a small portion of Zend_Db_Table's functionality here. However, we will be using most of its features as we progress through the book. If you are eager to fully understand Zend_Db_Table at this point, then please consult the reference manual as it contains very good and detailed documentation for Zend_Db_Table. This can be found at http://framework.zend.com/manual/en/zend.db.table.html.

Zend_Db_Table basic usage

To use `Zend_Db_Table`, we simply need to subclass the `Zend_Db_Table_Abstract` class. This class contains all the functionality we need to query, insert, and update rows in our database tables.

Next, we must tell `Zend_Db_Table` what table we want it to represent, which is done by adding a protected property called `$_name`:

```
protected $_name = 'product';
```

If we did not specify the `$_name` property, then `Zend_Db_Table` would use the class name as the table name. However, in our case we have namespaced our classes with the prefix `Strorefront_Resource` so we must explicitly specify the table name.

Our next step is to tell `Zend_Db_Table` what the primary key field is for the table. All classes that use `Zend_Db_Table` **must** have a primary key defined. We specify the primary key using the protected `$_primary` property.

```
protected $_primary   = 'productId';
```

It is important to remember that the primary key does not necessarily have to be an integer like in the storefront database. For `Zend_Db_Table` to function, it only needs a way to uniquely identify a single row. Therefore, your primary key field can be of any type as long as it is unique. However, by default, `Zend_Db_Table` does expect the field to be auto-incrementing or for us to handle sequencing for it. For more information on handling sequences and primary keys, please consult the reference manual.

Zend_Db_Table relationships

If we now go back to our basic Model Resources, we can see that `Storefront_Resource_Product` is now configured and ready to use. However, `Storefront_Resource_ProductImage` and `Storefront_Resource_Category` have the extra setting `$_referenceMap`. In addition to providing a way to read, insert, update, and delete data from a database table, `Zend_Db_Table` can also handle table relationships and dependencies. Relationships allow us to look up referenced table rows, and dependencies allow us to cascade update and delete operations.

To define a table reference, we use the protected `$_referenceMap` property. This expects an associative array containing the reference information for the table.

```
protected $_referenceMap = array(
    'Image' => array()
);
```

For `Storefront_Resource_ProductImage`, we need to first add a new rule key to the `$_referenceMap` array. This is used to uniquely identify the reference. In this case, we use `Image` as the relationship that will be used to lookup the products images. Next, we add the rule keys for the reference.

```
protected $_referenceMap = array(
    'Image' => array(
        'columns' => 'productId',
        'refTableClass' => 'Storefront_Resource_Product',
        'refColumns' => 'productId',
    )
);
```

Our first rule is `columns`. This defines the column, or columns (use an array for multiple columns), for the current table that should be used to match the related rows. In case of `Storefront_Resource_ProductImage`, this is the `productId` field of the `productImage` table.

Our second rule is `refTableClass`. This defines the parent class that this class references. In case of `Storefront_Resource_ProductImage`, the parent class is `Storefront_Resource_Product`.

Our third rule is `refColumns`. This defines the parent column, or columns of the parent table that should be used to match the related rows. In case of `Storefront_Resource_ProductImage`, this is the `productId` field of the `product` table.

Optionally, we can also supply `onDelete` and `onUpdate` rules. These are used if you are not using a database that supports declarative referential integrity such as SQLite or MySQL® MyISAM tables.

Model Resource Items

We now have our main Model Resource classes created. However, we are going to abstract our design even further by using Model Resource Items. Internally, `Zend_Db_Table` uses the row data gateway pattern to represent a single row in a database table. The row data gateway pattern is defined as:

Row data gateway

An object that acts as a gateway to a single record in a data source. There is one instance per row.

Martin Fowler—Patterns of Enterprise Application Architecture
http://martinfowler.com/eaaCatalog/rowDataGateway.html

Therefore, a row returned by `Zend_Db_Table` is an instance of the `Zend_Db_Table_Row` class. For our purpose, we do not want to use `Zend_Db_Table_Row` to represent our rows. This is because we are trying to implement a 'has-a' relationship with the data sources. To achieve this, we introduce another class per table to represent our row. We have generically named these classes Model Resource Items.

To implement our design, we need to edit the Model Resource classes to make them aware of our soon to be created Model Resource Items classes. Let's add the following to the Model Resource classes:

application/modules/storefront/models/resources/Product.php

```
class Storefront_Resource_Product extends Zend_Db_Table_Abstract
{
    protected $_name    = 'product';
    protected $_primary = 'productId';
    protected $_rowClass = 'Storefront_Resource_Product_Item';
```

application/modules/storefront/models/resources/ProductImage.php

```
class Storefront_Resource_ProductImage extends Zend_Db_Table_Abstract
{
    protected $_name = 'productImage';
    protected $_primary = 'imageId';
    protected $_rowClass = 'Storefront_Resource_ProductImage_Item';
```

application/modules/storefront/models/resources/Category.php

```
class Storefront_Resource_Category extends Zend_Db_Table_Abstract
{
    protected $_name = 'category';
    protected $_primary = 'categoryId';
    protected $_rowClass = 'Storefront_Resource_Category_Item';
```

For each of our Model Resources we have added the protected `$_rowClass` property. This will tell `Zend_Db_Table` to use the specified class instead of `Zend_Db_Table_Row`.

SF_Model_Resource_Db_Table_Row_Abstract

Before we create our Resource Model Item classes, we must first look at part of the SF library—namely the `SF_Model_Resource_Db_Table_Row_Abstract`. We will use this abstract class to provide the base functionality for all of our Model Resource Items. The main purpose of the SF Row Abstract is to provide a has-a relationship (composition) with the row instance (`Zend_Db_Table_Row`) and provide lazy loading of item level properties.

Below is the `SF_Model_Resource_Db_Table_Row_Abstract` class with the method body removed for brevity:

`library/SF/Model/Resource/Db/Table/Row/Abstract.php`

```
abstract class SF_Model_Resource_Db_Table_Row_Abstract
{
    protected $_row = null;

    public function __construct(array $config = array())

    public function __get($columnName)

    public function __isset($columnName)

    public function __set($columnName, $value)

    public function getRow()

    public function setRow(array $config = array())

    public function __call($method, array $arguments)
}
```

Let's look at each method:

- `__construct()`: The constructor will be called when `Zend_Db_Table` creates a new row. When instantiation occurs, `Zend_Db_Table` passes in a `$config` array. This array contains the data for the row. This is then passed onto the `setRow()` method.

- `setRow()`: The `setRow()` method is responsible for creating a new row instance that will be used by the Model Resource Item. By default, this is `Zend_Db_Table_Row`.

- `getRow()`: The `getRow()` method is simply an accessor for the `$_row` property that contains the `Zend_Db_Table_Row` instance.

- `__get()`, `__set()`, `__isset()`, and `__call()`: All of these methods simply proxy to the row instance stored in `$_row`. This provides an easy way to composite `Zend_Db_Table_Row` with our Model Resource Item.

- `__get()`: The `__get()` method also provides lazy loading of item level properties. This is done by checking the class for getter methods that match the queried property. For example, if our Model Resource Item has the method `getImages()` and this method gets a dependent row for instance, we can access this data using `$item->images` rather than using `$item->getImages()`. We will cover more on this later when we implement the full Catalog Model.

Creating the Model Resource Items

Creating our Model Resource Items is very straightforward. All we need to do is subclass the `SF_Model_Resource_Db_Table_Row_Abstract` class.

Create the following files and directories:

application/modules/storefront/models/resources/Product/Item.php

```
class Storefront_Resource_Product_Item extends SF_Model_Resource_Db_
Table_Row_Abstract
{
}
```

application/modules/storefront/models/resources/ProductImage/Item.php

```
class Storefront_Resource_ProductImage_Item extends SF_Model_Resource_
Db_Table_Row_Abstract
{
}
```

application/modules/storefront/models/resources/Category/Item.php

```
class Storefront_Resource_Category_Item extends SF_Model_Resource_Db_
Table_Row_Abstract
{
}
```

Nice and easy! We now have the basic structure for our Model Resources created. Next, we will need to add the business logic to our Models.

Implementing the Catalog Model

Now that we have our Model Resources created, we can start implementing the Catalog Models business logic.

Model Resource interfaces

Before using our Model Resources we need to define what they will do. To help with this, we are going to add interfaces for both Model Resources and Model Resource Items. The reason for this is that we can decouple our Model from its resources and move as much database-specific code as possible into the resources.

As we continue, let's create the following interfaces for the Model Resources.

application/modules/storefront/models/resources/Category/Interface.php

```
interface Storefront_Resource_Category_Interface
{
    public function getCategoriesByParentId($parentId);
    public function getCategoryByIdent($ident);
    public function getCategoryById($id);
}
```

application/modules/storefront/models/resources/Category/Item/
Interface.php

```
interface Storefront_Resource_Category_Item_Interface
{
    public function getParentCategory();
}
```

application/modules/storefront/models/resources/Product/Interface.php

```
interface Storefront_Resource_Product_Interface
{
    public function getProductById($id);
    public function getProductByIdent($ident);
    public function getProductsByCategory($categoryId, $paged=null,
        $order=null);
    public function saveProduct($info);
}
```

application/modules/storefront/models/resources/Product/Item/
Interface.php

```
interface Storefront_Resource_Product_Item_Interface
{
    public function getImages($includeDefault=false);
    public function getDefaultImage();
    public function getPrice($withDiscount=true,$withTax=true);
    public function isDiscounted();
    public function isTaxable();
}
```

application/modules/storefront/models/resources/ProductImage/
Interface.php

```
interface Storefront_Resource_ProductImage_Interface
{}
```

application/modules/storefront/models/resources/ProductImage/Item/
Interface.php

```
interface Storefront_Resource_ProductImage_Item_Interface
{
    public function thumbnail();
    public function full();
    public function isDefault();
}
```

We now have clear interfaces that will be used as contracts between the Model and the Model Resources. Looking at each interface, we can clearly see what functionality is provided by each resource. For example, the Product Resource Item has the method isTaxable() that we can use to check whether to add tax or not.

Each Model Resource now needs to implement these contracts and edit the resources. Doing so causes them to implement their respective interface.

application/modules/storefront/models/resources/Category.php

```
class Storefront_Resource_Category extends Zend_Db_Table_Abstract
implements Storefront_Resource_Category_Interface
```

application/modules/storefront/models/resources/Category/Item.php

```
class Storefront_Resource_Category_Item extends
SF_Model_Resource_Db_Table_Row_Abstract implements
Storefront_Resource_Category_Item_Interface
```

application/modules/storefront/models/resources/Product.php

```
class Storefront_Resource_Product extends Zend_Db_Table_Abstract
implements Storefront_Resource_Product_Interface
```

application/modules/storefront/models/resources/Product/Item.php

```
class Storefront_Resource_Product_Item extends
SF_Model_Resource_Db_Table_Row_Abstract implements
Storefront_Resource_Product_Item_Interface
```

application/modules/storefront/models/resources/ProductImage.php

```
class Storefront_Resource_ProductImage extends Zend_Db_Table_Abstract
implements Storefront_Resource_ProductImage_Item_Interface
```

application/modules/storefront/models/resources/ProductImage/Item/
Interface.php

```
class Storefront_Resource_ProductImage_Item extends
SF_Model_Resource_Db_Table_Row_Abstract implements
Storefront_Resource_ProductImage_Item_Interface
```

Our resources now must implement the methods specified in our new interfaces. These methods will access the database, and in the case of Resource Items, contain limited business logic.

Before we continue, we must be aware that there are some disadvantages to this design. The main ones are:

- We have more files to maintain
- We have business logic in more than one place, Models and Model Resource Items

Our first issue really comes down to a personal preference of mine. I like the use of interfaces as they help to define clear boundaries between objects. We could ditch the interfaces if we wanted with no real adverse affects.

Our second issue is a little more complex and is a consequence of the choice to include business logic with our Model Resource Item objects. By doing this, we almost have two Models or one split into at least two!

For example, we have `Storefront_Model_Catalog` and `Storefront_Resource_Product_Item`. Now, both of these contain business logic for products. As we can see, this could cause confusion. We could correct this by having a separate Product and Category Model. This would certainly make things clearer. We could also not put any business logic into the Model Resource Item and run everything through the Catalog Model. However, by not including any business logic in the Model Resource Items, all of them will simply become data containers that will need to be passed back to the Model for business operations to occur. Our final option would be to move further toward a Domain Model. However, this would require more infrastructure to be created and for the purposes of this book and indeed the storefront would probably be a step too far.

The design choices here vary from project to project, and we could easily refactor later on to correct some of these downfalls. The most important thing is that we are aware of them.

Model Resource implementation

Now that our resources are implementing their respective interfaces, we need to implement all the methods defined by them. Let's go through and add these now. We will explain the functionality as we go.

Category Model Resource

To start, we will create the `getCategoriesByParentId()` method.

application/modules/storefront/models/resources/Category.php

```
public function getCategoriesByParentId($parentId)
{
    $select = $this->select()
                    ->where('parentId = ?', $parentId)
                    ->order('name');

    return $this->fetchAll($select);
}
```

We will need to be able to fetch all categories within a category. We do this by getting all records that match the passed in `$parentId` parameter. To do this, we need to create a select statement that we can use to find the records. As our resource is a subclass of `Zend_Db_Table_Abstract`, we already have all the tools we need contained within this class.

We start by getting a new `Zend_Db_Table_Select` instance using the `select()` method of `Zend_Db_Table_Abstract`. `Zend_Db_Table_Select` and `Zend_Db_Select` allow us to programmatically create select statements. This means we don't have to worry too much about the actual SQL created as they do this for us. Moreover, they handle escaping for us as well, so we are safe to pass in dirty data.

We can create very complex statements using the `Zend_Db_Select` classes. This is done by calling the corresponding method to the SQL clause we want. For example, if we want to join table, then we use `$select->join(...)` or add a having clause by using `$select->having(...)`. A full detailed description of the various select methods are available in the reference manual, though we will be covering many of them as we progress.

In `getCategoriesByParentId()`, we add a WHERE and an ORDER BY clause to create the SQL:

```
WHERE parentId='1'
ORDER BY name DESC, using the where() and order() methods.
```

The final part of our method is to actually run the SQL statement and fetch all the rows that match. We do this by calling the `fetchAll()` method and passing it the `Zend_Db_Table_Select` stored in the `$select` variable.

application/modules/storefront/models/resources/Category.php

```
public function getCategoryByIdent($ident)
{
    $select = $this->select()
                    ->where('ident = ?', $ident);

    return $this->fetchRow($select);
}
```

Each of our categories will have a unique identity string that will be used to create nice URLs like catalog/hats. The `getCategoryByIdent()` method, just like `getCategoriesByParentId()`, creates a select statement and then returns the result. However, this time we use `fetchRow()` instead of `fetchAll()` that, as its name suggests, fetches a single row from the database. The return value type will be a `Storefront_Resource_Category_Item` instance, just as we specified in the `$_rowClass` property.

application/modules/storefront/models/resources/Category.php

```
public function getCategoryById($id)
{
    $select = $this->select()
                    ->where('categoryId = ?', $id);

    return $this->fetchRow($select);
}
```

The `getCategoryById()` method simply finds a category by its categoryId field and works just like the `getCategoryByIdent()` method.

Category Resource Item

Next, we need to create the `getParentCategory()` method for our Resource Item.

application/modules/storefront/models/resources/Category/Item.php

```
public function getParentCategory()
{
    return $this->findParentRow(
        'Storefront_Resource_Category',
        'SubCategory'
    );
}
```

This will be used to find a category's parent category. Here we are using another nice feature of `Zend_Db_Table` which is the table relationships. The `findParentRow()` uses the `subCategory` table relationship we defined in the Category Resource earlier. The `subCategory` relationship defines a self-reference on the category table. By using this, we can easily find a rows parent. To fetch a parent row, we must specify two things. They are: the table class that the reference is set in, and the name of the rule to use (in our case, this is `Storefront_Resource_Category` and `SubCategory`).

Product Model Resource

Now we need to create the product methods. We start by creating the `getProductById()` method.

application/modules/storefront/models/resources/Product.php

```
public function getProductById($id)
{
    return $this->find($id)->current();
}
```

The `getProductById()` method simply fetches a product by its `productId` field. This works exactly as in the Category Model Resource's `getCategoryById()` method. The only difference here is that we use the `find()` method instead of creating our own select statement by using `find()`. The `Zend_Db_Table` will automatically create a select statement that matches the tables primary key field (`productId`). The `find()` method will return a `Zend_Db_Table_Rowset` instance. Therefore, as we want a `Storefront_Resource_Product_Item` instance, we use `current()` to get the first row from the rowset.

application/modules/storefront/models/resources/Product.php

```
public function getProductByIdent($ident)
{
    return $this->fetchRow(
        $this->select()->where('ident = ?', $ident)
    );
}
```

The getProductByIdent() method is exactly the same as the getCategoryByIdent() method in the Category Resource, the only slight difference is in the syntax style we have used. Usually, we would keep the style consistent, but in this case, we just wanted to demonstrate the different styles.

application/modules/storefront/models/resources/Product.php

```php
public function getProductsByCategory($categoryId, $paged=null,
        $order=null)
{
    $select = $this->select();
    $select->from('product')
            ->where("categoryId IN(?)", $categoryId);

    if (true === is_array($order)) {
        $select->order($order);
    }

    if (null !== $paged) {
        $adapter = new Zend_Paginator_Adapter_DbTableSelect($select);

        $count = clone $select;
        $count->reset(Zend_Db_Select::COLUMNS);
        $count->reset(Zend_Db_Select::FROM);
        $count->from(
            'product',
            new Zend_Db_Expr(
                'COUNT(*) AS `zend_paginator_row_count`'
            )
        );
        $adapter->setRowCount($count);

        $paginator = new Zend_Paginator($adapter);
        $paginator->setItemCountPerPage(5)
                ->setCurrentPageNumber((int) $paged);
        return $paginator;
    }

    return $this->fetchAll($select);
}
```

The getProductsByCategory() is our main method that fetches our product listings. There is quite a bit of code here, but it really breaks down to two areas—creating the select statement and paginating the result.

We create the select statement in the same way that we did in the previous methods. However, this time we are using an `IN` clause as we want to be able to get products from multiple categories at once. When creating clauses that can have multiple values like `IN`, we can pass the `where()` method an array as its second parameter. `Zend_Db_Select` will then escape each item and add them into our SQL. The ordering of the result is optional, so we have wrapped the order clause within an `if` statement that checks if the order clause array has been passed in or not. The order array is simply an array containing order by clauses, for example, `array('name ASC', 'price DESC')`.

Pagination will be handled by the `Zend_Paginator`. The `$paged` parameter is used to either switch pagination on or off and can either be null (off), or an integer (on) that contains the current page number. To use `Zend_Paginator`, we first set up an adapter to configure our paginator instance. Currently `Zend_Paginator` has the following adapters:

- `Zend_Paginator_Adapter_Array`: Paginates an array
- `Zend_Paginator_Adapter_DbSelect`: Paginates a `Zend_Db_Select` result
- `Zend_Paginator_Adapter_DbTableSelect`: Paginates a `Zend_Db_Table_Select` result
- `Zend_Paginator_Adapter_Iterator`: Paginates an object that implements the PHP SPL Iterator interface
- `Zend_Paginator_Adapter_Null`: Does not calculate anything, but you can still use the related View Helper

For our purpose, we use the `DbTableSelect` adapter as we are using `Zend_Db_Table`. We start by creating a new instance of, and passing in, the `$select` variable we created earlier.

```
new Zend_Paginator_Adapter_DbTableSelect($select);
```

Next, we create a select statement that will be used to count the total amount of rows returned by the main select statement. This is optional, as `Zend_Paginator`, by default, will augment the main select statement to count the total rows. However, by using our own, we have more control over query performance. To create the count query, we need to duplicate, and then edit, the main select object.

```
$count = clone $select;
$count->reset(Zend_Db_Select::COLUMNS);
$count->reset(Zend_Db_Select::FROM);  .
$count->from(
    'product',
    new Zend_Db_Expr(
        'COUNT(*) AS `zend_paginator_row_count`'
    )
);
```

Here we first `clone` the `$select` variable that contains our main query. This is important as we do not want to affect the main select statement. We then start to edit the cloned select statement. Using the `reset()` method, we reset, or clear, the `columns` and `from` parts of the select statement. We do this so that we can inject the count query without affecting the `where` parts. Finally, we create the count expression by adding a new `from` part to the select statement and using `Zend_Db_Expr` (expression) to add the count clause.

```
$adapter->setRowCount($count);

$paginator = new Zend_Paginator($adapter);
$paginator->setItemCountPerPage(5)
        ->setCurrentPageNumber((int) $paged);
return $paginator;
```

Once we have our count query created, we set it on the adapter using `setRowCount()`. We can then create a new `Zend_Paginator` instance and pass in the adapter. Our final bit of configuration is to set the number of items per page (`setItemCountPerPage()`), and set the current page number (`setCurrentPageNumber()`). With the paginator now fully configured, we then return it. Therefore, when pagination is used, `getProductsByCategory()` will return a `Zend_Paginator` instance rather than a `Zend_Db_Table_Rowset` instance.

Product Resource Item

Now, we need to create the Product Resource Item. This will represent a single product.

`application/modules/storefront/models/resources/Product/Item.php`

```
public function getImages()
{
    return $this->findDependentRowset(
        'Storefront_Resource_ProductImage',
        'Image'
    );
}
```

We have already determined that our products will have images. Therefore, each product item will need to be able to access the images that go along with it. The `getImages()` method gets the current item's related image rows using the `findDependentRowset()` rowset method. This works in the same way as we used `findParentRow()` in `getParentCategory()`. To find the dependent rowset, we need to specify the table class that the relationship is defined in (`Storefront_Resource_ProductImage`) and the name of the relationship we want to use (`Image`). This will return either `null` (no images found), or a `Zend_Db_Table_Rowset` instance.

application/modules/storefront/models/resources/Product/Item.php

```
public function getDefaultImage()
{
    $row = $this->findDependentRowset(
        'Storefront_Resource_ProductImage',
        'Image',
        $this->select()
            ->where('isDefault = ?', 'Yes')
            ->limit(1)
    )->current();

    return $row;
}
```

The getDefaultImage() method simply finds the default image for the current item. We can see that this works in pretty much the same way as the getImages() method. However, this time we restrict the findDependentRowset() query by passing in a Zend_Db_Select instance as the third parameter. This simply limits the query to one row where isDefault is equal to 'Yes'. As findDependentRowset() returns a Zend_Db_Table_Rowset instance, we also get the current() item from it and return a single Storefront_Resource_ProductImage_Item instance.

application/modules/storefront/models/resources/Product/Item.php

```
public function getPrice($withDiscount=true,$withTax=true)
{
    $price = $this->getRow()->price;
    if (true === $this->isDiscounted()
        && true === $withDiscount)
    {
        $discount = $this->getRow()->discountPercent;
        $discounted = ($price*$discount)/100;
        $price = round($price - $discounted, 2);
    }
    if (true === $this->isTaxable() && true === $withTax) {
        $taxService = new Storefront_Service_Taxation();
        $price = $taxService->addTax($price);
    }
    return $price;
}
```

Our product items all have a price and the price can be discounted. We also need to add tax if the item is a taxable good. The getPrice() method provides the logic to calculate the price based on these criteria.

```
$price = $this->getRow()->price;
```

To calculate the price, we first retrieve the price field from the item's table row. This gives us the base price from which we can apply our calculations.

```
if (true === $this->isDiscounted()
    && true === $withDiscount)
{
    $discount = $this->getRow()->discountPercent;
    $discounted = ($price*$discount)/100;
    $price = round($price - $discounted, 2);
}
```

Next, we need to calculate the discount that may be applied to the base price. The isDiscounted() method will return true if the discount percentage of the row is greater than zero. Also, we check the $withDiscount parameter. By default, this is set to true so that the price includes the discount. However, there maybe times when we just want the base price so we can set the $withDiscount parameter to false and skip the discount calculation.

The actual discount calculation is just a very simple percentage calculation. We get the discountPercent from the row, work out the discount amount, and finally subtract the amount from the base price setting this in the $price variable.

```
if (true === $this->isTaxable() && true === $withTax) {
    $taxService = new Storefront_Service_Taxation();
    $price = $taxService->addTax($price);
}
```

The tax calculation works in a very similar way to the discount calculation. Again, we check if the item is taxable (isTaxable()) and whether the tax calculation is wanted ($withTax). However, this time we are using a Service to calculate the tax percentage. The reason for this is mainly an example of a Service. However, Services play an important role within our Model/Domain. The idea of a Service is that they provide functionality that does not logically fit within our Model. In the case of our product, the actual calculation of tax is not really Product related. Also, tax calculation could become complex and may in the future have its own Model. For example, if the storefront was to sell to multiple regions, then tax may need to be calculated on a regional basis.

To use the taxation service, we will need to create it. All of our services for the storefront will be placed within the services directory within the storefront module directory. Let's create the taxation service now:

application/modules/storefront/services/Taxation.php

```
class Storefront_Service_Taxation
{
```

```
const TAXRATE = 15;

public function addTax($amount)
{
    $tax = ($amount*self::TAXRATE)/100;
    $amount = round($amount + $tax,2);

    return $amount;
}
}
```

The Taxation Service class is very simple. It has one class constant TAXRATE that contains the tax rate, and one method addTax() that adds the tax amount to the passed in amount.

The final two methods in the Product Resource Item are simply used to check if the item has a discount and if the item is taxable.

application/modules/storefront/models/resources/Product/Item.php

```
public function isDiscounted()
{
    return 0 == $this->getRow()->discountPercent ? false : true;
}

public function isTaxable()
{
    return 'Yes' == $this->getRow()->taxable ? true : false;
}
```

The isDiscounted() method will return true if the rows discount percentage is above 0. The isTaxable() method will return true if the rows taxable field is 'Yes'.

ProductImage Resource Item

Our final Resource Item is product image. We need to create the various images related methods for this item.

application/modules/storefront/models/resources/ProductImage/Item.php

```
public function getThumbnail()
{
    return $this->getRow()->thumbnail;
}
```

The getThumbnail() method is a simple accessor to the rows thumbnail field, which contains the filename for the thumbnail image.

application/modules/storefront/models/resources/ProductImage/Item.php

```
public function getFull()
{
    return $this->getRow()->full;
}
```

The getFull() method is a simple accessor to the rows full field, which contains the filename for the full-size image.

application/modules/storefront/models/resources/ProductImage/Item.php

```
public function isDefault()
{
    return 'Yes' === $this->getRow()->isDefault ? true : false;
}
```

The isDefault() method simply checks if the current item is the default image or not.

Catalog Model

With all our Model's resources created, we can now implement the methods in the Catalog Model skeleton we created earlier. Let's go through and implement each method in turn.

application/modules/storefront/models/Catalog.php

```
public function getCategoriesByParentId($parentID)
{
    $parentID = (int) $parentID;

    return $this->getResource('Category')
                ->getCategoriesByParentId($parentID);
}
```

This method returns all the categories that match the passed in parentId. It is used to find all the categories under another category. We first cast the $parentID parameter to an integer, and then return the output of the Category Model Resource's getCategoriesByParentId() method. To access the Category Model Resource, we use the getResource() method which is defined in the Model Abstract. By passing in the name of the Model Resource we want, the Category Model Resource instance is returned.

application/modules/storefront/models/Catalog.php

```php
    public function getCategoryByIdent($ident)
    {
        return $this->getResource('Category')
                    ->getCategoryByIdent($ident);
    }
```

Here we are doing just the same as in the `getCategoriesByParentId()` method. We simply return `getResource()`, and then return the `getCategoryByIdent()` method output.

application/modules/storefront/models/Catalog.php

```php
    public function getProductById($id)
    {
        $id = (int) $id;

        return $this->getResource('Product')->getProductById($id);
    }
```

Ok, you are probably getting the idea now. Get the Model Resource and return the Model Resource methods output. Here we are using the Product Model Resource and the `getProductById()` method:

application/modules/storefront/models/Catalog.php

```php
    public function getProductByIdent($ident)
    {
        return $this->getResource('Product')
                    ->getProductByIdent($ident);
    }
```

And again, we get the Product Model Resource and return the output of the `getProductByIdent()` method:

application/modules/storefront/models/Catalog.php

```php
    public function getProductsByCategory($category, $paged=false,
        $order=null, $deep=true)
    {
        if (is_string($category)) {
            $cat = $this->getResource('Category')
                        ->getCategoryByIdent($category);
            $categoryId = null === $cat ? 0 : $cat->categoryId;
        } else {
            $categoryId = (int) $category;
        }
```

```
if (true === $deep) {
    $ids = $this->getCategoryChildrenIds(
        $categoryId, true
    );
    $ids[] = $categoryId;
    $categoryId = null === $ids ? $categoryId : $ids;
}

return $this->getResource('Product')
            ->getProductsByCategory(
                $categoryId,
                $paged,
                $order
            );
}
```

Now this method has much more logic for us to look at. This method is used to get all products within or below a category. The method accepts the following four parameters:

- $category: Can either be an integer (categoryId) or a string (ident).
- $paged: Is a switch to either get paginated (Zend_Paginator) result or not.
- $order: Can be an array containing the order SQL clause(s).
- $deep: A switch to either get all products from a category branch or get products from a single category only.

The logic with this method is to split into three areas—getting the categoryId, getting the category children, and returning the Model Resource output.

As the $category parameter can be either a string or an integer, the first section tests if the $category is a string. If the is_string() test returns true, then we then query the Category Model Resource to get the category by its ident. If a Category is found for that ident, then we extract the categoryId from it and set it in the $categoryId variable. Conversely, if the is_string() test return false, then we simply set the $categoryId variable to the $category parameters value.

The second section is only executed if the $deep parameter is true. If it is, then we use the getCategoryChildrenIds() method to get an array containing all the category IDs that are below the category being queried. This functionality will become much clearer when we implement the controllers and views.

The third section simply returns the output of the Product Model Resource's `getProductsByCategory()` method, just like in the previous methods.

`application/modules/storefront/models/Catalog.php`

```php
public function getCategoryChildrenIds($categoryId,
        $recursive = false)
{
    $categories = $this->getCategoriesByParentId($categoryId);
    $cats = array();

    foreach ($categories as $category) {
        $cats[] = $category->categoryId;
        if (true === $recursive) {
            $cats = array_merge(
                $cats,
                $this->getCategoryChildrenIds(
                    $category->categoryId, true
                )
            );
        }
    }

    return $cats;
}
```

This method is a helper method used by the previous `getProductsByCategory()` method. It accepts the following two parameters:

- `$categoryId`: The categoryId of the category that we want the child category IDs from.
- `$recursive`: Whether we want to recursively get the category IDs or not.

We use this method to recursively get an array of the category IDs that are below the given category.

`application/modules/storefront/models/Catalog.php`

```php
public function getParentCategories($category)
{
    $cats = array($category);

    if (0 == $category->parentId) {
        return $cats;
    }

    $parent = $category->getParentCategory();
    $cats[] = $parent;
```

```
        if (0 != $parent->parentId) {
            $cats = array_merge(
                $cats,
                $this->getParentCategories($parent)
            );
        }

        return $cats;
    }
```

The getParentCategories() works in the opposite direction as the getCategoryChildrenIds(), going up the category tree instead of down. Again, we use recursion to traverse the category tree by having the method call itself. Additionally, this method returns actual category items rather than an ID array.

Loading Models and other assets

Before we create our Controllers, we are going to need to configure the autoloader to load our Models and other assets.

Configuring the Autoloader

We now have all our Models, Model Resources, and services created. However, we will need a way to load these classes when they are required. To do this, we are going to use the Zend_Application_Module_Autoloader component. This component is a subclass of the Zend_Loader_Autoloader_Resource component that we looked at in Chapter 4. The Zend_Application_Module_Autoloader provides a convenient way to create an autoloader for a particular module as it comes with a standard set of autoloader resource types preconfigured.

To enable the module autoloader, we need to add a bootstrap class resource to the Bootstrap class. Add the following resource **after** the logging resource:

application/bootstrap/Bootstrap.php

```
    protected function _initDefaultModuleAutoloader()
    {
        $this->_logger->info('Bootstrap ' . __METHOD__);

        $this->_resourceLoader = new
                Zend_Application_Module_Autoloader(array(
                    'namespace' => 'Storefront',
                    'basePath'  => APPLICATION_PATH .
                        '/modules/storefront',
        )));
```

```
$this->_resourceLoader->addResourceTypes(array(
    'modelResource' => array(
        'path'      => 'models/resources',
        'namespace' => 'Resource',
    ),
    'service' => array(
        'path'      => 'services',
        'namespace' => 'Service',
    ),
));
}
```

Our `DefaultModuleAutoloader` bootstrap resource first instantiates a new
`Zend_Application_Module_Autoloader` instance, assigning it to the protected
`$_resourceLoader` property. During instantiation, we pass in an array of options
defining the `namespace` and `basePath` from which the autoloader will operate. In
this case, this is `Storefront` and the path to the storefront module directory. The
autoloader will now be registered and will have the default resource types added.
The default resource types are as follows:

Autoloader Resource	Namespace	Path
dbtable	Storefront_Model_DbTable	APPLICATION_PATH . '/modules/storefront/models/DbTable'
form	Storefront_Form	APPLICATION_PATH . '/modules/storefront/forms'
model	Storefront_Model	APPLICATION_PATH . '/modules/storefront/models'
plugin	Storefront_Plugin	APPLICATION_PATH . '/modules/storefront/plugins'
api	Storefront_Api	APPLICATION_PATH . '/modules/storefront/apis'

After we have instantiated `Zend_Application_Module_Autoloader`, we need
to customize the default set of autoloader resource types and add two new types
using the `addResourceTypes()` method. The types we add are `modelResource`
and `service`. These will be used to autoload our Model Resources and Services
respectively. The new resource types will have the following properties:

Autoloader Resource	Namespace	Path
modelResource	Storefront_Resource	APPLICATION_PATH . '/modules/storefront/models/resources'
service	Storefront_Service	APPLICATION_PATH . '/modules/storefront/services'

The Zend_Db_Table bug

The autoloader will now automatically include any class the first time it is used. We assume this will also work for classes that `Zend_Db_Table` needs when it loads dependent table classes. However, this is not the case. All `Zend_Db_Table` components explicitly use `Zend_Loader::loadClass()` to load their dependent classes. Currently, the `loadClass()` method does not trigger the autoloader, meaning that we need to explicitly include any class that a `Zend_Db_Table` class requires.

As a workaround to this issue, we need to edit our Model Resources. Add the following to the top of each Model Resource file.

application/modules/storefront/models/resources/Category.php

```
if (!class_exists('Storefront_Resource_Category_Item')) {
    require_once dirname(__FILE__) . '/Category/Item.php';
}
```

application/modules/storefront/models/resources/Product.php

```
if (!class_exists('Storefront_Resource_ProductImage')) {
    require_once dirname(__FILE__) . '/ProductImage.php';
}

if (!class_exists('Storefront_Resource_Product_Item')) {
    require_once dirname(__FILE__) . '/Product/Item.php';
}
```

application/modules/storefront/models/resources/ProductImage.php

```
if (!class_exists('Storefront_Resource_ProductImage_Item')) {
    require_once dirname(__FILE__) . '/ProductImage/Item.php';
}

if (!class_exists('Storefront_Resource_Product')) {
    require_once dirname(__FILE__) . '/Product.php';
}
```

Here we have added a `require_once` statement to each file that includes the classes, that the Model Resource depends on. For example, `Storefront_Resource_Product` class needs to have its corresponding Resource Item (`Storefront_Resource_Product_Item`) included as well as the `productImage` table class that it uses when finding dependent image rows from the database. We also wrap the `require_once` statement in a `class_exists` if statement. The `class_exists` function will check the autoloader for the class, meaning that the `require_once` will not be called and will save us processing time as `require_once` is slow.

Hopefully, this issue will be fixed in later versions of the Zend Framework. It is worth checking this before applying the workaround.

Creating the Catalog Controllers

It is time to move on to our Action Controllers. Remember that we are using the Fat Model Skinny Controller method. As a result, our controllers are very simple and merely pass information to the Models and Views.

CategoryController

The CategoryController is used to populate our static top-level category menu, which is situated in the lefthand column of the main template. This list needs to be populated at each request because it appears on all of the pages. To achieve this, we are going to use the Action Stack Plugin and the Response Object.

> The Action Stack can be performance-degrading. See the *Storefront Optimization* chapter for details.

application/modules/storefront/controllers/CategoryController.php

```
class Storefront_CategoryController extends Zend_Controller_Action
{
    public function indexAction()
    {
        $id = $this->_getParam('categoryId', 0);
        $catalogModel = new Storefront_Model_Catalog();

        $this->view->categories =
            $catalogModel->getCategoriesByParentId($id);

        $this->_helper
            ->viewRenderer
            ->setResponseSegment(
                $this->_getParam('responseSegment')
            );
    }
}
```

Here we have a standard Action Controller, just as we created earlier for the Hello Zend application. The Storefront_CategoryController has only one action, (indexAction). This will control our top-level category menu population.

Looking at the indexAction, we see that we first get the categoryId parameter assigning it to the $id variable using the _getParam() method. We also specify a default value of 0 (zero) to the _getParam() call so that if the categoryId parameter is not set, it will default to the top-level categories where they all have parentId of 0 (zero).

Next, we instantiate a new Storefront_Model_Catalog instance and assign it to the $catalogModel variable. This class will be automatically loaded by the autoloader we configured earlier.

Once we have the Catalog Model instance, we can then assign the category list to the view. We do this by calling the getCategoriesByParentId() method and assigning its returned value to the categories view variable. The return type of the getCategoiresByParentId() method will be a Zend_Db_Table_Rowset instance. We will use this later to iterate over the records stored inside the row object to produce our menu in the View.

The final part of the indexAction is different from what you would usually find in a normal Controller. As the category top-level menu will be global in our application, we don't want to accidentally overwrite the $this->view->categories property. Therefore, we need a way to segregate the top-level menu data from all the other views. We do this using a Response Object Segment. We have covered these briefly in Chapter 2, so let's look at how we use them:

```
$this->_helper
    ->viewRenderer
    ->setResponseSegment(
        $this->_getParam('responseSegment')
    );
```

To write to a Response Segment from within an Action Controller, we use the viewRenderer Action Helper's setResponseSegment() method. This method accepts one parameter, $name. This should be a string containing the name of the segment we want to write to. The viewRenderer will then write the output of the Action to the named Response Segment in the Response Object.

For extra flexibility we have inserted a user parameter, responseSegment, to specify the segment name. We can then easily change the segment without needing to change our Action Controller.

Action Stack Front Controller Plugin

Now that we have a Controller for the category top-level menu, we are going to need a way to call it on every request. For this, we are going to use the Action Stack.

The Action Stack is an extension of the Request Dispatch process. Its purpose is to contain a stack of requests that will be executed once the normal requests have finished. Therefore, it is processed at the postDispatch event in the Front Controller. It will not be processed until all normal requests are completed. If we forward a request, it will wait until that has been completed before the Action Stack is processed.

As we want to add to the Action Stack on each request, we are going to create a Front Controller Plugin that hooks into the dispatchLoopStartup hook:

library/SF/Plugin/Action.php

```
class SF_Plugin_Action extends Zend_Controller_Plugin_Abstract
{
  protected $_stack;
    public function
dispatchLoopStartup(Zend_Controller_Request_Abstract $request)
    {
        $stack = $this->getStack();

        // category menu
        $categoryRequest = new Zend_Controller_Request_Simple();
        $categoryRequest->setControllerName('category')
                        ->setActionName('index')
                        ->setParam(
                            'responseSegment',
                            'categoryMain'
                        );
        // push requests into the stack
        $stack->pushStack($categoryRequest);
    }
    public function getStack()
    {
        if (null === $this->_stack) {
            $front = Zend_Controller_Front::getInstance();
            if (!$front->hasPlugin(
                    'Zend_Controller_Plugin_ActionStack'
            )) {
                $stack = new Zend_Controller_Plugin_ActionStack();
                $front->registerPlugin($stack);
            } else {
                $stack = $front->getPlugin('ActionStack');
            }
            $this->_stack = $stack;
        }
        return $this->_stack;
    }
}
```

Our SF_PluginAction class has two methods, dispatchLoopStartup() and getStack(), which hook into the dispatchLoopStartup hook and get the Action Stack plugin from the Front Controller respectively. If we look at the dispatchLoopStartup() method, we first see that, we get the Action Stack plugin and assign it to the $stack variable. We then create a new instance of the Zend_Controller_Request_Simple class. This class is the most basic Request Object available in the Zend Framework, and we use it because we do not want all the extra functionality related to the HTTP Request Object type. Once we have the Request instance, we create our request:

```
$categoryRequest->setControllerName('category')
                ->setActionName('index')
                ->setParam(
                    'responseSegment',
                    'categoryMain'
                );
```

Here, we set the Action Controller to call using setControllerName(), set the Action to call using setActionName(), and set the user parameter that specifies the name of the Response Segment using setParam(). This will then give the Dispatcher all the information it needs to execute our request.

The final job is to add the newly created Request Object to the Action Stack using $stack->pushStack($categoryRequest). When adding to the Action Stack, it is important to remember that the stack is executed using a **Last In First Out (LIFO)** order.

With our Front Controller Plugin created, we have one small job to do before it will work. We need to register the plugin with the Front Controller. To do this, add the following to the store.ini file.

application/config/store.ini

```
resources.frontcontroller.moduledirectory = APPLICATION_PATH"/modules"
resources.frontcontroller.defaultmodule = "storefront"
resources.frontcontroller.throwerrors = false
resources.frontcontroller.params.prefixDefaultModule = true
resources.frontcontroller.plugins.action = "SF_Plugin_Action"
```

In this case, we simply add a new option to the frontcontroller bootstrap plugin resource plugins. This option accepts an array of Front Controller Plugin classes to register.

CatalogController

The CatalogController is our main Controller and contains the majority of our control logic for the storefront (currently) and is responsible for the listing and viewing of products. To start, let's create the basic structure and add each action one at a time.

application/modules/storefront/controllers/CatalogController.php

```
class Storefront_CatalogController extends Zend_Controller_Action
{
    protected $_catalogModel;

    public function init()
    {
        $this->_catalogModel = new Storefront_Model_Catalog();
    }
}
```

This is our basic controller structure. We have a protected the $_catalogModel property and a single init() method. The init() method is a Zend Framework standard and is called every time the Action Controller class is instantiated. Therefore, we use this to set up our controller-wide properties. In the Catalog Controller's case, we use init() to set the $_catalogModel property. To this property, we assign a new Storefront_Model_Catalog instance.

With the basic structure created, let's add the Actions.

application/modules/storefront/controllers/CatalogController.php

```
public function indexAction()
{
    $products = $this->_catalogModel->getProductsByCategory(
        $this->_getParam('categoryIdent', 0),
        $this->_getParam('page', 1),
        array('name')
    );
    $category = $this->_catalogModel
                    ->getCategoryByIdent(
                        $this->_getParam('categoryIdent', '')
                    );

    if (null === $category) {
        throw new SF_Exception_404(
            'Unknown category ' .
            $this->_getParam('categoryIdent')
        );
```

```
        }

        $subs = $this->_catalogModel
                        ->getCategoriesByParentId(
                            $category->categoryId
                        );
        $this->getBreadcrumb($category);

        $this->view->assign(array(
            'category' => $category,
            'subCategories' => $subs,
            'products' => $products
            )
        );
    }
```

The `indexAction` is responsible for listing our products. It also needs to page these results and filter them by category. Our first task then is to get the products from the Model and assign them to the `$products` variable. We do this by calling the Catalog Models `getProductsByCategory()` method and passing in three parameters. This will return all products in the current category, plus any products contained within this category subcategories.

The parameters here are important. For the first parameter, we pass in `$this->_getParam('categoryIdent', 0)`, which will get the `categoryIdent` user parameter from the URI. Therefore, our URI will look something like /catalog/ aCategoryIdent. For the second parameter, we pass in `$this->_getParam('page', 1)`. This will get the current page for the paginator to use. Therefore, our URI will look like /catalog/aCategoryIdent/page/1. The third parameter is an array containing the order by field(s). In this case, we have hardcoded it to order by the name field. For the user parameters to work, we will need to create some routes that the router can use to match our URIs. We will create these shortly. For now, let's look at the rest of the `indexAction`.

We need to get the category so that our view can display its name, and so that we can throw a 404 exception if the category does not exist. We do this by calling the `getCategoryByIdent()` method and passing in the `categoryIdent` user parameter. Then, we need to check if the result is null. If it is, then we throw an `SF_Exception_404` exception. This exception is contained within the SF library. For this to work, we also need to edit the `ErrorController` so that it knows what to do with this exception type. Add the following to the errorAction's switch statement:

application/modules/storefront/controllers/ErrorController.php

```
case 'SF_Exception_404':
    // send 404
    $this->getResponse()
        ->setRawHeader('HTTP/1.1 404 Not Found');
    $this->view->message = $errors->exception->getMessage();
    break;
```

Going back to the Catalog Controllers `indexAction`, our next task is to fetch the current categories subcategories. To do this, we again access our Model to retrieve the data. We call the `getCategoriesByParentId()` method and pass in the current categories `categoryId` field (`$category->categoryId`), storing the result in the `$subs` variable.

Our listing will also need a breadcrumb so the user can easily navigate the catalog structure. To retrieve the breadcrumb data, we use the `getBreadcrumb()` method passing in the `$category` object. When we call the `getBreadcrumb()` method, it will assign the `bread` View property for us.

Our final task is to assign all the data to the View. We do this by using the `assign()` method, which accepts a match-pair array of variables to assign to the View. With this done, our View now has access to all the data we retrieved earlier.

application/modules/storefront/controllers/CatalogController.php

```
public function viewAction()
{
    $product = $this->_catalogModel->getProductByIdent(
        $this->_getParam('productIdent', 0)
    );

    if (null === $product) {
        throw new SF_Exception_404('Unknown product ' .
            $this->_getParam('productIdent'));
    }

    $category = $this->_catalogModel->getCategoryByIdent(
        $this->_getParam('categoryIdent', '')
    );
    $this->getBreadcrumb($category);

    $this->view->assign(array(
        'product' => $product,
        )
    );
}
```

The `viewAction` is very similar to the `indexAction` and is responsible for displaying the product information to the user. The main operation is to get the product information from the database using the `getProductByIdent()` method. To do this, we pass in the `productIdent` user parameter. Again, the user parameter will be taken from the URI. This means our URIs will look similar to `/catalog/aCategoryIdent/aProductIdent`. The product object will be stored in the `$product` variable. We check if this is null, and if it is, we throw another 404 exception. After this, just like in the `indexAction`, we get the current category by its ident and use this to retrieve the breadcrumb data. We then simply assign the `$product` object to the View.

`application/modules/storefront/controllers/CatalogController.php`

```
public function getBreadcrumb($category)
{
    $this->view->bread = $this->_catalogModel
                            ->getParentCategories($category);
}
```

As mentioned earlier, the `getBreadcrumb()` method is a helper used by the `indexAction` and `viewAction` methods. It simply sets the list of parent categories for the current category in the bread View property.

Storefront routes

To access, and pass in the correct variables to our Controllers, we need to create some routes that parse the URI to retrieve this information. We will need to create a new method within the Bootstrap class that configures the routes and adds them into the Router.

`application/bootstrap/Bootstrap.php`

```
protected function _initRoutes()
{
    $this->_logger->info('Bootstrap ' . __METHOD__);
    $this->bootstrap('frontController');

    $router = $this->frontController->getRouter();

    // catalog category product route
    $route = new Zend_Controller_Router_Route(
        'catalog/:categoryIdent/:productIdent',
        array(
            'action'        => 'view',
            'controller'    => 'catalog',
            'module'        => 'storefront',
```

```
                'categoryIdent' => '',
            ),
            array(
                'categoryIdent' => '[a-zA-Z-_0-9]+',
                'productIdent'  => '[a-zA-Z-_0-9]+'
            )
        );

        $router->addRoute('catalog_category_product', $route);

        // catalog category route
        $route = new Zend_Controller_Router_Route(
            'catalog/:categoryIdent/:page',
            array(
                'action'        => 'index',
                'controller'    => 'catalog',
                'module'        => 'storefront',
                'categoryIdent' => '',
                'page'          => 1
            ),
            array(
                'categoryIdent' => '[a-zA-Z-_0-9]+',
                'page'          => '\d+'
            )
        );

        $router->addRoute('catalog_category', $route);
    }
```

Here we have added a new bootstrap class resource called Routes. This resource will add two routes for use: catalog_category_product and catalog_category.

The first route will match the URIs to display our product information, for example, catalog/scarves/a-silk-scarf. To define the route, we instantiate a new Zend_Controller_Router_Route route passing in the route definition, which states that:

- The first segment must be the string catalog
- The second segment must be a string that matches the regex [a-zA-Z-_0-9]+, will be stored in the categoryIdent user parameter, and will default to an empty string
- The third segment must be a string that matches the regex [a-zA-Z-_0-9]+ and will be stored in the productIdent user parameter
- If the URI is matched, then the request should be routed to the view Action of the Catalog Controller in the storefront module

The second route matches our product listing and defines that:

- The first segment must be the string catalog
- The second segment must be a string that matches the regex [a-zA-Z-_0-9]+, will be stored in the categoryIdent user parameter, and will default to an empty string
- The third segment must be a number and will be stored in the page user parameter and defaults to 1 (one)
- If the URI is matched, then the request should be routed to the index Action of the Catalog Controller in the storefront module

> When adding routes, beware of the order in which you add them. Routes are matched in LIFO order. This means that you should put most generic at the top and the least generic at the bottom.

Once the routes are defined, we need to add them to the Router. We do this by using the addRoute() method. This method accepts two parameters, the name of the route and the route instance. The naming of the route is very important, as we will use it later when creating links in our views. A good practice is to name them so that they describe what they match.

Creating the Catalog Views

We are reaching the end of our implementation now. All that is left to do is make the Views display the information. The Views are generally straightforward, so we will try to get through them as quickly as possible and cover just the important points as we go along. In addition, the HTML does not format nicely in print, so you may find it easier to open the View files in your editor to get a clearer picture.

Category views

Let's start by creating the category view that shows the category menu items:

application/modules/storefront/views/scripts/category/index.phtml

```
<div class="sub-nav">
<h3>select <span>category</span></h3>
    <ul>
        <? foreach ($this->categories as $category): ?>
        <li><a href="<?=$this->url(array('categoryIdent'
                    => $category->ident), 'catalog_category',
                    true );?>"><?=$category->name; ?></a></li>
        <? endforeach; ?>
    </ul>
</div>
```

The category `index.phtml` script is rendered by the Category Controller. This view iterates over the categories property that contains `Storefront_Resource_Category_Item` instances and creates the top-level category menu.

The most important part of this is the way we create our URIs for the anchor tags `href` attribute. For this we use the URL View Helper.

```
$this->url(array(
        'categoryIdent' => $category->ident
    ),
    'catalog_category',
    true
);
```

When we link to a category, we want it to be in the format that our routes we created earlier can match. The first parameter we pass is an array containing the user parameters to set in the route. In this case, it is `categoryIdent`. The second parameter is the name of the route to create the URL from. This will then go back to the route and create the URL from it. The final parameter tells the route to replace the route defaults with the passed in user parameters.

Catalog views

Next, let's create a Catalog view:

`application/modules/storefront/views/scripts/category/index.phtml`

```
<h3><?= $this->Escape($this->category->name); ?></h3>
<p>
    <?= $this->breadcrumb(); ?>
</p>
<? foreach($this->products as $product):  ?>
<div class="productitem clearfix">
    <?=$this->productImage($product->defaultImage, array('class'
      => 'right'))->thumbnail(); ?>
    <h4><a href="<?=$this->url(array('productIdent'
        => $product->ident,
                        'categoryIdent' => $this->category->ident),
                        'catalog_category_product');
  ?>"><?=$this->Escape($product->name); ?></a></h4>
    <p><?=$this->Escape($product->shortDescription); ?></p>
    <p><?=$this->productPrice($product); ?></p>
</div>
<? endforeach; ?>
<? if($this->products instanceof Zend_Paginator): ?>
<?= $this->paginationControl($this->products,
                        'Sliding',
                        'catalog/_paginator.phtml'); ?>
<? endif ?>
```

The Catalog `index.phtml` script is used to display our product listing. This is split into the following four parts:

- **Displaying the current category**: This is simple and all we need to do is echo out the `$this->category->name` property, while making sure that we escape the output.

- **Displaying the breadcrumb**: To display it, we use the breadcrumb View Helper, a custom Helper that we will create shortly.

- **Displaying the product**: This works in exactly the same way as the categories. We iterate over the Views product's property using the URL helper to create the links to the product items. We also use other custom View Helpers, productPrice, and productImage. The productPrice helper is used to display the price information including things like discounts and so on, and the productImage helper is used to fetch the correct product image.

- **Displaying the pagination links**: This checks if the products View property is an instance of the `Zend_Pagintor` class. If it is, then we use the paginationControl View Helper to display the pagination controls. The pagination control requires a view script that contains the controls HTML. We place this inside the catalog view directory. The script is taken directly from the online reference manual and the only modification we make is to add the route name into the URL Helper calls. **You will need to copy this file from the example files**.

application/modules/storefront/views/scripts/category/view.phtml

```
<?=$this->productImage($this->product->defaultImage, array('class'
    => 'right'))->full(); ?>
<h3><?=$this->Escape($this->product->name); ?></h3>
<p>
    <?= $this->breadcrumb($this->product); ?>
</p>

<div>
    <p><?=$this->product->description; ?></p>
    <p><?=$this->productPrice($this->product); ?></p>
</div>

<div class="clearfix">
    <? foreach ($this->product->images as $image): ?>
        <? if (!$image->isDefault()): ?>
            <?=$this->productImage($image, array('class' => 'left'))
            ->thumbnail(); ?>
        <? endif; ?>
    <? endforeach; ?>
</div>
```

The Catalog `view.phtml` script is used to display single product's information. Here, we are echoing out the `Storefront_Resource_Product_Item` instances properties, stored within the Views product property. One important operation is when we get the product's images using `foreach ($this->product->images as $image)`. This is using the lazy loading functionality `SF_Model_Resource_Db_Table_Row_Abstract`. When we access the images property on the `Storefront_Resource_Product_Item` instance, it will proxy to the `getImages()` method and will automatically fetch the related image data for us.

`application/layouts/scripts/main.phtml`

```
<div id="contentWrap" class="clearfix">
    <div class="left categorylist">
        <?= $this->layout()->categoryMain; ?>
        <? if (0 < count($this->subCategories)):?>
        <div class="sub-nav">
        <h3>in this <span>category</span></h3>
            <ul>
            <? foreach ($this->subCategories as $category): ?>
            <li><a href="<?=$this->url(array('categoryIdent'
                => $category->ident), 'catalog_category', true
                );?>"><?=$category->name; ?></a></li>
            <? endforeach; ?>
            </ul>
        </div>
        <? endif; ?>
    </div>
    <div class="content left">
        <?= $this->layout()->content ?>
    </div>
</div>
```

To complete our view creation, we need to edit the main layout script. Here, we have added the top-level category menu, and the subcategory menu. To render the top-level menu, we echo out the Response Segment that we created in the Category Controller using `$this->layout()->categoryMain;`. To render the subcategory menu, we first check if the subCategory's View property is set, and then simply iterate over it to create the subcategory menu.

Catalog View Helpers

During our View creation, we have used various View Helpers. We will need to create these helpers for our Views to function. View Helpers are used to encapsulate common View-related tasks, and help keep our Views tidy and reduce the amount of duplication.

View Helper creation

The creation of a View Helper is very easy. At the minimum, all we need to do is subclass the `Zend_View_Helper_Abstract` and name the class correctly. For the storefront, all our View Helpers are stored within `application/modules/storefront/views/helpers`. Paths can also be customized, or added, through the View instance.

Example View Helper—`Myhelper.php`

```
class Zend_View_Helper_Myhelper extends Zend_View_Helper_Abstract
{
    public function myhelper()
    {
        // code here...
    }
}
```

Here we have created a basic View Helper example. This has the following three important aspects to it:

- It subclasses the `Zend_View_Helper_Abstract` class. We can also subclass other View Helpers and extend their functionality.

- It is prefixed with the `Zend_View_Helper_` prefix. Prefixes can also be customized.

- It has a public method that has the same name as the Helper (MyHelper), and the filename matches the class name (minus the prefix).

Best practices

A common question about View Helpers is whether they can access Models directly. The short answer is, yes they can. However, there are some important rules to follow when dealing with View and Models. If we go back to our Application Stack, we remember that User Interface is at the top of the stack and the Domain/Model is below this and that dependencies go in a downward direction. Therefore, it is fine for our View to depend on a Model, but a Model should not depend on a View. From this we can surmise the general rule of thumb that:

- View Helpers can instantiate Models and use them

- View to Model access should be encapsulated within a View Helper

- Views should not update the Model (this would create an upwards dependency)

- View to Model access should be avoided if at all possible, and should be well documented

Creating the Catalog View Helpers

Let's now look at the storefront's View Helpers. We will again go through as quickly as possible, looking at the important parts used within the View Helpers, as most of the logic is created by HTML.

application/modules/storefront/views/helpers/Breadcrumb.php

```
class Zend_View_Helper_Breadcrumb extends Zend_View_Helper_Abstract
{
    public function breadcrumb($product = null)
    {
        if ($this->view->bread) {
            $bread = $this->view->bread;
            $crumbs = array();
            $bread = array_reverse($bread);

            foreach ($bread as $category) {
                $href = $this->view->url(array(
                    'categoryIdent' => $category->ident,
                    ),
                    'catalog_category'
                );
                $crumbs[] = '<a href="' . $href . '">' .
                    $this->view->Escape($category->name) . '</a>';
            }

            if (null !== $product) {
                $crumbs[] = $this->view->Escape($product->name);
            }

            return join(' &raquo; ', $crumbs);
        }
    }
}
```

The breadcrumb Helper is used to create the HTML for the breadcrumb navigation. We can see that we automatically have access to the View from our Helpers through the Helper's view property (`$this->view`). This also means that we can use other View Helpers from within our Helper. For example, we use the URL View Helper to create our links, and the Escape View Helper to escape our output (`$this->view->url()` and `$this->view->Escape()`).

application/modules/storefront/views/helpers/ProductImage.php

```
class Zend_View_Helper_ProductImage extends
Zend_View_Helper_HtmlElement
{
    protected $_image;
```

```
    protected $_attribs;

public function productImage(Storefront_Resource_ProductImage_Item
$image = null, $attribs = false)
    {
        $this->_image = $image;
        $this->_attribs = $attribs;
        return $this;
    }

    public function thumbnail()
    {
        if (null !== $this->_image) {
            return $this->_createImgTag($this->_image->thumbnail);
        }
    }


    public function full()
    {
        if (null !== $this->_image) {
            return $this->_createImgTag($this->_image->full);
        }
    }


    protected function _createImgTag($file)
    {
        if ($this->_attribs) {
            $attribs = $this->_htmlAttribs($this->_attribs);
        } else {
            $attribs = '';
        }

        $tag = 'img src="' . $this->view->baseUrl('images/product/'
                . $file) . '" ';
        return '<' . $tag . $attribs . $this->getClosingBracket()
                . self::EOL;
    }
}
```

The productImage Helper is used to create an img HTML tag for our product
images. This helper differs from our previous example because this time, we subclass
the Zend_View_Helper_HtmlElement class. The HtmlElement Helper is a standard
helper that is included with the Zend Framework and provides functionality to help
create HTML elements. By subclassing it, we gain access to ways to easily handle
things like HTML attributes, and so on.

The first thing to note in this helper is that in the `productImage()` method, we return a reference of the helper (`$this`). By doing this, we can provide access to other public methods within the helper. For example, we can access the `full()` method from within our View scripts using `$this->productImage()->full()`. Have another look at the View scripts for the full usage.

The second thing to note is the protected `_createImgTag()` method. This method will actually create the HTML for us and uses some of its parent class functionality. The first method we use is `_htmlAttribs()`. This method accepts an array containing a matched-pair array of HTML attributes and will return a string ready to use in our tag. Next, we have the `getClosingBracket()` method. This will close our tag and use the correct method for the doctype we have set for our View.

We also use the BaseUrl View Helper. I have taken this from a proposal by Geoffrey Tran and Robin Skoglund. This helper simply makes sure that when we link to files, the path will be correct. **When doing this, remember to copy this helper from the example files**.

application/modules/storefront/views/helpers/ProductPrice.php

```
class Zend_View_Helper_ProductPrice extends Zend_View_Helper_Abstract
{
    public function productPrice(Storefront_Resource_Product_Item
                                 $product)
    {
        $currency = new Zend_Currency();
        $formatted = $currency->toCurrency($product->getPrice());

        if ($product->isDiscounted()) {
            $formatted .= ' was <del>' . $currency->
                toCurrency($product->getPrice(false)) . '</del>';
        }

        return $formatted;
    }
}
```

Our final helper is used to display the price of a product. When displaying the price, we want two things, to display the currency symbol and to display any discount. To help display the price correctly, we are using `Zend_Currency`. `Zend_Currency` is a locale aware component that will display the correct currency symbol and formatting for the current locale. Therefore, to use `Zend_Currency`, we need to configure our locale, which we do in the `Boostrap` class.

application/boostrap/bootstrap.php

```
protected function _initLocale()
{
    $this->_logger->info('Bootstrap ' . __METHOD__);
```

```
$locale = new Zend_Locale('en_GB');
Zend_Registry::set('Zend_Locale', $locale);
}
```

Here, we simply instantiate a new `Zend_Locale` instance by passing in our required locale and then adding the instance to the registry. By adding the locale instance to the registry using the `Zend_Locale` key, all Zend Framework components that are locale aware will now use this instance.

Building and running the storefront

With our implementation complete, we can now run a build and see if everything has worked. Again to run a build, simply change into the build directory and run the ant command.

We should then be able to browse our local machine, and if everything goes well, then we should see the following screenshot:

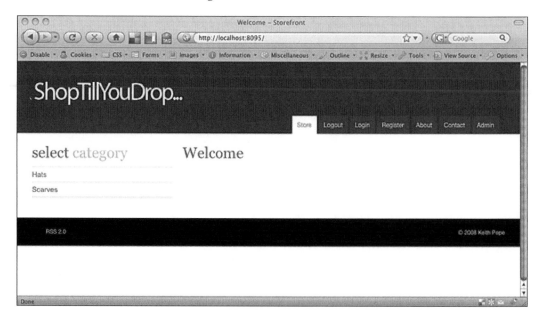

Additionally, we should now be able to browse our product catalog:

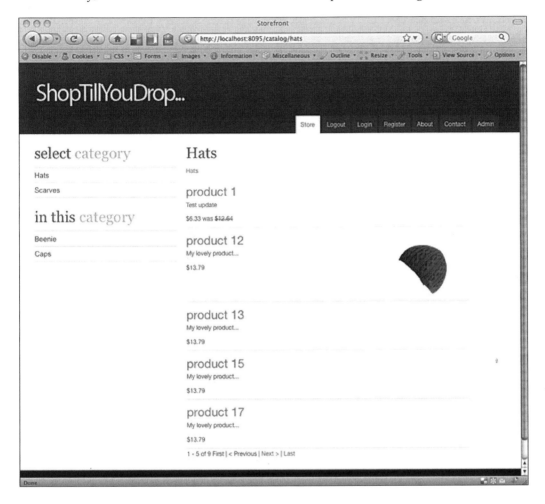

Summary

Hurray, we have a working application! It has been a long one but it was all worth it in the end. We have covered a lot here, so let's recap the major topics we have covered.

The implementation of the Model and its Resources took up the majority of this chapter. Here, we looked at creating Model Data Sources using `Zend_Db_Table`; creating Model Resources so that we can implement the has-a relationship between the Model, Model Resources and Data Sources, and finally creating the Model. This was by far the most important part of this chapter, and maybe even the book. These classes, and their design, form the heart of our application and the conventions used here will be used throughout the rest of the book. Take some time to digest the process we undertook to create our Model. It can be a little daunting to start with, but we will be implementing more Models in the coming chapters so we will get plenty of practice!

We also created our Catalog Controllers, and tried to keep to the Fat Model Skinny Controller methodology. We pushed as much functionality as possible into the Model, used the Controllers to simply call the Model methods, and assign data to the View. We also looked at how we can have global elements such as the top-level category menu by using the Action Stack and a Front Controller Plugin.

Our final task was to implement the Views so that we could display the data set by our Controllers. We looked at how to create Views scripts and View Helpers to encapsulate common behavior shared among our Views.

Now that we have our Catalog working, we can move on to create the Customer related functionality for the storefront.

6
Implementing User Accounts

With our main Catalog functionality completed, we are going to move on and create the user functionality. The main task here is to provide users with a way to register at the Storefront so that they can purchase products.

In this chapter, we will cover:

- Implementing the user model and resources
- Implementing the Customer Controller
- Using Zend_Form to create forms
- Implementing the Customer Views

As we can see, this follows very much the same process as Chapter 5. The main focus here is to cover the Zend_Form component and persist our Model data.

Creating the user model and resources

To start us off, we are going to create the user model and its related resources. This will be exactly as we did in Chapter 5 when we created the Catalog Model. The good news is, now that we understand how the Model's and Resources work, we can create our Model very quickly.

User model

First, we create a new file in our `models` directory called `User.php` containing the `Storefront_Model_User` class.

application/modules/storefront/models/User.php

```
class Storefront_Model_User extends SF_Model_Abstract
{
    public function getUserById($id)
    {
        $id = (int) $id;
        return $this->getResource('User')->getUserById($id);
    }

    public function getUserByEmail($email, $ignoreUser=null)
    {
        return $this->getResource('User')
                    ->getUserByEmail($email, $ignoreUser);
    }

    public function getUsers($paged=false, $order=null)
    {
        return $this->getResource('User')
                    ->getUsers($paged, $order);
    }

    public function registerUser($post)
    {
        $form = $this->getForm('userRegister');
        return $this->_save(
            $form,
            $post,
            array('role' => 'Customer')
        );
    }

    public function saveUser($post)
    {
        $form = $this->getForm('userEdit');
        return $this->_save($form, $post);
    }

    protected function _save(Zend_Form $form, array $info,
                            $defaults=array())
    {
        if (!$form->isValid($info)) {
            return false;
        }
        // get filtered values
```

```php
        $data = $form->getValues();

        // password hashing
        if (array_key_exists('passwd', $data)
            && '' != $data['passwd']
        ) {
            $data['salt'] = md5($this->createSalt());
            $data['passwd'] = sha1($data['passwd']
                            .$data['salt']);
        } else {
            unset($data['passwd']);
        }

        // apply any defaults
        foreach ($defaults as $col => $value) {
            $data[$col] = $value;
        }

        $user = array_key_exists('userId', $data) ?
            $this->getResource('User')
                ->getUserById($data['userId']) : null;

        return $this->getResource('User')
                    ->saveRow($data, $user);
    }
    private function createSalt()
    {
        $salt = '';
        for ($i = 0; $i < 50; $i++) {
            $salt .= chr(rand(33, 126));
        }
        return $salt;
    }
}
```

The user model contains the following methods:

- getUserById(): Fetches a user matched by the userId field
- getUserByEmail(): Fetches a user matched by the email field. Optionally, this method accepts a second parameter that specifies a User to not match
- getUsers(): Fetches all users
- saveUser(): Creates or updates a User row in the database
- registerUser(): Registers a new user
- save(): Used internally to perform insert/updates
- createSalt(): Creates a salt string to use when hashing our passwords

The `getUserById()`, `getUserByEmail()`, and `getUsers()` methods are all very much like the previous Catalog Model methods, and simply return the output of the User Model Resource. Therefore, we will concentrate on the methods that are used to create and update our users, `registerUser()`, `saveUser()`, and `save()`.

When saving User data, we are going to have the following four different contexts when performing these actions:

1. A User registers to the site
2. A registered User edits their details
3. An administrator adds a new User
4. An administrator updates a User's details

To accommodate these rules, we have three data saving methods, `registerUser()`, `saveUser()`, and `save()`. The reason we use three methods is so that we can have different input filtering, validation, and default values that meet our contextual requirements.

The `registerUser()` method will be used when a new user registers to the site. This method accepts one parameter, `$post`, which will contain the HTTP POST data sent from the registration form. If we look at the `registerUser()` methods body, we see that we first get a `Zend_Form` instance using the `getForm()` method. This method is defined in the `SF_Model_Abstract` class and simply instantiates the requested form class for us (in this case, this is the `Storefront_Form_User_Register` class). When requesting a form using `getForm()`, we use a camel-cased name, `$this->getForm('userRegister')`. This will be rewritten for us by the Model base class to `User_Register`.

Now, you may be thinking that we are breaking our dependency rule because Model **should not** depend on Interface as `Zend_Form` is used for display. This assumption is completely founded when first looking at this. However, `Zend_Form` internally is split into three parts, that is, display, input filtering, and validation. This means that we can simply use the input filtering and validation parts and not worry about the display. By doing this, we gain a rather handy way to apply input filtering and validation to our Models. You could even rename the `getForm()` method to something like `getInputFilter()` so that it speaks of its purpose more clearly.

Going back to the `registerUser()` method, we return the result of the `save()` method next, passing in the `$form` to use, the `$post` data, and an array containing the default user role.

The `saveUser()` method will be used when Users update their details and when administrators create users or update user information. Currently, this works in exactly the same way as the `registerUser()` method and just uses a different form instance. We will need to change this when we come to implement the administration and security aspects of the Storefront. Currently, we have a major problem in that users can update other user information by passing another `userId` in the post! However, we will need authentication and access control to fix this, so for now we will leave it as it is.

Our final method is `save()`, which is a protected method that is only used internally by the class and provides the common functionality for all our user related data persistence requirements. The `save()` method accepts three arguments, `$form`, `$info`, and optionally `$defaults`. These should be a `Zend_Form` instance, an array containing the column data, and any default values respectively.

In the `save()` method body, we first perform data validation:

```
if (!$form->isValid($info)) {
    return false;
}
```

Here we use the `isValid()` method of `Zend_Form` to run the validation chain. This will make sure that we have all the fields required to create a valid User. We will look at how validation works when we create our form classes. If the data passed is not valid, then it will simply return a false value.

Next, we need to filter our data. We do this by using the `getValues()` method.

```
$data = $form->getValues();
```

The `getValue()` method of `Zend_Form` will filter out any values that are not defined as form elements as well as apply any transformations. All this is defined when we create the form classes, so we will look at this in detail again when we create them.

Once we have the filtered data, we move on to hashing our passwords. This is done to add an extra layer of security to our passwords. By hashing our passwords and using a salt, it hinders a hacker from easily extracting user passwords if the database is compromised. The salt actually adds a random element to the hashing so that a hacker cannot use a hash database to brute force the passwords. However, this method is still weak to dictionary attacks. So if your users have weak passwords, then they can be easily cracked.

The control statement we use for the password hashing first checks whether the password is present and is not blank. If it is blank then we unset it, as when updating a record we don't want to overwrite the user's password. If a password is present, then we apply the hashing algorithm to the password and set this as the `passwd` field's value.

After this, we apply any defaults that have been passed in, which will either overwrite or create fields that are not present.

Our final task is to save the data to the database. To do this, we first need to check if we are updating or inserting a record.

```
$user = array_key_exists('userId', $data) ?
        $this->getResource('User')
            ->getUserById($data['userId']) : null;
return $this->getResource('User')
            ->saveRow($data, $user);
```

Here, we first try to retrieve a user from the database if the `userId` field is set. If not, then we set `User` to `null`. We then pass this to the `saveRow()` method along with the `$data` array. The user instance will then be used to determine if we should be updating or inserting. The `saveRow()` method is defined in the `SF_Model_Db_Table_Abstract` and is used by all database Models to save data.

User Model Resources

With our User Model created, we can move on to creating the Model Resources. We will not cover these in detail here, as the functionality was covered in Chapter 5.

application/modules/storefront/models/resources/User/Item/
Interface.php

```
interface Storefront_Resource_User_Item_Interface
{
    public function getFullname();
}
```

application/modules/storefront/models/resources/User/Item.php

```
class Storefront_Resource_User_Item extends
    SF_Model_Resource_Db_Table_Row_Abstract implements
    Storefront_Resource_User_Item_Interface
{
    public function getFullname()
    {
        return $this->getRow()->title .
            ' ' .
            $this->getRow()->firstname .
```

```
                ' ' .
            $this->getRow()->lastname;
    }
}
```

application/modules/storefront/models/resources/User/Interface.php

```
interface Storefront_Resource_User_Interface extends SF_Model_
Resource_Db_Interface
{
    public function getUserById($id);
    public function getUserByEmail($email);
    public function getUsers($paged=false, $order=null);
}
```

application/modules/storefront/models/resources/User.php

```
require_once dirname(__FILE__) . '/User/Item.php';

class Storefront_Resource_User extends
        SF_Model_Resource_Db_Table_Abstract implements
        Storefront_Resource_User_Interface
{
    protected $_name = 'user';
    protected $_primary = 'userId';
    protected $_rowClass = 'Storefront_Resource_User_Item';
    public function getUserById($id)
    {
        return $this->find($id)->current();
    }
    public function getUserByEmail($email, $ignoreUser=null)
    {
        $select = $this->select();
        $select->where('email = ?', $email);

        if (null !== $ignoreUser) {
            $select->where('email != ?', $ignoreUser->email);
        }

        return $this->fetchRow($select);
    }
    public function getUsers($paged=false, $order=null)
    {
        if (true === is_array($order)) {
            $select->order($order);
```

```
        }
        if (null !== $paged) {
            $adapter = new
                    Zend_Paginator_Adapter_DbTableSelect($select);
            $count = clone $select;
            $count->reset(Zend_Db_Select::COLUMNS);
            $count->reset(Zend_Db_Select::FROM);
            $count->from('user', new Zend_Db_Expr('COUNT(*) AS
                    `zend_paginator_row_count`'));
            $adapter->setRowCount($count);

            $paginator = new Zend_Paginator($adapter);
            $paginator->setItemCountPerPage(15)
                    ->setCurrentPageNumber((int) $paged);
            return $paginator;
        }
        return $this->fetchAll($select);
    }
}
```

Here we can see that we have used exactly the same process as in Chapter 5. We
have defined our interfaces so that we have tight contracts for our Model Resources
and have created a Model Resource and a Model Resource item.

Creating the Customer Controller

Now that we have our Model completed, let's move on and create our Customer
Controller. The Customer Controller is straightforward as we are using the Fat
Model Skinny Controller principle. Let's create the Controller now.

application/modules/storefront/controllers/CustomerController.php

```
class Storefront_CustomerController extends Zend_Controller_Action
{
    protected $_model;

    public function init()
    {
        // get the default model
        $this->_model = new Storefront_Model_User();

        // add forms
        $this->view
                ->registerForm = $this->getRegistrationForm();
        $this->view
                ->loginForm = $this->getLoginForm();
```

```
    $this->view
        ->userForm = $this->getUserForm();
}
```

We use the `init()` method to instantiate our User Model and to assign our forms to the view.

```
public function indexAction()
{
    $userId = 1; //will be from session
    $this->view
        ->user = $this->_model->getUserById($userId);
    $this->view
        ->userForm = $this->getUserForm()->populate(
                        $this->view->user->toArray()
                    );
}
```

The `indexAction` is used by a user to update their information and displays the user edit form. Currently, we have hardcoded the `$userId` variable to the value of 1 as this will need to come from the session when we add the authentication part of the Storefront. When assigning the `userForm` to the View, we populate the form with the user information from the `Storefront_Resource_User_Item` that is stored in the user property of the View. To populate the form, we use the `populate()` method of `Zend_Form`. This method accepts an array of values that will be assigned to the form. Therefore, we also need to transform the `Storefront_Resource_User_Item` into an array using the `toArray()` method.

```
public function saveAction()
{
    $request = $this->getRequest();

    if (!$request->isPost()) {
        return $this->_helper->redirector('index');
    }

    if (false === $this->_model->saveUser(
        $request->getPost())
    ) {
        return $this->render('index');
    }
}
```

The `saveAction` is used to update user information so that the form displayed in `indexAction` posts its data to this action. This is the first time we have used one of our User Model's data persistence methods, so let's take a close look at what we have done here.

First, we get the `Zend_Controller_Request_Http` object and assign it to the `$request` variable using the `getRequest()` method. This contains all the data sent through the form. We then make sure that we actually have some post data using the Request objects `isPost()` method. If there is no post data, then we redirect the user back to the `indexAction`. To perform the redirect, we use the redirector Action Helper. This is a standard Action Helper and is generally the best way to perform HTTP redirects within our Controllers. It is also route aware. Therefore, we can easily create redirects based on a route in the router.

Next, we try to save the User information to the database using the User Models `saveUser()` method. Here, we simply check if the `saveUser()` method returns `false`. If it does, then we render the index View (`index.phtml`). Notice how we do not redirect! This is because, if we redirect, then it will create a new HTTP request, meaning we lose all of our error data. Now when `saveUser()` returns `false`, it means that the form validation has failed. As a result, we re-display the index View so that we can show the user the form errors. All errors are handled through `Zend_Form` so all we need to do is render the form again. Any other errors such as a database exception will be passed down to the error controller and displayed to the user.

This is a good example of the **Fat Model Skinny Controller** principle; the `saveAction` is completely dumb and does nothing to the data apart from passing it to the Model and deciding what should be called or rendered. Our aim is to make all of our controllers work in this fashion.

```
public function registerAction()
{}
```

The `registerAction` is the way we like our Controller Actions, completely blank. All this action does is it simply renders the register View (`register.phtml`).

```
public function completeRegistrationAction()
{
    $request = $this->getRequest();

    if (!$request->isPost()) {
        return $this->_helper->redirector('register');
    }

    if (false === ($id = $this->_model
        ->registerUser($request->getPost()))
    ) {
        return $this->render('register');
    }
}
```

The completeRegistrationAction follows the same process as the saveAction. The only real difference is that is uses a different Model method (registerUser()) and redirects and renders the register View.

```
public function getRegistrationForm()
{
    $urlHelper = $this->_helper->getHelper('url');

    $this->_forms['register'] = $this->_model->getForm
                                ('userRegister');
    $this->_forms['register']->setAction($urlHelper->url(array(
        'controller' => 'customer' ,
        'action' => 'complete-registration'
        ),
        'default'
    ));
    $this->_forms['register']->setMethod('post');

    return $this->_forms['register'];
}

public function getUserForm()
{
    $urlHelper = $this->_helper->getHelper('url');

    $this->_forms['userEdit'] = $this->_model->getForm
                                ('userEdit');
    $this->_forms['userEdit']->setAction($urlHelper->url(array(
        'controller' => 'customer' ,
        'action' => 'save'
        ),
        'default'
    ));
    $this->_forms['userEdit']->setMethod('post');

    return $this->_forms['userEdit'];
}
```

Our final two methods are not Actions but helpers for setting up our form instances. When we create our forms we do not hardcode the action or method attributes. Therefore, we need to set these attributes once we have the form instance. If we look at the getUserForm() method for example, we first retrieve the URL Action Helper and set in the $urlHelper variable, which will be used to create the action attribute. Next, we retrieve the actual form instance from the User Model.

```
$this->_forms['userEdit'] = $this->_model->getForm('userEdit');
```

Here we are assigning the return value of `getForm()` to the `'userEdit'` element of the `$_forms` array, this will be an instance of the `Storefront_Form_User_Edit` class.

Once we have our `Storefront_Form_User_Edit` instance, we can then set the required attributes. The first attribute we set is action. To create the URL for the action, we are going to use the URL Action Helper.

```
$this->_forms['userEdit']->setAction(
    $urlHelper->url(array(
        'controller' => 'customer' ,
        'action' => 'save'
        ),
        'default'
    )
);
```

This will create a URL to the customer controller's `save` Action using the default route, which is `/customer/save`.

To set the forms method attribute, we simply use the `setMethod()` form method and pass in the string `'post'`. We then return the newly configured form instance.

Zend_Form

So far, we have used quite a bit of the functionality of `Zend_Form`. We have used it to validate and filter our data in our Model and we have configured our form instances. Now that we know what it can do and how we can use it, we are going to look at how `Zend_Form` works and create our User forms.

Basic forms

Before we start creating our User forms, let's first start by looking at what `Zend_Form` is.

What is a Form?

This is an important question, as we need to know what exactly `Zend_Form` does. A form created using `Zend_Form` is comprised of three main areas. They are display, validation, and filtering. The following image illustrates this:

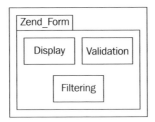

`Zend_Form` uses `Zend_View` for display, `Zend_Validate` for validation, and `Zend_Filter` for filtering. Therefore, `Zend_Form` is used to manage these three areas. If we wanted to, we could create our own form handling functionality by simply using these by themselves. However, using `Zend_Form` is much easier and encapsulates all this into one manageable component.

The management of these components is handled through the elements of `Zend_Form`. Every `Zend_Form` will have elements that we define, and each element carries its own validation, filtering, and display information.

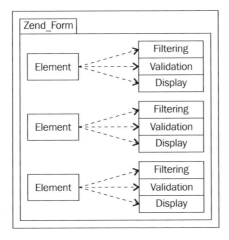

The previous screenshot shows how elements are handled by Zend_Form. When creating a form, we will need to define each element and additionally configure its display, validation, and filtering properties.

Creating a Form

There are two ways to create a form using Zend_Form, that is, through a Zend_Form instance or through inheritance. To start, let's create a standalone script that will create a form using a Zend_Form instance:

```php
<?php
require_once 'Zend/Loader.php';
Zend_Loader::registerAutoload();

$view = new Zend_View();
$form = new Zend_Form();

$form->setAction('login');
$form->setMethod('post');

$form->addElement('text', 'username', array(
    'label' => 'Username:',
));
$form->addElement('password', 'password', array(
    'label' => 'Password:',
));
$form->addElement('submit', 'submit', array(
    'label' => 'Login',
    'ignore' => true
));
echo $form->render($view);
```

Here we first instantiate a Zend_View and Zend_Form instance. The View instance is required to render the form as Zend_Form uses the Zend_View form View Helpers to create the form element's HTML. We then set the action and method attributes of the form using the setAction() and setMethod() methods respectively. Next we start adding the form's elements using the addElement() method. This method accepts three parameters. They are the type of element, the element name, and an array of options. For example, for the username field we specify that the element should be a text input with the name username and the label Username. We will get to the full set of options a little later.

Finally, we render our form using the `render()` method. This will output the following HTML:

```html
<form method="post"
      action="login"
      enctype="application/x-www-form-urlencoded">
    <dl class="zend_form">
        <dt id="username-label">
            <label class="optional" for="username">Username:</label>
        </dt>
    <dd id="username-element">
        <input type="text" value="" id="username" name="username"/>
    </dd>
    <dt id="password-label">
        <label class="optional" for="password">Password:</label>
    </dt>
    <dd id="password-element">
        <input type="password" value="" id="password"
               name="password"/>
    </dd>
    <dt id="submit-label"></dt>
    <dd id="submit-element">
        <input type="submit" value="Login" id="submit"
               name="submit"/>
    </dd>
    </dd>
    </dl>
</form>
```

Now we have our first `Zend_Form`. Currently, it has no validation and if you look at the HTML, it is not exactly perfect but we have a form nonetheless. Now, let's create the same form using inheritance.

```php
class LoginForm extends Zend_Form
{
    public function init()
    {
        $this->setAction('login');
        $this->setMethod('post');

        $this->addElement('text', 'username', array(
            'label' => 'Username:',
        ));
        $this->addElement('password', 'password', array(
            'label' => 'Password:',
        ));
        $this->addElement('submit', 'submit', array(
            'label' => 'Login',
            'ignore' => true
        ));
    }
}
```

We can see that the `LoginForm` class simply subclasses the form `Zend_Form` and uses the special `init()` method to create the form internally. The `init()` method is called in the `Zend_Form` class constructor. To configure the form and add its elements, we use exactly the same method as before, apart from the use of `$this->addElement()`, as this will produce exactly the same HTML as before.

Customizing Zend_Form's output

Before we move on and create our User forms, we are going to stick with our simple login form example and look at customizing the `Zend_Form` display. This is a very common requirement, and a lot of people have trouble understanding how the display layer works. However, once you get the hang of it, it is actually very easy.

You may have noticed that the HTML produced earlier was not exactly how we would want it. If we look closely, then we see that we have an empty `<dt>` tag for our **submit** button.

```
<dt id="submit-label"></dt>
```

So how do we fix this? Well the answer is decorators, not the sugary, tea-drinking type but the objects that are used to decorate the form and its elements. The reason we call them decorators is because they implement the Decorator design pattern, so this is probably a good place to start.

The Decorator pattern

The Decorator pattern allows us to add functionality to an object dynamically at runtime. This is achieved by wrapping the object to be decorated with a decorator class. The decorator class will have the same API as the wrapped object. By wrapping the object and replacing calls to that object with calls to the decorator, the decorator is able to change the behavior of the object. To clarify this, let's look at an example decorator. We will start by creating the class that will be decorated.

```
abstract class Math
{
    abstract public function execute();
}

class base extends Math
{
    public function execute()
    {
        return 0;
    }
}
```

Here we have one abstract class named `Math` that is used to define the object's API and a concrete class `base` which we want to decorate. Next we create our abstract decorator class, which will be used when we create our concrete decorators.

```
abstract class MathDecorator extends Math
{
    protected $_math;

    public function __construct(Math $math = null)
    {
        $this->_math = $math;
    }
}
```

Our abstract decorator's constructor accepts one parameter, $math, which is used to pass in the object we are wrapping. Now we can create our decorators:

```
class AddOneDecorator extends MathDecorator
{
    public function execute()
    {
        return $this->_math->execute()+1;
    }
}

class MinusTwoDecorator extends MathDecorator
{
    public function execute()
    {
        return $this->_math->execute()-2;
    }
}
```

Here we have two decorators, `AddOneDecorator` and `MinusTwoDecorator`. These can now be used to decorate the base classe's functionality.

```
$d = new MinusTwoDecorator(
        new AddOneDecorator(
            new AddOneDecorator(
                new AddOneDecorator(
                    new base()
                )
            )
        )
    );
echo $d->execute();
```

Here we are using the decorators to change the behavior of the base classes `execute()` method. We can see that we are able to chain the decorators together to decorate the object many times. This example will output the value 1 (one), which is `0 + 1 + 1 + 1 - 2`.

Zend_Form's Decorators

Right, so now that we have a basic understanding of the Decorator pattern, let's look at what this means for `Zend_Form`. The `Zend_Form` uses decorators to create the DOM elements that make up the form. The form is split into parts, which are elements, the form, display groups, and subforms. Each of these parts has their own set of default decorators that combine to make up the complete form.

Form elements

Elements have five standard decorators, and these are:

- ViewHelper
- Errors
- Description (only renders if a description is set)
- HtmlTag
- Label

These decorators are registered in the order shown here. Therefore, when an element is rendered, the call is similar to `label( HtmlTag( Description( Errors( ViewHelper() ) ) ) )`. This is pseudo code, but you can see how this is the same method as in our decorator pattern example. The following screenshot illustrates the rendering of a `Zend_Form` element:

Here we can see the HTML produced for each element, the decorators used, and the order in which the decorators are called, and therefore the order in which the HTML is created.

Each decorator also has a set of options. These options define how the decorator behaves. By default, the element's decorators have the following options applied to them:

- **ViewHelper**: placement = APPEND
- **Errors**: placement = APPEND
- **Description**: placement = APPEND, tag = p, class = description
- **HtmlTag**: tag = dd, id = (element name)
- **Label**: placement = PREPEND, tag = dt

We can now see how these settings produce the HTML elements. For example, the HtmlTag decorator is set to use the <dd> tag to wrap the previous decorator's output. We have also introduced another important aspect of the decorators here, which is **placement**. Placement tells the decorator whether we want it to apply itself to the start, end, or wrap the previous decorator's output. All decorators support the placement option apart from the ViewHelper. There are of course many options for each decorator. For a full list, use the reference manual.

The Form

The Form has three default decorators:

- FormElements
- HtmlTag (tag=dl)
- Form

The following screenshot illustrates the rendering of the Form:

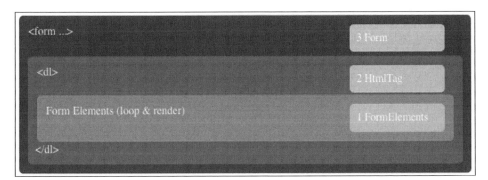

We can see that this is very similar to a form element. The most important decorator here is `FormElements`. This decorator will iterate over all the form elements, display groups, and subforms registered with the `Zend_Form` instance rendering each element, which in turn renders all the form element decorators.

Display Groups and Subforms

Display Groups and Subforms have the following default decorators:

- FormElements
- HtmlTag (tag=dl)
- Fieldset
- DtDdWrapper

The following screenshot illustrates the rendering of a Display Group or Subform:

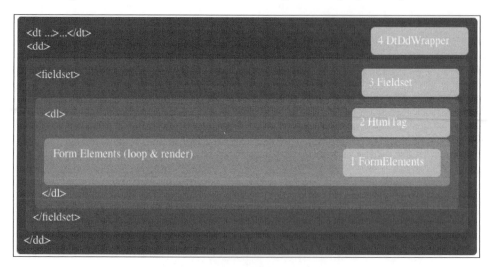

Fixing the login forms HTML

If we go back to our simple login form example, we can now customize the submit element's decorators to fix the empty `<dt>` tag.

Using our first `Zend_Form` example and a `Zend_Form` instance, update the submit element.

```
$form->addElement('submit', 'submit', array(
    'label' => 'Login',
    'ignore' => true,
    'decorators' => array(
        'ViewHelper',
```

```
            array(
                'HtmlTag',
                array(
                    'tag' => 'dd',
                    'id' => 'form-submit'
                )
            )
        )
    ));
```

So here we have changed the submit element's decorators from:

- ViewHelper
- Errors
- Description
- HtmlTag
- Label

To:

- ViewHelper
- HtmlTag

We have removed three decorators (Errors, Description, and Label). This will now produce the following HTML:

```
<dd id="form-submit">
    <input type="submit" value="Login" id="submit" name="submit"/>
</dd>
```

By doing this, we have now removed the empty `<dt>` tag. Before we continue though, let's look at the code we used to define the new set of decorators. To define the decorators, we add the `'decorators'` key to the options array when adding the element with `addElement()` and pass in the following array:

```
array(
    'ViewHelper',
    array(
        'HtmlTag',
        array(
            'tag' => 'dd',
            'id' => 'form-submit'
        )
    )
)
```

This is where decorators can be confusing, but I promise this becomes easier as you progress. So here, we have an array containing our decorators. The first decorator we define is `ViewHelper`, and this does not need to be configured so we simply supply the string `ViewHelper` as an array value. Next, we need to define the `HtmlTag` decorator that will wrap the `ViewHelper` in a `<dd>` tag. As this needs configuration, we pass in another array instead of a string.

```
array(
    'HtmlTag',
    array(
        'tag' => 'dd',
        'id' => 'form-submit'
    )
)
```

The first element in the array is the string `'HtmlTag'`, which defines the decorator to use. The second element is an array containing the options for the `HtmlTag` decorator, and these options will be passed to the decorator when it is called. The options we set are `tag` and `id`. The `tag` defines the HTML tag that the `ViewHelper` will be wrapped in and the `id` will set the ID attribute on the tag.

Decorators give us great control over the way `Zend_Form` creates the HTML forms. With a bit of perseverance, we can create highly customized layouts. Always try to keep in mind what the default decorators are, and from there it becomes a lot easier to create a custom layout.

The User forms

Now that we have completed a few examples, let's move on and create the User forms. To achieve this, we are going to create a few form classes that will be used by our User Model. We already know that the validation, filtering, and display needs to be slightly different depending on what operation the Model is performing. For example, when registering, the form will have fewer fields than when an administrator is editing a user. Therefore, we will first create a base form class and then use inheritance to specialize our forms.

application/modules/storefront/forms/User/Base.php

```
class Storefront_Form_User_Base extends Zend_Form
{
    public function init()
    {
        // add path to custom validators
        $this->addElementPrefixPath(
            'Storefront_Validate',
```

```
        APPLICATION_PATH .
        '/modules/storefront/models/validate/',
        'validate'
);

$this->addElement('select', 'title', array(
        'required'    => true,
        'label'       => 'Title',
        'multiOptions' => array('Mr' => 'Mr','Ms' => 'Ms','Miss'
                      => 'Miss','Mrs' => 'Mrs'),
));

$this->addElement('text', 'firstname', array(
        'filters'     => array('StringTrim'),
        'validators' => array(
            'Alpha',
            array('StringLength', true, array(3, 128))
        ),
        'required'    => true,
        'label'       => 'Firstname',
));

$this->addElement('text', 'lastname', array(
        'filters'     => array('StringTrim'),
        'validators' => array(
            'Alpha',
            array('StringLength', true, array(3, 128))
        ),
        'required'    => true,
        'label'       => 'lastname',
));

$this->addElement('text', 'email', array(
        'filters'     => array('StringTrim', 'StringToLower'),
        'validators' => array(
            array('StringLength', true, array(3, 128)),
            array('EmailAddress'),
            array('UniqueEmail', false, array(new
                Storefront_Model_User())),
        ),
        'required'    => true,
        'label'       => 'Email',
));

$this->addElement('password', 'passwd', array(
        'filters'     => array('StringTrim'),
        'validators' => array(
```

```
                        array('StringLength', true, array(6, 128))
            ),
            'required'    => true,
            'label'       => 'Password',
        ));

        $this->addElement('password', 'passwdVerify', array(
            'filters'     => array('StringTrim'),
            'validators'  => array(
                'PasswordVerification',
            ),
            'required'    => true,
            'label'       => 'Confirm Password',
        ));

        $this->addElement('submit', 'submit', array(
            'required' => false,
            'ignore'   => true,
            'decorators' => array('ViewHelper',array('HtmlTag',
                    array('tag' => 'dd', 'id' => 'form-submit')))
        ));

         $this->addElement('hidden', 'userId', array(
            'filters'     => array('StringTrim'),
            'required'    => true,
            'decorators' => array('viewHelper',array('HtmlTag',
                    array('tag' => 'dd', 'class' => 'noDisplay')))
        ));
    }
}
```

This is our base user form. It includes all of the elements that we require for our user forms. All of our other user forms will extend from this form. The base form has the following elements:

- title
- firstname
- lastname
- email
- passwd
- passwdVerify
- submit
- userId

Looking at the base form, we see that we are adding elements in the same way as we did in the example of our earlier login form. However, this time we have included more options with each element. Let's go through and look at the important aspects here.

A Typical Form element

To start, we will look at the `firstname` element. This element has quite a standard configuration that most of our other elements follow and will serve as a good example for us.

```
$this->addElement('text', 'firstname', array(
    'filters'    => array('StringTrim'),
    'validators' => array(
        'Alpha',
        array('StringLength', true, array(3, 128))
    ),
    'required'   => true,
    'label'      => 'Firstname',
));
```

Here we are creating a text input element with the name `firstname`. We also pass in an options array that defines our filters, validators, and other settings.

The first item in our options array is **filters**. Filters are `Zend_Filter` classes that are used to filter the input. The `firstname` element has one filter named `StringTrim`. This filter uses the `trim()` function to remove extra whitespace from the input. We can define as many filters as we wish by providing their names within the filters array. This works much the same way as defining decorators that we looked at earlier.

Our second item is **validators**. Validators are `Zend_Validate` classes and are used to validate the input. We have two validators defined for the `firstname` element, `Alpha` and `StringLength`. The `Alpha` validator will make sure the input is alphanumeric and the `StringLength` validator will make sure that the string is between 3 and 128 characters long. When defining the `StringLength` validator, we need to pass in options for that validator. In order to do this, we use an array instead of a string just like we did when defining decorators that require options. The first option we pass to the `StringLength` validator is a Boolean value (`true`). This tells the validator to stop processing the validation chain if validation fails. The validation chain is the stack of validators we define in the validators array. If we had further validators after `StringLength`, then they would not run if `StringLength` failed. The second option, which we pass to `StringLength` is an array containing the parameters for the validator. These will then be used when the validator is instantiated, and in this case, we set the `min` and `max` parameters for the `StringLength` validator.

Our third item is `required`. The `required` option tells the form whether the item is required or not. Our final option is `label` that simply defines the text to use in the label tag.

Custom validators

Now that we have looked at an example of a typical form element, let's look at some of the special elements in the base form that use custom validators. Zend_Form provides a great number of validators. However, there are always cases where we need our own validation functionality. Adding this is easy. All we need to do is create our own validator class that extends from the Zend_Validate_Abstract class. In the user form, we use two custom validators, namely, UniqueEmail and PasswordVerification.

Unique email validator

To start, we will create the unique email validator. This will check that the email is unique when creating a new user. We do this because the users will authenticate themselves with their email and password.

application/modules/storefront/models/validate/UniqueEmail.php

```
class Storefront_Validate_UniqueEmail extends Zend_Validate_Abstract
{
    const EMAIL_EXISTS = 'emailExists';

    protected $_messageTemplates = array(
        self::EMAIL_EXISTS =>
            'Email "%value%" already exists in our system',
    );

    public function __construct(Storefront_Model_User $model)
    {
        $this->_model = $model;
    }

    public function isValid($value, $context = null)
    {
        $this->_setValue($value);

        $currentUser = isset($context['userId']) ?
            $this->_model->getUserById($context['userId']) : null;

        $user = $this->_model->getUserByEmail($value, $currentUser);

        if (null === $user) {
            return true;
        }

        $this->_error(self::EMAIL_EXISTS);
        return false;
    }
}
```

Firstly, we have created a new directory for our custom validators within the models directory called validate, and we will store all storefront validators here. Next, we create the Storefront_Validate_UniqueEmail class, which subclasses the Zend_Validate_Abstract. All validators follow the same convention and have two main aspects, namely, errors and validation.

When creating our error types and error messages, we need to define them in a standard way because each error type and error message can be changed through setMessage().

```
const EMAIL_EXISTS = 'emailExists';

protected $_messageTemplates = array(
    self::EMAIL_EXISTS =>
        'Email "%value%" already exists in our system',
);
```

To define an error type, we create a class constant that contains a string, which will be used to uniquely identify the error. In this case, we create the EMAIL_EXISTS constant with the value of emailExists. To define the error message for an error type, we add an item to the $_messageTemplates array. This item should use the error type constant as its key and then a string containing the error message as its value. For the EMAIL_EXISTS error type, we define the error message "Email "%value%" already exists in our system". When creating an error message, we can use the placeholder %value%, which will be replaced by the value being validated.

To add validation to our validator, we use the isValid() method, which is defined by the Zend_Validate_Interface. The isValid() method will be called when the validator is executed in the validation chain and will have the value to be validated passed to it.

```
public function isValid($value, $context = null)
{
    $this->_setValue($value);

    $currentUser = isset($context['userId']) ?
        $this->_model->getUserById($context['userId']) : null;

    $user = $this->_model->getUserByEmail($value, $currentUser);

    if (null === $user) {
        return true;
    }

    $this->_error(self::EMAIL_EXISTS);
    return false;
}
```

For the `UniqueEmail` validator, we first set the value to be validated using the `_setValue()` method. This will also clear any previous error messages for this validator. Next we access our User Model. The User Model is set in the protected `$_model` property when the validator is instantiated. The first thing we do with the User Model is to check whether the `userId` is set in the post data. The post data will be stored in the `$context` parameter of the `isValid()` method. If the `userId` is set, then we get the User that matches that `userId`. This will then be used by the `getUserByEmail()` method.

After we have the `$currentUser`, which will either be a `Storefront_Resource_User_Item` instance or `null`, we need to find out if the email is already in use. To do this, we query the User Model using the `getUserByEmail()` method and pass in the `$value` and `$currentUser` variables. The `$value` will be the email address, and the `$currentUser` will be used to ignore the current user from the query if we are editing a user.

To validate, we simply check whether `$user` is `null`, and if it is, then the email does not exist and we return `true`. If the `$user` is not `null`, then we set the error using the `_error()` method and return `false`.

Password verification validator

Our second validator is the password verification validator, which is used to make sure that when a user enters his/her password that he/she has not typed it incorrectly, by getting them to enter their password twice in the form.

`application/modules/storefront/models/validate/PasswordVerification.php`

```
class Storefront_Validate_PasswordVerification extends
Zend_Validate_Abstract
{
    const NOT_MATCH = 'notMatch';

    protected $_messageTemplates = array(
        self::NOT_MATCH => 'Passwords do not match'
    );

    public function isValid($value, $context = null)
    {
        $value = (string) $value;
        $this->_setValue($value);

        if (is_array($context)) {
            if (isset($context['passwd'])
                && ($value == $context['passwd']))
            {
                return true;
```

```
        }
    } elseif (is_string($context) && ($value == $context)) {
        return true;
    }

    $this->_error(self::NOT_MATCH);
    return false;
    }
}
```

The `PasswordVerification` validator works in exactly the same way as the `UniqueEmail` so we will not go back over it. Generally, we are checking to see if the `passwdVerify` field is equal to the `passwd` field.

Using custom validators, filters, and decorators

Now that we have created our validators, we need to first make our form elements know where they are. We do this by adding the `application/modules/storefront/models/validate` directory to each element of the Plugin Loader. The Plugin Loader is used internally to load the validators.

```
$this->addElementPrefixPath(
    'Storefront_Validate',
    APPLICATION_PATH .
    '/modules/storefront/models/validate/',
    'validate'
);
```

Here we add the path to all the elements in the form using the `addElementPrefixPath()` method. This accepts three parameters, namely, the validator class name prefix, the path, and the path type. The type can be either `validate`, `filter`, or `decorator`.

With our elements aware of the path to the validators, we can now use them to create elements just like using the standard validators.

```
            $this->addElement('text', 'email', array(
                'filters'    => array('StringTrim', 'StringToLower'),
                'validators' => array(
                    array('StringLength', true, array(3, 128)),
                    array('EmailAddress'),
                    array('UniqueEmail', false, array(new
                            Storefront_Model_User())),
                ),
                'required'   => true,
                'label'      => 'Email',
            ));
```

Here is the email element. We can see that we have used the `UniqueEmail` validator when creating this element. We give the validator an options array containing a new `Storefront_Model_User` instance so that the validator can query the database.

Base form decorators

The final interesting aspect of the base form are the decorators that we use on `submit` and `hidden` form elements.

```
$this->addElement('submit', 'submit', array(
    'required' => false,
    'ignore'   => true,
    'decorators' => array(
        'ViewHelper',
        array(
            'HtmlTag',
            array('tag' => 'dd', 'id' => 'form-submit')
        )
    ),
));

$this->addElement('hidden', 'userId', array(
    'filters'    => array('StringTrim'),
    'required'   => true,
    'decorators' => array(
        'viewHelper',
        array(
            'HtmlTag',
            array('tag' => 'dd', 'class' => 'noDisplay')
        )
    ),
));
```

The `submit` element uses the same set of decorators that we used in the login form example to get rid of the empty `<dt>` tag. For the `hidden` element, we need to do something a little differently. Here we come to a bug in `Zend_Form`, by default, the `hidden` elements are treated the same as any other element, meaning that they have a `<dt>` and `<dd>` tag. By adding these, we get gaps in the layout wherever we use `hidden` elements. Currently there is no way to change this, but this may be fixed in the future so that `hidden` elements are appended to the HTML after the `<dl>` part. Therefore, to fix this we need to do our own workaround, and the way we do it is by using a CSS class that hides the `<dd>` that warps the hidden input element.

The decorators used for the hidden `userId` element are:

- `viewHelper`
- `HtmlTag` (tag = dd, class = noDisplay)

Again, like in the submit decorators, we drop the label decorator (<dt>). For the `HtmlTag`, we use a <dd> tag but this time we add the CSS class `noDisplay`. This CSS class will hide the <dd> tag for us to get rid of our layout gaps.

If we were using many hidden elements, then we would probably want to define the decorators for this in a method that all our forms could access and simply call that when adding hidden elements.

```
$this->addElement('hidden', 'userId', array(
    'filters'    => array('StringTrim'),
    'required'   => true,
    'decorators' => $this->_hiddenDecorators()
));
```

Specializing forms

We have our base form but there are going to be situations where we need the form to behave in a slightly different way. For example, editing a user is very different from registering a user. To do this we are going to use inheritance, which is a good way to specialize our form classes using polymorphism. However, remember that inheritance has its problems in the fact that you need to maintain the entire inheritance tree. So changes higher up can affect all the classes below. If we were to have many different uses, then it may be better to use a Decorator Pattern to apply the specializations.

Let's now create our two form context classes:

application/modules/storefront/forms/User/Register.php

```
class Storefront_Form_User_Register extends Storefront_Form_User_Base
{
    public function init()
    {
        // make sure parent is called!
        parent::init();

        // specialize this form
        $this->removeElement('userId');
        $this->getElement('submit')->setLabel('Register');
    }
}
```

`application/modules/storefront/forms/User/Edit.php`

```
class Storefront_Form_User_Edit extends Storefront_Form_User_Register
{
    public function init()
    {
        // make sure parent is called!
        parent::init();

        // specialize this form
        $this->getElement('passwd')->setRequired(false);
        $this->getElement('passwdVerify')->setRequired(false);
        $this->getElement('submit')->setLabel('Save User');
    }
}
```

These are our two forms that will be used by the storefront. They both subclass the `Storefront_Form_User_Base` form, and therefore already have all the elements defined by the base form. To specialize our forms, we again use the `init()` method. However, this time we must call the `parent::init()` method to first create the base form elements. If we do not do this, then the form will not work. After we have called the parents `init()` method, we can start to specialize our forms.

For the Register form, we apply the following specializations:

- Remove the `userId` element
- Change the `'submit'` button's label to `'Register'`

For the Edit form, we apply the following specializations:

- Set the `passwd` element to `optional`
- Set the `passwdVerify` element to `optional`
- Change the `'submit'` button's label to `'Save User'`

We can see that the forms are very easy to specialize in this way, and we can quickly make changes to the base form elements. By doing this, we also give our Models the ability to understand the different contexts that they are being used in, by the type of form that is used.

Creating the Customer Views

Now that we have our Models and Forms created, let's quickly create the Views for the customers. This is simple, as `Zend_Form` is doing most of the work for us!

application/modules/storefront/views/scripts/customer/index.phtml

```
<h3>your <span>account</span></h3>
<p>
    You can edit your account details below:
</p>
<?=$this->userForm;?>
```

application/modules/storefront/views/scripts/customer/complete-registration.phtml

```
<h3>thank <span>you</span></h3>
<p>You are now registered and can login.</p>
```

application/modules/storefront/views/scripts/customer/register.phtml

```
<h3>new <span>customer</span></h3>
<p>Please complete the form below to register to the site.</p>
<?=$this->registerForm ?>
```

Building the application

Right, that's it, done! It's time to build a view to the site. You should now be able to register at `/register` and edit the user with `userId=1` at `/customer`. If for some reason you don't have a user with the `userId` of 1, then change the `$userID` variable in the `indexAction` of the `CustomerController` class.

Summary

In this chapter, we have looked at creating some of the functionality for our Customers. Our Customers can now register to the site. However, the main focus has been to understand how we can use `Zend_Form`. With our Customer functionality complete, we have successfully created our forms, customized them using decorators, added custom validation, and used `Zend_Form` as an input filter for our Models. Over the next few chapters, we will be looking at creating the shopping cart and the administration area, and at adding user authentication and authorization to complete our basic storefront.

7
The Shopping Cart

Our next task in creating the storefront is to create the shopping cart. This will allow users to select the products they wish to purchase. Users will be able to select, edit, and delete items from their shopping cart.

In this chapter, we will cover:

- Creating Models that do not use a database as a data source
- Using `Zend_Session_Namespace`
- More Forms, View Helpers, and so on
- Implementing the Cart Views and Controllers

Creating the Cart Model and Resources

We will start by creating our model and model resources. The Cart Model differs from our previous model in the fact that it will use the session to store its data instead of the database.

Cart Model

The Cart Model will store the products that they wish to purchase. Therefore, the Cart Model will contain Cart Items that will be stored in the session. Let's create this class now.

application/modules/storefront/models/Cart.php

```
class Storefront_Model_Cart extends SF_Model_Abstract implements
SeekableIterator, Countable, ArrayAccess
{
    protected $_items = array();

    protected $_subTotal = 0;
```

```php
    protected $_total = 0;

    protected $_shipping = 0;

    protected $_sessionNamespace;

    public function init()
    {
        $this->loadSession();
    }

    public function addItem(
        Storefront_Resource_Product_Item_Interface $product,
        $qty
    )
    {
        if (0 > $qty) {
            return false;
        }

        if (0 == $qty) {
            $this->removeItem($product);
            return false;
        }

        $item = new Storefront_Resource_Cart_Item(
            $product, $qty
        );
        $this->_items[$item->productId] = $item;
        $this->persist();
        return $item;
    }

    public function removeItem($product)
    {
        if (is_int($product)) {
            unset($this->_items[$product]);
        }

        if ($product instanceof
            Storefront_Resource_Product_Item_Interface) {
            unset($this->_items[$product->productId]);
        }

        $this->persist();
    }

    public function setSessionNs(Zend_Session_Namespace $ns)
    {
```

```
        $this->_sessionNamespace = $ns;
    }

    public function getSessionNs()
    {
        if (null === $this->_sessionNamespace) {
            $this->setSessionNs(new
                    Zend_Session_Namespace(__CLASS__));
        }
        return $this->_sessionNamespace;
    }

    public function persist()
    {
        $this->getSessionNs()->items = $this->_items;
        $this->getSessionNs()->shipping = $this->getShippingCost();
    }

    public function loadSession()
    {
        if (isset($this->getSessionNs()->items)) {
            $this->_items = $this->getSessionNs()->items;
        }
        if (isset($this->getSessionNs()->shipping)) {
            $this->setShippingCost($this->getSessionNs()->shipping);
        }
    }

    public function CalculateTotals()
    {
        $sub = 0;
        foreach ($this as $item) {
            $sub = $sub + $item->getLineCost();
        }

        $this->_subTotal = $sub;
        $this->_total = $this->_subTotal + (float) $this->_shipping;
    }

    public function setShippingCost($cost)
    {
        $this->_shipping = $cost;
        $this->CalculateTotals();
        $this->persist();
    }

    public function getShippingCost()
    {
```

```
            $this->CalculateTotals();
            return $this->_shipping;
    }

    public function getSubTotal()
    {
            $this->CalculateTotals();
            return $this->_subTotal;
    }

    public function getTotal()
    {
            $this->CalculateTotals();
            return $this->_total;
    }
/*...*/
}
```

We can see that the Cart Model class is fairly weighty and in fact, we have not included the full class here. The reason we have slightly truncated the class is that we are implementing the SeekableIterator, Countable, and ArrayAccess interfaces. These interfaces are defined by PHP's SPL Library and we use them to provide a better way to interact with the cart data. For the complete code, copy the methods below getTotal() from the example files for this chapter. We will look at what each method does shortly in the *Cart Model implementation* section, but first, let's look at what functionality the SPL interfaces allow us to add.

Cart Model interfaces

The SeekableIterator interface allows us to access our cart data in these ways:

```
// iterate over the cart
foreach($cart as $item) {}

// seek an item at a position
$cart->seek(1);

// standard iterator access
$cart->rewind();
$cart->next();
$cart->current();
```

The Countable interface allows us to count the items in our cart:

```
count($cart);
```

The ArrayAccess interface allows us to access our cart like an array:

```
$cart[0];
```

Obviously, the interfaces provide no concrete implementation for the functionality, so we have to provide it on our own. The methods not listed in the previous code listing are:

- `offsetExists($key)`
- `offsetGet($key)`
- `offsetSet($key, $value)`
- `offsetUnset($key)`
- `current()`
- `key()`
- `next()`
- `rewind()`
- `valid()`
- `seek($index)`
- `count()`

We will not cover the actual implementation of these interfaces, as they are standard to PHP. However, you will need to copy all these methods from the example files to get the Cart Model working.

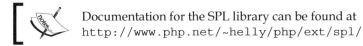

> Documentation for the SPL library can be found at
> `http://www.php.net/~helly/php/ext/spl/`

Cart Model implementation

Going back to our code listing, let's now look at how the Cart Model is implemented. Let's start by looking at the properties and methods of the class.

The Cart Model has the following class properties:

- `$_items`: An array of cart items
- `$_subTotal`: Monetary total of cart items
- `$_total`: Monetary total of cart items plus shipping
- `$_shipping`: The shipping cost
- `$_sessionNamespace`: The session store

The Cart Model has the following methods:

- `init()`: Called during construct and loads the session data
- `addItem(Storefront_Resource_Product_Item_Interface $product, $qty)`: Adds or updates items in the cart
- `removeItem($product)`: Removes a cart item
- `setSessionNs(Zend_Session_Namespace $ns)`: Sets the session instance to use for storage
- `getSessionNs()`: Gets the current session instance
- `persist()`: Saves the cart data to the session
- `loadSession()`: Loads the stored session values
- `calculateTotals()`: Calculates the cart totals
- `setShippingCost($cost)`: Sets the shipping cost
- `getShippingCost()`: Gets the shipping cost
- `getSubTotal()`: Gets the total cost for items in the cart (not including the shipping)
- `getTotal()`: Gets the subtotal plus the shipping cost

When we instantiate a new Cart Model instance, the `init()` method is called. This is defined in the `SF_Model_Abstract` class and is called by the `__construct()` method. This enables us to easily extend the class's instantiation process without having to override the constructor.

The `init()` method simply calls the `loadSession()` method. This method populates the model with the cart items and shipping information stored in the session. The Cart Model uses `Zend_Session_Namespace` to store this data, which provides an easy-to-use interface to the `$_SESSION` variable. If we look at the `loadSession()` method, we see that it tests whether the items and shipping properties are set in the session namespace. If they are, then we set these values on the Cart Model.

To get the session namespace, we use the `getSessionNs()` method. This method checks if the `$_sessionNs` property is set and returns it. Otherwise it will lazyload a new `Zend_Session_Namespace` instance for us. When using `Zend_Session_Namespace`, we must provide a string to its constructor that defines the name of the namespace to store our data in. This will then create a clean place to add variables to, without worrying about variable name clashes. For the Cart Model, the default namespace will be `Storefront_Model_Cart`.

The `Zend_Session_Namespace` component provides a range of functionality that we can use to control the session. For example, we can set the expiration time as follows:

```
$ns = new Zend_Session_Namespace('test');
$ns->setExpirationSeconds(60, 'items');
$ns->setExpirationHops(10);
$ns->setExpirationSeconds(120);
```

This code would set the item's property expiration to 60 seconds and the namespaces expiration to 10 hops (requests) or 120 seconds, whichever is reached first. The useful thing about this is that the expiration is not global. Therefore, we can have specialized expiration per session namespace. There is a full list of `Zend_Session_Namespace` functionalities in the reference manual.

> **Testing with `Zend_Session` and `Zend_Session_Namespace`**
>
> Testing with the session components can be fairly difficult. For the Cart Model, we use the `setSessionNs()` method to allow us to inject a mock object for testing, which you can see in the Cart Model unit tests. There are plans to rewrite the session components to make testing easier in the future, so keep an eye out for those updates.

To add an item to the cart, we use the `addItem()` method. This method accepts two parameters, `$product` and `$qty`. The `$product` parameter must be an instance of the `Storefront_Resource_Product_Item` class, and the `$qty` parameter must be an integer that defines the quantity that the customer wants to order.

If the `addItem()` method receives a valid `$qty`, then it will create a new `Storefront_Resource_Cart_Item` and add it to the `$_items` array using the `productId` as the array key. We then call the `persist()` method. This method simply stores all the relevant cart data in the session namespace for us. You will notice that we are not using a Model Resource in the Cart Model and instead we are directly instantiating a Model Resource Item. This is because the Model Resources represent store items and the Cart Model is already doing this for us so it is not needed.

To remove an item, we use the `removeItem()` method. This accepts a single parameter `$product` which can be either an integer or a `Storefront_Resource_Product_Item` instance. The matching cart item will be removed from the `$_items` array and the data will be saved to the session. Also, `addItem()` will call `removeItem()` if the quantity is set to zero.

The other methods in the Cart Model are used to calculate the monetary totals for the cart and to set the shipping. We will not cover these in detail here as they are fairly simple mathematical calculations.

Cart Model Resources

Now that we have our Model created, let's create the Resource Interface and concrete Resource class for our Model to use.

application/modules/storefront/models/resources/Cart/Item/Interface.php

```
interface Storefront_Resource_Cart_Item_Interface
{
    public function getLineCost();
}
```

The Cart Resource Item has a very simple interface that has one method, getLineCost(). This method is used when calculating the cart totals in the Cart Model.

application/modules/storefront/models/resources/Cart/Item.php

```
class Storefront_Resource_Cart_Item implements Storefront_Resource_
Cart_Item_Interface
{
    public $productId;
    public $name;
    public $price;
    public $taxable;
    public $discountPercent;
    public $qty;

    public function __construct(Storefront_Resource_Product_Item_
            Interface $product, $qty)
    {
        $this->productId = (int) $product->productId;
        $this->name      = $product->name;
        $this->price     = (float) $product->getPrice(false,false);
        $this->taxable   = $product->taxable;
        $this->discountPercent  = (int) $product->discountPercent;
        $this->qty       = (int) $qty;
    }

    public function getLineCost()
    {
        $price = $this->price;

        if (0 !== $this->discountPercent) {
            $discounted = ($price*$this->discountPercent)/100;
            $price = round($price - $discounted, 2);
        }

        if ('Yes' === $this->taxable) {
```

```
            $taxService = new Storefront_Service_Taxation();
            $price = $taxService->addTax($price);
        }

        return $price * $this->qty;
    }
}
```

The concrete Cart Resource Item has two methods `__construct()` and `getLineCost()`. The constructor accepts two parameters `$product` and `$qty` that must be a `Storefront_Resource_Product_Item_Interface` instance and integer respectively. This method will then simply copy the values from the product instance and store them in the matching public properties. We do this because we do not want to simply store the product instance because it has all the database connection data contained within. This object will be serialized and stored in the session.

The `getLineCost()` method simply calculates the cost of the product adding tax and discounts and then multiplies it by the given quantity.

Shipping Model

We also need to create a Shipping Model so that the user can select what type of shipping they would like. This Model will simply act as a data store for some predefined shipping values.

`application/modules/storefront/models/Shipping.php`

```
    class Storefront_Model_Shipping extends SF_Model_Abstract
    {
        protected $_shippingData = array(
            'Standard' => 1.99,
            'Special'  => 5.99,
        );

        public function getShippingOptions()
        {
            return $this->_shippingData;
        }
    }
```

The shipping Model is very simple and only contains the shipping options and a single method to retrieve them. In a normal application, shipping would usually be stored in the database and most likely have its own set of business rules. For the Storefront, we are not creating a complete ordering process so we do not need these complications.

Creating the Cart Controller

With our Model and Model Resources created, we can now start wiring the application layer together. The Cart will have a single Controller, CartController that will be used to add, view, and update cart items stored in the Cart Model.

application/modules/storefront/controllers/CartController.php

```
class Storefront_CartController extends Zend_Controller_Action
{
    protected $_cartModel;
    protected $_catalogModel;

    public function init()
    {
        $this->_cartModel = new Storefront_Model_Cart();
        $this->_catalogModel = new Storefront_Model_Catalog();
    }

    public function addAction()
    {
        $product = $this->_catalogModel->getProductById(
            $this->_getParam('productId')
        );

        if(null === $product) {
          throw new SF_Exception(
            'Product could not be added to cart as it does not exist'
            );
        }

        $this->_cartModel->addItem(
            $product, $this->_getParam('qty')
        );

        $return = rtrim(
            $this->getRequest()->getBaseUrl(), '/'
        ) . $this->_getParam('returnto');

        $redirector = $this->getHelper('redirector');

        return $redirector->gotoUrl($return);
    }

    public function viewAction()
    {
        $this->view->cartModel = $this->_cartModel;
    }
```

```
public function updateAction()
{
    foreach($this->_getParam('quantity') as $id => $value)
    {
        $product = $this->_catalogModel
                            ->getProductById($id);
        if (null !== $product) {
            $this->_cartModel->addItem($product, $value);
        }
    }
    $this->_cartModel->setShippingCost(
        $this->_getParam('shipping')
    );

    return $this->_helper->redirector('view');
}
}
```

The Cart Controller has three actions that provide a way to:

- **add**: add cart items
- **view**: view the cart contents
- **update**: update cart items

The addAction() first tries to find the product to be added to the cart. This is done by searching for the product by its productId field, which is passed either in the URL or by post using the Catalog Model. If the product is not found, then we throw an SF_Exception stating so. Next, we add the product to the cart using the addItem() method. When adding the product, we also pass in the qty. The qty can again be either in the URL or post.

Once the product has been successfully added to the cart, we then need to redirect back to the page where the product was added. As we can have multiple locations, we send a returnto variable with the add request. This will contain the URL to redirect back to, once the item has been added to the cart. To stop people from being able to redirect away from the storefront, we prepend the baseurl to the redirect string. To perform the actual redirect, we use the redirector Action Helper's gotoUrl() method. This will create an HTTP redirect for us.

The viewAction() simply assigns the Cart Model to the cartModel View property. Most of the cart viewing functionality has been pushed to the Cart View Helper and Forms, which we will create shortly.

The updateAction() is used to update the Cart Items already stored in the cart. The first part of this updates the quantities. The quantities will be posted to the Action as an array in the quantity parameter. The array will contain the productId as the array key, and the quantity as the value. Therefore, we iterate over the array finding the product by its ID and adding it to the cart. The addItem() method will then update the quantity for us if the item exists and remove any with a zero quantity. Once we have updated the cart quantities, we set the shipping and redirect back to the viewAction.

Creating the Cart Views and Forms

Now that we have our Model and Controller created, we can now start putting everything together and get the cart working.

Cart forms

The Cart will use two forms Storefront_Form_Cart_Add and Storefront_Form_Cart_Table. The add form is displayed next to the products so users can add items to the Cart, and the table form is used to display all the items in the cart so users can edit them.

Add form

The add form can be used by customers browsing the store to quickly add items to their shopping cart. This form will look like the one shown in the screenshot below when it is rendered:

Let's add the code to create the add form now.

application/modules/storefront/forms/Cart/Add.php

```php
class Storefront_Form_Cart_Add extends SF_Form_Abstract
{
    public function init()
    {
        $this->setDisableLoadDefaultDecorators(true);

        $this->setMethod('post');
        $this->setAction('');

        $this->setDecorators(array(
            'FormElements',
            'Form'
        ));

        $this->addElement('text', 'qty', array(
            'decorators' => array(
                'ViewHelper'
            ),
            'style' => 'width: 20px;',
            'value' => 1
        ));

        $this->addElement('submit', 'buy-item', array(
            'decorators' => array(
                'ViewHelper'
            ),
            'label' => 'Add to cart'
        ));

        $this->addElement('hidden', 'productId', array(
            'decorators' => array(
                'ViewHelper'
            ),
        ));
        $this->addElement('hidden', 'returnto', array(
            'decorators' => array(
                'ViewHelper'
            ),
        ));
    }
}
```

The add form contains four elements—qty, buy-item, productId, and returnto. We can see that it is much like the other forms we have created previously. The only major difference here is that we use the setDisableLoadDefaultDecorators() method to disable the default decorators for the form (not the elements). We do this because we do not want the form to contain the default definition list markup (<dl>). We also only use the ViewHelper decorator on each element so that the <dt> and <dd> tags are omitted.

Table form

The table form is going to form the customer shopping cart. Customers will use this form to view, update, and remove items from their cart. This form will look similar to the one showed below when it is rendered:

Let's add the code for the table form now:

application/modules/storefront/forms/Cart/Table.php

```php
class Storefront_Form_Cart_Table extends SF_Form_Abstract
{
    public function init()
    {
        $this->setDisableLoadDefaultDecorators(true);

        $this->setDecorators(array(
            array(
                'ViewScript',
                array('viewScript' => 'cart/_cart.phtml')
            ),
            'Form'
        ));

        $this->setMethod('post');
        $this->setAction('');
```

```
$this->addElement('submit', 'update-cart', array(
    'decorators' => array(
        'ViewHelper'
    ),
    'label' => 'Update'
));
    }
}
```

The table form is highly specialized. Therefore, we have chosen to use a
`ViewScript` decorator. To do this, we first disable the default decorators
using the `setDisableLoadDefaultDecorators()`.

We then need to configure the forms decorators. We will only have two decorators
for the form, `ViewScript` and `Form`. This means that if we render the form, the
`update-cart` element will not be rendered because we have not included the
`FormElements` decorator. This is where the `ViewScript` decorator comes in. We
can use this decorator to render a View script, in this case `cart/_cart.phtml`.
We then have access to all the elements within the form inside this View script,
meaning we can create highly specialized markup without needing to use lots of
complicated decorators.

Also, the table form will need to have fields dynamically added to it as we need a
form element for each cart item. We will look at this shortly when we create the
View Helper and Views for the Cart.

The ViewScript decorator uses a View Partial to render its view script.
This has an overhead as it clones the view instance. Generally, partials
should be avoided in large numbers so do not over use them or the
ViewScript decorator.

SF_Form_Abstract

You may have noticed that our forms did not subclass `Zend_Form` as in our previous
examples. Also, this time we have extended from the `SF_Form_Abstract` class. This
is because we have done some minor refactoring to the SF library so that we can
inject the Model into the form.

`library/SF/Form/Abstract.php`

```
class SF_Form_Abstract extends Zend_Form
{
    protected $_model;

    public function setModel(SF_Model_Interface $model)
    {
```

```
        $this->_model = $model;
    }

    public function getModel()
    {
        return $this->_model;
    }
}
```

The new SF_Form_Abstract class subclasses Zend_Form and adds two new methods, setModel() and getModel(). These simply set, and get, the protected $_model property. This then means that when we instantiate the form, we can pass in the model inside the options array.

```
$form = new SF_Form_Abstract(array('model' => new myModel()));
```

Here we are taking advantage of the fact that the setOptions() method will look for setters that match elements in the options array. In our case, the setOptions() class will find the setModel() method, call it, and pass in the model. This type of functionality is very common in Zend Framework components. It is always worth checking the setOptions() methods on components to see if you can extend them in this way.

To get the model injected on instantiation, we also need to make a minor change to the SF_Model_Abstract.

library/SF/Model/Abstract.php

```
    public function getForm($name)
    {
        if (!isset($this->_forms[$name])) {
            $class = join('_', array(
                    $this->_getNamespace(),
                    'Form',
                    $this->_getInflected($name)
            ));
            $this->_forms[$name] = new $class(
                array('model' => $this)
            );
        }
        return $this->_forms[$name];
    }
```

Here, we simply pass in an array containing the model ($this) when we first instantiate the form class. We now have access to our Model from within our forms.

Cart View Helper

The Cart View Helper is responsible for creating many of the display elements for the cart. Therefore, we will break it down and look at each method in turn.

application/modules/storefront/views/helpers/Cart.php

```php
class Zend_View_Helper_Cart extends Zend_View_Helper_Abstract
{
    public $cartModel;

    public function Cart()
    {
        $this->cartModel = new Storefront_Model_Cart();

        return $this;
    }
}
```

The main `Cart()` method instantiates a new Cart Model and then returns a reference to itself so that we can chain calls to the other methods.

application/modules/storefront/views/helpers/Cart.php

```php
    public function getSummary()
    {
        $currency = new Zend_Currency();
        $itemCount = count($this->cartModel);

        if (0 == $itemCount) {
            return '<p>No Items</p>';
        }

        $html  = '<p>Items: ' . $itemCount;
        $html .= ' | Total: '.$currency->toCurrency
                    ($this->cartModel->getSubTotal());
        $html .= '<br /><a href="';
        $html .= $this->view->url(array(
            'controller' => 'cart',
            'action' => 'view',
            'module' => 'storefront'
            ),
            'default',
            true
        );
        $html .= '">View Cart</a></p>';

        return $html;
    }
```

The getSummary() method creates the HTML that will be used to display a summary of the cart items and subtotal to the user. This will be displayed below the main category menus.

application/modules/storefront/views/helpers/Cart.php

```
public function addForm(Storefront_Resource_Product_Item
                            $product)
{
    $form = $this->cartModel->getForm('cartAdd');
    $form->populate(array(
        'productId' => $product->productId,
        'returnto' => $this->view->url()
    ));
    $form->setAction($this->view->url(array(
        'controller' => 'cart',
        'action' => 'add',
        'module' => 'storefront'
        ),
        'default',
        true
    ));
    return $form;
}
```

The addForm() method will return a form for adding a single product to the cart. This method accepts one parameter $product that must be an instance of Storefront_Resource_Product_Item. We will use this to render individual **add to cart** forms for each product.

application/modules/storefront/views/helpers/Cart.php

```
public function cartTable()
{
    $cartTable = $this->cartModel->getForm('cartTable');
    $cartTable->setAction($this->view->url(array(
        'controller' => 'cart' ,
        'action' => 'update'
        ),
        'default'
    ));

    $qtys = new Zend_Form_SubForm();

    foreach($this->cartModel as $item) {
        $qtys->addElement('text', (string) $item->productId,
            array(
```

```
                        'value' => $item->qty,
                        'belongsTo' => 'quantity',
                        'style' => 'width: 20px;',
                        'decorators' => array(
                            'ViewHelper'
                        ),
                    )
                );
        }
        $cartTable->addSubForm($qtys, 'qtys');

        // add shipping options
        $cartTable->addElement('select', 'shipping', array(
            'decorators' => array(
                'ViewHelper'
            ),
            'MultiOptions' => $this->_getShippingMultiOptions(),
            'onChange' => 'this.form.submit();',
            'value' => $this->cartModel->getShippingCost()
        ));

        return $cartTable;
    }
```

The `cartTable()` method will return the table containing all our cart items, their costs, and totals. This will be used to update items in the cart. We create a subform to dynamically add the cart items quantity elements at runtime. The reason we use a subform is so we can easily get the whole set of quantity fields from the form, and later iterate over them in the View script.

The form will need to contain an array of quantity text elements so that we can iterate over them in the `updateAction` in the controller. To create this array, we pass the `belongsTo` option to the `addElement()` method, which will tell the form that these elements are an array with the name quantity. We also set the value of the element to the `qty` held in the cart item. We also need a way of passing the `productId` for each cart item. To do this, we set the element name to the `productId` of the item. This also helps us by providing a unique name for each element (we have to cast this to a string). It will create a set of text form elements like:

```
<input type="text" style="width: 20px;" value="1" id="quantity-21"
name="quantity[21]"/>

<input type="text" style="width: 20px;" value="5" id="quantity-10"
name="quantity[10]"/>
```

Once we have all the quantity elements in the subform, we then add the whole subform to the main table form using the addSubForm() method. We give this the name of qtys, which we will use in the View script later to retrieve the elements.

We also add the shipping options to the main table form. Here, we use the _getShippingMultiOptions() method to populate the select elements options and set the value to the currently selected shipping option of the cart.

application/modules/storefront/views/helpers/Cart.php

```
public function formatAmount($amount)
{
    $currency = new Zend_Currency();
    return $currency->toCurrency($amount);
}
```

The formatAmount() method is a little helper method we use to display amounts from the Cart. This may not be necessary in the future as there is a proposal for a currency View Helper that we would use instead.

application/modules/storefront/views/helpers/Cart.php

```
private function _getShippingMultiOptions()
{
    $currency = new Zend_Currency();
    $shipping = new Storefront_Model_Shipping();
    $options = array(0 => 'Please Select');

    foreach($shipping->getShippingOptions() as $key => $value) {
        $options["$value"] = $key . ' - ' . $currency-
        >toCurrency($value);
    }

    return $options;
}
```

Our final method is the private _getShippingMultiOptions() method. This is used internally by the cartTable() method to populate the shipping select element's options. This method gets the shipping options from the Shipping Model and creates an array suitable for the multiOptions option.

Cart View scripts

Now that we have all the tools created that we will need to build our cart, we can start creating the user interface.

Cart view.phtml

The `view.phtml` is the View that is rendered by the `viewAction` of the
`CartController`. This View includes a title and renders the `cartTable` form.

application/modules/storefront/views/scripts/cart/view.phtml

```
<h3>shopping <span>cart</span></h3>
<?=$this->Cart()->cartTable();?>
```

Cart _cart.phtml

The `ViewScript` decorator attached to the table form will render the `_cart.phtml`
View. When it renders, the ViewScript decorator will create a view partial and pass
in the form as the element property for this View script.

application/modules/storefront/views/scripts/cart/_cart.phtml

```
<div style="padding: 8px;">
  <table style="width: 100%;">
    <tbody>
        <?
        $i = 0;
        foreach($this->element->getModel() as $item):
        ?>
        <tr <? if($i % 2){ echo 'class="odd"';};?>>
            <td><?=$this->Escape($item->name); ?></td>
            <td><?=$this->element->qtys->getElement
                ($item->productId); ?></td>
            <td class="rt"><?=$this->Cart()->formatAmount
                ($item->getLineCost()); ?></td>
        </tr>
        <?
        ++$i;
        endforeach;
        ?>
        <tr>
            <td colspan="2" class="rt">SubTotal:</td>
            <td class="rt colRight"><?=$this->Cart()
              ->formatAmount($this->element->getModel()
              ->getSubTotal()); ?></td>
        </tr>
        <tr>
            <td colspan="2" class="rt">Shipping: <?=$this->element
              ->getElement('shipping');?></td>
            <td class="rt colRight"><?=$this->Cart()
              ->formatAmount($this->element->getModel()
              ->getShippingCost()); ?></td>
        </tr>
```

```
        <tr>
            <td colspan="2" class="rt">Total:</td>
            <td class="rt"><?=$this->Cart()->formatAmount($this
                ->element->getModel()->getTotal()); ?></td>
        </tr>
    </tbody>
</table>
<?=$this->element->getElement('update-cart'); ?>
</div>
```

The HTML produced by this script will look similar to the following screenshot:

name	1	£12.64
product 12	1	£13.79
product 10	1	£13.79
SubTotal:		£40.22
Shipping: Standard – £1.99		£1.99
Total:		£42.21
Update		

The main aspect here is the line items. We need to iterate over the cart and display each product line item.

```
<?
$i = 0;
foreach($this->element->getModel() as $item):
?>
    <tr <? if($i % 2){ echo 'class="odd"';};?>>
        <td><?=$this->Escape($item->name); ?></td>
        <td>
<?=$this->element->qtys->getElement($item->productId); ?>
        </td>
        <td class="rt">
<?=$this->Cart()->formatAmount($item->getLineCost()); ?>
        </td>
    </tr>
<?
++$i;
endforeach;
?>
```

Here, we get the Cart Model from the form using our new `getModel()` method that we created earlier in the `SF_Form_Abstract` and iterate over it. As we iterate over the Cart Model, we display all the products and line costs. We also get the quantity form elements. To retrieve the correct quantity form element for each product, we access the `qtys` subform and use the `getElement()` method. We pass in the items `productId` as we named our quantity form elements using the `productId` earlier.

All of the other form data is rendered in a similar way. We either get data from the Cart Model, or get elements from the form itself. By using the `ViewScript` decorator, we can see that it is much easier to mix form and non-form elements.

Layout main.phtml

`application/layouts/scripts/main.phtml`

```
<div class="left categorylist">
    <?= $this->layout()->categoryMain; ?>
    <? if (0 < count($this->subCategories)):?>
    <div class="sub-nav">
    <h3>in this <span>category</span></h3>
        <ul>
            <? foreach ($this->subCategories as $category): ?>
            <li><a href="<?=$this->url(array('categoryIdent' =>
                $category->ident), 'catalog_category', true
                );?>"><?=$category->name; ?></a></li>
            <? endforeach; ?>
        </ul>
    </div>
    <? endif; ?>
    <div>
    <h3>in your <span>cart</span></h3>
    <?= $this->Cart()->getSummary(); ?>
    </div>
</div>
```

We need to display the cart summary to the users so that they can see a brief overview of the items in their cart. To do this, we will use the Cart View Helper and the `getSummary()` method that looks similar to the following screenshot:

Catalog index.phtml

application/modules/storefront/view/scripts/catalog/index.phtml

```
<p><?=$this->productPrice($product); ?></p>
<?=$this->Cart()->addForm($product); ?>
```

When displaying a list of products, we want the user to be able to add the product to their cart at that point. To do this, we render the cart add form under the price. This will make our catalog listing look like the one shown below:

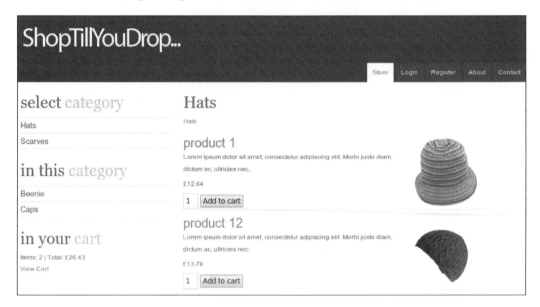

Catalog view.phtml

application/modules/storefront/view/scripts/catalog/view.phtml

```
<p><?=$this->productPrice($this->product); ?></p>
<?=$this->Cart()->addForm($this->product); ?>
```

Just like the `index.phtml`, we need to render the cart add form after the product price. This will make our details page look like this:

Summary

In this chapter, we have looked at creating Models that do not use a database, using Zend_Form to create highly customized form layouts, injecting the Model into the Form instances, and adding dynamic data to our forms. In the next chapter, we will look at authorization and authentication by adding the security layer to the storefront.

8
Authentication and Authorization

We are now reaching the end of the Storefront development. In this chapter, we will focus on how we can control access to parts of the application and how users can log in to use the services provided by the Storefront.

We will cover the following topics in this chapter:

- Authentication and Authorization
- Using `Zend_Auth` and `Zend_Acl`
- Integrating the ACL into our Models

Authentication versus Authorization

Before we go any further, we need to first look at what exactly authentication and authorization is, as they are often misunderstood.

Authorization is the process of allowing someone or something to actually do something. For example, if I go into a data centre, then the security guards control my authorization to the data centre and would, for instance, not allow me access to the server room if I was just a visitor but would if I worked there as a system admin.

Authentication is the process of confirming someone or something's identity. For example, when I go to into the data centre the security guards will ask me for my identity, which most probably would be a card with my name and photo on. They use this to authenticate my identity.

These concepts are very important so make sure you understand the difference. This is how I remember them:

Authorization: Can they do this?

Authentication: Are they who they say they are?

Authentication with Zend_Auth

To provide our authentication layer, we are going to use `Zend_Auth`. It provides an easy way to authenticate a request, obtain a result, and then store the identity of that authentication request.

Zend_Auth

`Zend_Auth` has three main areas—authentication adapters, authentication results, and identity persistence.

Authentication adapters

Authentication adapters work in a similar way to database adapters. We configure the adapter and then pass it to the `Zend_Auth` instance, which then uses it to authenticate the request.

The following concrete adapters are provided by default:

- HTTP Digest authentication
- HTTP Basic authentication
- Database Table authentication
- LDAP authentication
- OpenID authentication
- InfoCard authentication

All of these adapters implement the `Zend_Auth_Adapter_Interface`, meaning we can create our own adapters by implementing this interface.

Authentication results

All authentication adapters return a `Zend_Auth_Result` instance, which stores the result of the authentication request. The stored data includes whether the authentication request was successful, an identity if the request was successful, and any failure messages, if unsuccessful.

Identity persistence

The default persistence used is the PHP session. It uses `Zend_Session_Namespace` to store the identity information in the `Zend_Auth` namespace. There is one other type of storage available named `NonPersistent`, which is used for HTTP authentication. We can also create our own storage by implementing the `Zend_Auth_Storage_Interface`.

Authentication Service

We are going to create an Authentication Service that will handle authentication requests. We are using a service to keep the authentication logic away from our User Model. Let's create this class now:

application/modules/storefront/services/Authentication.php

```
class Storefront_Service_Authentication
{
    protected $_authAdapter;
    protected $_userModel;
    protected $_auth;

    public function __construct(Storefront_Model_User
            $userModel = null)
    {
        $this->_userModel = null === $userModel ?
            new Storefront_Model_User() : $userModel;
    }

    public function authenticate($credentials)
    {
        $adapter = $this->getAuthAdapter($credentials);
        $auth    = $this->getAuth();
        $result  = $auth->authenticate($adapter);

        if (!$result->isValid()) {
            return false;
        }

        $user = $this->_userModel
                    ->getUserByEmail($credentials['email']);

        $auth->getStorage()->write($user);

        return true;
    }

    public function getAuth()
    {
```

```
        if (null === $this->_auth) {
            $this->_auth = Zend_Auth::getInstance();
        }
        return $this->_auth;
    }

    public function getIdentity()
    {
        $auth = $this->getAuth();
        if ($auth->hasIdentity()) {
            return $auth->getIdentity();
        }
        return false;
    }

    public function clear()
    {
        $this->getAuth()->clearIdentity();
    }

    public function setAuthAdapter(Zend_Auth_Adapter_Interface
                                    $adapter)
    {
        $this->_authAdapter = $adapter;
    }

    public function getAuthAdapter($values)
    {
        if (null === $this->_authAdapter) {
            $authAdapter = new Zend_Auth_Adapter_DbTable(
                Zend_Db_Table_Abstract::getDefaultAdapter(),
                'user',
                'email',
                'passwd'
            );
            $this->setAuthAdapter($authAdapter);
            $this->_authAdapter
                ->setIdentity($values['email']);
            $this->_authAdapter
                ->setCredential($values['passwd']);
            $this->_authAdapter
                ->setCredentialTreatment(
                    'SHA1(CONCAT(?,salt))'
                );
        }
        return $this->_authAdapter;
    }
}
```

The Authentication Service contains the following methods:

- `__constuct`: Creates or sets the User Model instance
- `authenticate`: Processes the authentication request
- `getAuth`: Returns the `Zend_Auth` instance
- `getIdentity`: Returns the stored identity
- `clear`: Clears the identity (log out)
- `setAuthAdapter`: Sets the authentication adapter to use
- `getAuthAdapter`: Returns the authentication adapter

The Service is really separated into three areas. They are getting the `Zend_Auth` instance, configuring the adapter, and authenticating the request using `Zend_Auth` and the Adapter.

To get the `Zend_Auth` instance, we have the `getAuth()` method. This method retrieves the singleton `Zend_Auth` instance and sets it on the `$_auth` property. It is important to remember that `Zend_Auth` is a singleton class, meaning that there can only ever be one instance of it.

To configure the adapter, we have the `getAuthAdapter()` method. By default, we are going to use the `Zend_Auth_Adapter_DbTable` adapter to authenticate the request. However, we can also override this by setting another adapter using the `setAuthAdapter()` method. This is useful for adding authenticate strategies and testing. The configuration of the `DbTable` adapter is important here, so let's have a look at that code:

```
$authAdapter = new Zend_Auth_Adapter_DbTable(
    Zend_Db_Table_Abstract::getDefaultAdapter(),
    'user',
    'email',
    'passwd',
    'SHA1(CONCAT(?,salt))'
);
$this->setAuthAdapter($authAdapter);
$this->_authAdapter->setIdentity($values['email']);
$this->_authAdapter->setCredential($values['passwd']);
```

The `Zend_Auth_Adapter_DbTable` constructor accepts five parameters. They are database adapter, database table, table name, identity column, and credential treatment. For our adapter, we supply the default database adapter for our table classes using the `getDefaultAdapter()` method, the user table, the email column, the passwd column, and the encryption and salting SQL for the password. Once we have our configured adapter, we set the identity and credential properties. These will then be used during authentication.

To authenticate the request, we use the authenticate method.

```
$adapter = $this->getAuthAdapter($credentials);
$auth    = $this->getAuth();
$result  = $auth->authenticate($adapter);

if (!$result->isValid()) {
    return false;
}

$user = $this->_userModel
               ->getUserByEmail($credentials['email']);

$auth->getStorage()->write($user);

return true;
```

Here we first get the configured adapter, get the Zend_Auth instance, and then fetch the result using Zend_Auth's authenticate method, while passing in the configured adapter. We then check that the authentication request was successful using the isValid() method. At this point, we can also choose to handle different kinds of failures using the getCode() method. This will return one of the following constants:

```
Zend_Auth_Result::SUCCESS
Zend_Auth_Result::FAILURE
Zend_Auth_Result::FAILURE_IDENTITY_NOT_FOUND
Zend_Auth_Result::FAILURE_IDENTITY_AMBIGUOUS
Zend_Auth_Result::FAILURE_CREDENTIAL_INVALID
Zend_Auth_Result::FAILURE_UNCATEGORIZED
```

By using these, we could switch and handle each error in a different way. However, for our purposes, this is not necessary.

If the authentication request was successful, we then retrieve a Storefront_Resource_User_Item instance from the User Model and then write this object to Zend_Auth's persistence layer by getting the storage instance using getStorage() and writing to it using write(). This will then store the user in the session so that we can retrieve the user information throughout the session.

Our Authentication Service is now complete, and we can start using it to create a login system for the Storefront.

Customer Controller

To use our new Authentication Service, we need to add the following to the Customer Controller:

application/modules/storefront/controllers/CustomerController.php

```
public function init()
{
    // get the default model
    $this->_model = new Storefront_Model_User();
    $this->_authService =
        new Storefront_Service_Authentication();
    // add forms
    $this->view->registerForm = $this->getRegistrationForm();
    $this->view->loginForm = $this->getLoginForm();
    $this->view->userForm = $this->getUserForm();
}
public function loginAction()
{}
public function authenticateAction()
{
    $request = $this->getRequest();
    if (!$request->isPost()) {
        return $this->_helper->redirector('login');
    }
    // Validate
    $form = $this->_forms['login'];
    if (!$form->isValid($request->getPost())) {
        return $this->render('login');
    }
    if (false === $this->_authService->authenticate
                        ($form->getValues())) {
        $form->setDescription('Login failed, please try again.');
        return $this->render('login');
    }
    return $this->_helper->redirector('index');
}
public function logoutAction()
{
    $this->_authService->clear();
    return $this->_helper->redirector('index');
}
public function getLoginForm()
{
    $urlHelper = $this->_helper->getHelper('url');
    $this->_forms['login'] = $this->_model->getForm('userLogin');
```

```
    $this->_forms['login']->setAction($urlHelper->url(array(
        'controller' => 'customer',
        'action'     => 'authenticate',
        ),
        'default'
    ));
    $this->_forms['login']->setMethod('post');

    return $this->_forms['login'];
}
```

We have added three new methods to the Customer Controller—loginAction, authenticateAction, and getLoginForm. We have also updated the init() method to instantiate the Authentication Service and add the login form to the view.

The loginAction is used to display the login form to the user and simply renders the login.phtml view.

The authenticateAction validates the login form, authenticates the request, and then redirects the user to the indexAction if the request is successfully authenticated. If the authentication request fails, we set the description of the form to reflect this and then re-render the login form.

The getLoginForm method simply gets the login form from the User Model. We should already be familiar with the way this works.

Authentication View Helper

There are many times when our Views need to use information about the user to decide whether to display something or not. To help with this, we will create the AuthInfo View Helper.

application/modules/storefront/views/helpers/AuthInfo.php

```
class Zend_View_Helper_AuthInfo extends Zend_View_Helper_Abstract
{
    protected $_authService;
    public function authInfo ($info = null)
    {
        if (null === $this->_authService) {
            $this->_authService = new
                    Storefront_Service_Authentication();
        }
        if (null === $info) {
            return $this;
        }
        if (false === $this->isLoggedIn()) {
            return null;
```

```
        }
        return $this->_authService->getIdentity()->$info;
    }
    public function isLoggedIn()
    {
        return $this->_authService->getAuth()->hasIdentity();
    }
}
```

The `AuthInfo` Helper is pretty simple and wraps the functionality of the Authentication Service for us. Remember though just like Models, our View Helpers should only have read-only access to the Service.

We can use the `AuthInfo` Helper in two ways:

- To get some user information, we use:

  ```
  $this->authInfo('role');
  $this->authInfo('firstname');
  ```

  This would get the `role` and `firstname` of the currently authenticated user or null if they are not logged in.

- To check if the user is logged in or not, we use:

  ```
  $this->authInfo()->isLoggedIn();
  ```

  This will return `true` if they are logged in or `false` if they are not.

Other Authentication Service elements

With the main Authentication components created, all that is left to do is create the forms and update the Views. As we have covered this a few times already, we will not include the code listing here. Instead, copy the following updated or new files from the example files:

- `application/layouts/scripts/_topnav.phtml`: updates the menu to exclude certain items to non-logged in users.
- `application/modules/storefront/forms/User/Login.php`: new login form.
- `application/modules/storefront/views/scripts/customer/login.phtml`: new view to display the login form.

Of course, this would be a good chance for you to try and create these elements yourself. Once these are created, we should be able to log in by registering and then using the newly created user to authenticate with.

Authorization with Zend_Acl

We now have a way to check if a user is who he/she says he/she is. Next we need to stop certain users from accessing certain parts of the application. To do this, we are going to use the `Zend_Acl` component.

Zend_Acl introduction

ACL (Access Control List) lets us create a list that contains all the rules for accessing our system. In `Zend_Acl`, this list works like a tree enabling us to inherit from rule to rule, building up a fine-grained access control system.

There are two main concepts at work in `Zend_Acl` — Resources and Roles. A **Resource** is something that needs to be accessed and a **Role** is the thing that is trying to access the Resource. To have access to a resource, you need to have the correct Role.

To start us off, let's first look at a basic example. In this example, we are going to use the scenario of a data centre. In the data centre, we need to control access to the server room. Only people with the correct permissions will be able to access the server room.

To start, we need to create some Roles and Resources.

```
$visitor = new Zend_Acl_Role('Visitor');
$admin   = new Zend_Acl_Role('Admin');

$serverRoom = new Zend_Acl_Resource('ServerRoom');
```

Here we have created two Roles — Visitor and Admin and one Resource — ServerRoom. Next, we need to create the Access Control List.

```
$acl = new Zend_Acl();
$acl->addRole($visitor);
$acl->addRole($admin, $visitor);
$acl->add($serverRoom);
```

Here we instantiate a new `Zend_Acl` instance and add the two Roles and one new access rule. When we add the Roles, we make the Admin Role inherit from the Visitor Role. This means that Admin inherits all the access rules of the Visitor. We also add one new Rule containing the ServerRoom resource.

At this point, access to the server room is denied for both Visitors and Admins. We can change this by adding allow or deny rules:

- **Allow all to all resources**: `$acl->allow();`
- **Deny all to all resources**: `$acl->deny();`
- **Allow Admin and Deny Visitor to all resources**: `$acl->allow($admin);`
- **Allow Admin and Deny Visitor to ServerRoom resource**: `$acl->allow($admin, $serverRoom);`

When adding rules, we can also set permissions. These can be used to deny/allow access to parts of a Resource. For example, we may allow visitors to view the server room but not access the cabinets. To do this, we can add extra permission options to our rules.

Allow Visitor and Admin to view the ServerRoom, Deny Visitor cabinet access:

```
$acl->allow(visitor, $serverRoom, array('view'));
$acl->deny($visitor, $serverRoom, array('cabinet'));
```

Here we simply add the new permissions as an array containing the strings of the permissions we want to add to the ServerRoom resource.

Next we need to query the ACL. This is done through the `isAllowed()` method.

```
$acl->isAllowed($admin, $serverRoom, 'view');
// returns true

$acl->isAllowed($visitor, $serverRoom, 'view');
// returns true

$acl->isAllowed($visitor, $serverRoom, 'cabinet');
// returns false
```

As we can see, `Zend_Acl` provides us with an easy, lightweight way of controlling access to our systems resources. Next we will look at the ways in which we can use the ACL component in our MVC application.

ACL in MVC

When looking to implement ACL in MVC, we need to first think about how and where we implement the ACL in the MVC layers. The ACL by nature is centralized, meaning that all rules, permissions, and so on are kept in a central place from which we query them. However, do we really want this? What about when we introduce more than one module, do all modules use the same ACL? Also we need to think about where access control happens—is it in the Controller layer or the Model/Domain layer?

Using a centralized global ACL

A common way to implement the ACL is to use a centralized ACL with access controlled at the application level or outside the domain layer. To do this, we first create a centralized ACL. Typically, this would be done during the bootstrap process and the full ACL would be created including all rules, resources, and roles. This can then be placed within the Registry or passed as an invoke argument to the Front Controller. We would then intercept each request using a Front Controller plugin (preDispatch). This would check whether the request was authorized or not using the ACL. If the request was not valid, we would then redirect the request to an access denied controller/action.

This approach would base its rules on the controller/action being requested, so a rule using this may look something like:

```
$acl->allow('Customer', 'user', 'edit');
```

Here we would allow access for a Customer Role to the User Resource and the Edit permission. This would map to the user Controller, and the edit action or user/edit.

The advantages of using centralized global ACL are as follows:

- Centralized place to access and manage ACL rules, resources, and roles
- Maps nicely to the MVC controller/action architecture

The disadvantages are as follows:

- Centralized ACL could become large and hard to manage
- No means to handle modules
- We would need to re-implement access controls in order to use our Domain in a web service, as they are based on action/controller

Using module specific ACL's

The next logical step is to split the ACL so that we have one ACL per module. To do this, we would still create our ACL during bootstrap but this time we would create a separate ACL for each module, and then we would use an Action Helper instead of Front Controller plugin to intercept the request (preDispatch).

Advantages:

- Fixes our module handling problem with the previous approach
- Keeps things modular and smaller

Disadvantages:

- We still have the problem of having to re-implement access control if we use our Domain away from the controller/action context.

ACL in the Domain layer

To deal with our last concern about what if we need to use the Domain in another context outside the controller/action architecture, we have the option to move all the Access Control into the Domain itself. To do this, we would have one ACL per module but would push the management of this into the Model. The Models would then be responsible for handling their own access rules. This in effect will give us a de-centralized ACL, as the Models will add all rules to the ACL.

Advantages:

- We can use the Model in different contexts without the need to re-implement the access control rules.
- We can unit test the access control
- The rules will be based on Model methods and not depend on the application layer

Disadvantages:

- Adds complexity to the Domain/Models
- Being de-centralized, it could be harder to manage

For the Storefront, we have opted to use the Model based ACL approach. While it adds more complexity and implementation can be a little confusing, the advantages of being able to unit test and use the Models outside the application layer is a big advantage. It also gives us a chance to demonstrate some of the more advanced features of the ACL component.

Model based ACL

The first thing to look at is some of the main components that we need to implement a Model based ACL. The main elements here are as follows:

- **The ACL**: This stores the roles we want in the system and any global rules.
- **Resource(s)**: This will be our Model. The Model will become the Resource we wish to access.
- **Roles**: These are the actual roles we wish to use.

As we can see there is nothing new here, we are just going to be implementing them in a different way than in our earlier examples. To do this, we are going to need to create some new classes and refactor some old ones. We will start though by looking at the main ACL class and Roles.

The Storefront ACL

We will need a `Zend_Acl` instance for the storefront module. We will use this to store all our roles and rules.

`application/modules/storefront/models/Acl/Storefront.php`

```
class Storefront_Model_Acl_Storefront extends Zend_Acl implements
SF_Acl_Interface
{
    public function __construct()
    {
       $this->addRole(new Storefront_Model_Acl_Role_Guest)
            ->addRole(new Storefront_Model_Acl_Role_Customer, 'Guest')
            ->addRole(new Storefront_Model_Acl_Role_Admin, 'Customer');

        $this->deny();
    }
}
```

The `Storefront_Model_Acl_Storefront` class will store all the rules that the storefront module's Models add to it. This class subclasses the `Zend_Acl` class and using the constructor adds the available roles to the ACL tree. We add three roles to the ACL—Guest, Customer, and Admin. The Customer role inherits from the Guest and the Admin role inherits from the Customer. We then deny access to all resources using the `deny()` method with no parameters. This effectively creates a white-list, meaning that everything is denied unless we explicitly allow it.

We can see that the `Storefront_Model_Acl_Storefront` class is very simple and is only responsible for setting up the roles. The Models will define the resources and permissions later.

The Storefront roles

Previously, we added the three storefront user roles to the ACL. We will need to create the Role classes for each of them. To create a Role class, we need to implement the `Zend_Acl_Role_Interface` interface. This interface defines one method (`getRoleId()`), which should return the role identity string.

application/modules/storefront/models/Acl/Role/Admin.php

```
class Storefront_Model_Acl_Role_Admin implements
Zend_Acl_Role_Interface
{
    public function getRoleId()
    {
        return 'Admin';
    }
}
```

application/modules/storefront/models/Acl/Role/Customer.php

```
class Storefront_Model_Acl_Role_Customer implements
Zend_Acl_Role_Interface
{
    public function getRoleId()
    {
        return 'Customer';
    }
}
```

application/modules/storefront/models/Acl/Role/Guest.php

```
class Storefront_Model_Acl_Role_Guest implements
Zend_Acl_Role_Interface
{
    public function getRoleId()
    {
        return 'Guest';
    }
}
```

Here we have created the three roles available to the storefront (Admin, Customer, and Guest). Each one simply implements the `Zend_Acl_Role_Interface` and returns a string that uniquely identifies it. However, there is one more class that needs to implement the `Zend_Acl_Role_Interface`, which is the `Storefront_Resource_User_Item` class.

application/modules/storefront/models/resources/User/Item.php

```
class Storefront_Resource_User_Item extends
SF_Model_Resource_Db_Table_Row_Abstract implements
Storefront_Resource_User_Item_Interface, Zend_Acl_Role_Interface
{
    /*... */

    public function getRoleId()
    {
        if (null === $this->getRow()->role) {
            return 'Guest';
        }
        return $this->getRow()->role;
    }
}
```

Here we have updated our user model resource item to implement the `Zend_Acl_Role_Interface` and added the `getRoleId()` method. This method either returns the user's current role column or Guest if the role is not set. We do this because we are storing the user item in the `Zend_Auth` identity and will be passing this to the Models for them to use for authorization checks. We can then be sure that the Models are using a valid identity.

The Storefront resources

As we said before in this implementation, the Model will be the Resource. The way we achieve this is very simple. All we need to do is implement the `Zend_Acl_Resource_Interface`, and this will then turn our Models (or any class) into valid ACL Resources. Here is a basic example:

```
class MyClass implements Zend_Acl_Resource_Interface
{
    public function getResourceId()
    {
        return 'MyResource';
    }
}
```

Once our class has implemented the resource interface, we can use it with the ACL:

```
$resource = new MyClass();
$acl = new Zend_Acl();
$acl->add($resource);
```

We are half way to having the ACL integrated into our Models. Next, we will create some abstract classes and interfaces that our Models can use to fully implement all the required functionality.

The new base model

To fully use the ACL, our Models need access to the ACL, the resource, and the identity. In our implementation these are `Storefront_Model_Acl_Storefront`, the Model (`$this`), and `Storefront_Resource_User_Item` (stored in `Zend_Auth`). To make these available to the Model, we are going to need some extra functionality added to each of our Models. To encapsulate this, we are going to create a new abstract model class and some new interfaces.

`library/SF/Model/Acl/Interface.php`

```
interface SF_Model_Acl_Interface
{
    public function setIdentity($identity);
    public function getIdentity();
    public function setAcl(SF_Acl_Interface $acl);
    public function getAcl();
    public function checkAcl($action);
}
```

Here we have defined a new interface for our Models. This also introduces the `SF_Model_Acl` namespace. As not all of our Models will use the ACL, we will make it optional whether the Model uses the `SF_Model` or `SF_Modle_Acl` classes. The interface defines five methods. These will be used to set and get the identity and ACL and also to query the ACL.

`library/SF/Model/Acl/Abstract.php`

```
abstract class SF_Model_Acl_Abstract extends SF_Model_Abstract
implements SF_Model_Acl_Interface, Zend_Acl_Resource_Interface
{
    protected $_acl;

    protected $_identity;

    public function setIdentity($identity)
    {
        if (is_array($identity)) {
```

```
            if (!isset($identity['role'])) {
                $identity['role'] = 'Guest';
            }
            $identity = new Zend_Acl_Role($identity['role']);
        } elseif (is_scalar($identity) && !is_bool($identity)) {
            $identity = new Zend_Acl_Role($identity);
        } elseif (null === $identity) {
            $identity = new Zend_Acl_Role('Guest');
        } elseif (!$identity instanceof Zend_Acl_Role_Interface) {
            throw new SF_Model_Exception('Invalid identity
                                         provided');
        }
        $this->_identity = $identity;
        return $this;
    }

    public function getIdentity()
    {
        if (null === $this->_identity) {
            $auth = Zend_Auth::getInstance();
            if (!$auth->hasIdentity()) {
                return 'Guest';
            }
            $this->setIdentity($auth->getIdentity());
        }
        return $this->_identity;
    }

    public function checkAcl($action)
    {
        return $this->getAcl()->isAllowed(
            $this->getIdentity(),
            $this,
            $action
        );
    }
}
```

The SF_Model_Acl_Abstract class subclasses the SF_Model_Abstract and implements the SF_Model_Acl_Interface and Zend_Acl_Resource_Interface interfaces. All Models that need ACL support can now subclass the SF_Model_Acl_Abstract.

The setIdentity() method will accept either null, string, array, or a Zend_Acl_Role_Interface instance. The identity should contain the role to be used when checking the ACL. If no role is set, then we default to the Guest role.

The `getIdentity()` method is designed to lazy load the identity from `Zend_Auth`. Therefore, we first check if the `$_identity` property is null. If it is, then we retrieve the identity from `Zend_Auth` and set it on the Model using `setIdentity()`. The identity returned by `Zend_Auth` will be an instance of `Storefront_Resource_User_Item`. This implements the `Zend_Acl_Role_Interface` and as a result it is fine to set it on the Model. During normal use we would always rely on the lazy loading here. The only time we would not is during testing when we need to set the identity ourselves and not from the session.

The `checkAcl()` method is used to query the ACL. This method simply returns the result of the `isAllowed()` method of the `Zend_Acl` class. We can see that we pass the identity, the resource (`$this`/`$the` Model), and the action to `isAllowed()`. The action will be defined by us when we configure the ACL inside the concrete Models and simply represent the permission or the action that is trying to be undergone.

You will notice that we still have not implemented some of the methods defined in the `SF_Model_Acl_Interface` and `Zend_Acl_Resource_Interface` interfaces. These will need to be implemented inside the concrete Models as they contain Model specific settings.

Securing the User Model

Now that we have the base class created, we can start securing our application. To do this, we will edit the User Model. The first step is to have the Model subclass the `SF_Model_Acl_Abstract` class.

application/modules/storefront/models/User.php

```
class Storefront_Model_User extends SF_Model_Acl_Abstract
{
```

Once we have the User Model subclassing the `SF_Model_Acl_Abstract`, we then must implement the `getAcl()`, `setAcl()`, and `getResourceId()` methods.

application/modules/storefront/models/User.php

```
public function getResourceId()
{
    return 'User';
}
public function setAcl(SF_Acl_Interface $acl)
{
    if (!$acl->has($this->getResourceId())) {
        $acl->add($this)
            ->allow('Guest', $this, array('register'))
            ->allow('Customer', $this, array('saveUser'))
```

```
                    ->allow('Admin', $this);
        }
        $this->_acl = $acl;
        return $this;
    }

    public function getAcl()
    {
        if (null === $this->_acl) {
            $this->setAcl(new Storefront_Model_Acl_Storefront());
        }
        return $this->_acl;
    }
```

First we implement the getResourceId() method, which is defined by the Zend_Acl_Resource_Interface interface and simply returns the string identifying the resource (the Model) as User.

Next, we implement the setAcl() method, which is defined by the SF_Model_Acl_ Interface interface. This method is responsible for configuring our ACL by adding the Resources and Rules. We first check to see if the ACL has the Resource registered to it. If not, we then add the Resource ($this) and configure the rules for the User Model. The rules here are as follows:

- **Guest** can access register
- **Customer** can access register and saveUser
- **Admin** can access everything (we pass null as the action)

Once the ACL is configured, we set the ACL on the $_acl property and return $this to allow method chaining. Note that the permission names we use do not have to match method names.

Our final method is getAcl(). This again is defined by the SF_Model_Acl_ Interface interface. This method checks if the $_acl property has been set and then if not sets a new Storefront_Model_Acl_Storefront instance as the ACL to be used. We do this to help with testing later on, as it allows us to not use the default ACL and inject a mock one instead.

Now that we have implemented all of our required methods, we can start querying the ACL to deny or allow access to parts of the Model. Edit the User Model and add the following to the methods as shown.

application/modules/storefront/models/User.php

```
    public function saveUser($post, $validator = null)
    {
        if (!$this->checkAcl('saveUser')) {
            throw new SF_Acl_Exception("Insufficient rights");
```

```
    }
/*...*/

public function registerUser($post)
{
    if (!$this->checkAcl('register')) {
        throw new SF_Acl_Exception("Insufficient rights");
    }
/*...*/
```

To query the ACL, we simply need to call the `checkAcl()` method. This will then query the ACL for us and tell us if the current user has the correct access permissions. If the User does not have the correct permissions, then we throw an `SF_Acl_Exception`. You will need to copy this exception class from the example files.

We now have a fully working ACL that is integrated into the Domain layer of our MVC application and we are not depending on the Controller layer for this functionality, meaning we can use the Models outside the MVC context. It is important to note that we could also implement the ACL in this way for other entities within the application, such as Services. All we need to do is create the base classes for that namespace or create a more generic set of ACL base classes.

Non-Model ACL

With this implementation, we also have the ability to use the ACL in a more common way. We can still add other Resources to the ACL that are not Models, meaning we can control access to non-Model Resources.

For the next chapter, we will be creating the administrator functionality for the Storefront. The way we do this there will not be an `admin` Model. However, we still want to deny access to this area to anyone without the Admin Role. To deal with this requirement, we are going to create a new Resource and add it to the ACL. To start, create the following ACL resource class:

```
application/modules/storefront/models/Acl/Resources/Admin.php

class Storefront_Model_Acl_Resource_Admin implements
Zend_Acl_Resource_Interface
{
    public function getResourceId()
    {
        return 'Admin';
    }
}
```

Here we have simply created a new ACL Resource identified as `Admin`, which will represent the administration area. Next, we need to add the following code to the ACL:

`application/modules/storefront/models/Acl/Storefront.php`

```
class Storefront_Model_Acl_Storefront extends Zend_Acl implements
SF_Acl_Interface
{
    public function __construct()
    {
        $this->addRole(new Storefront_Model_Acl_Role_Guest)
            ->addRole(new Storefront_Model_Acl_Role_Customer,
                'Guest')
            ->addRole(new Storefront_Model_Acl_Role_Admin,
                'Customer');

        $this->deny();

    $this->add(new Storefront_Model_Acl_Resource_Admin)
        ->allow('Admin');
    }
}
```

Here we add the new Resource to the main ACL and allow admin access for all permissions. We now have the ACL configured and can query it to see if a user is allowed to access this Resource. In the next chapter, we will create an Action Helper to help us query the ACL from within our Controllers.

It is important to note that when we use the ACL like this it obviously creates a dependency on the application layer, so it is important that we only use it where necessary and make sure we push whatever we can into the Models. The Admin Resource only really exists within the Application layer and has no Model. This will become clearer when we implement the administration area.

Unit testing with ACL

One of the advantages of integrating the ACL into our Models is that we can now test security in our unit tests. There is a whole suite of unit tests included with the example files. Let's have a look at the User Model tests as well as one of the tests that makes use of the new ACL integration:

`tests/unit/Model/UserTest.php`

```
public function test_User_Can_Be_Edited_By_Customer_And_Admin()
{
    $post = array(
        'userId'      => 10,
```

```
            'title'      => 'Mr',
            'firstname' => 'keith',
            'lastname' => 'pope',
            'email'      => 'me@me.com'
        );

        // Guest
        try {
            $edit = $this->_model->saveUser($post);
            $this->fail('Guest should not be able to edit user');
        } catch (SF_Acl_Exception $e) {}

        // Customer
        try {
            $this->_model->setIdentity(array('role' => 'Customer'));
            $edit = $this->_model->saveUser($post);
        } catch (SF_Acl_Exception $e) {
            $this->fail('Customer should be able to edit user');
        }

        // Admin
        try {
            $this->_model->setIdentity(array('role' => 'Admin'));
            $edit = $this->_model->saveUser($post);
        } catch (SF_Acl_Exception $e) {
            $this->fail('Admin should be able to edit user');
        }

        $this->assertEquals(10, $edit);
    }
```

This test is used to validate the security of the User Model without going into too much detail on how PHPUnit works. We can have three main assertions in this test:

- Guest should not be able to saveUser
- Customer should be able to saveUser
- Admin should be able to saveUser

When we run the Guest assertion, we use the default identity created by our Models, which is Guest. This means that the $_model->saveUser() call should throw an SF_Acl_Exception. If it does not, then we fail the test.

When running the Customer and Admin assertions, we inject the role we wish to use by calling the setIdentity() method. Remember we have no Zend_Auth session, so we manually set the identity. We then fail the test if an SF_Acl_Exception is thrown as Customer and Admin should be allowed to saveUser.

As we can see, the Model-ACL implementation provides us with a flexible platform for testing and using the Models outside the MVC setting.

Summary

We now have a fully working authentication and authorization system integrated into the Storefront. In the first part of this chapter, we looked at authentication (are they who they say they are?) and used `Zend_Auth` to create the Authentication Service. This enabled our users to be authenticated by the Storefront and their identity stored for later use with the authorization systems.

In the second part of this chapter, we looked at authorization (can they do this?) and different ways of using `Zend_Acl`. We opted to integrate the authorization layer into our Models so that we could use the Models outside the typical MVC context. To implement this, we created a new base Model class for Models that need ACL support and then secured the User Model using this new functionality.

In the next chapter, we will look at adding some basic administrator functionality to the Storefront as well as allowing the addition of products to the catalog.

The Administration Area

We have now reached the final part of the Storefront development. In this chapter, we will focus on the creation of the functionality to administer the Storefront catalog.

We will cover the following topics in this chapter:

- Ways of implementing administration areas
- Adding products to the catalog
- Securing the administration area

What is an administration area?

The creation of an administration area is a very common use case for a web-based application. Typically we want to have an area where users with administrator privileges can have access to manage the application's settings. Also we probably want to use a different layout so that it is easier to navigate to things like users and products. Therefore, for the Storefront, we want to create a separate area from the main Storefront where Admin users can add, edit, and delete products and users.

Implementation options

When implementing an administration area to an application, we have two choices: We can create a module that is totally separate from our main module(s) or we can create a pseudo module that acts like a normal module but all functionality is actually held within our main module(s).

If we use a separate module, we will have a separate application layer from our main modules, meaning the administration area will have its own set of Controllers, Views, and so on.

Advantages of using a separate module:

- For large applications, having separate controllers can help reduce the size of the main module(s) controllers
- Less Views and Controller Actions in the main module(s)

Disadvantages of using a separate module:

- We have a module that could contain functionality that affects many other modules, and this could become confusing
- We have to solve cross module access problems

If we use a pseudo module, then all the administration Controllers, Views, and so on will be within our main module(s).

Advantages of using a pseudo module:

- Administration functionality is contained within the main module(s), which can be logically easier to understand. For example, the save operations for a module is contained within that module, not outside it.
- Modules become easier to reuse in other applications.

Disadvantage of using a pseudo module:

- Controllers can become large

Both of these approaches are equally valid. We just need to consider our options carefully before we implement them. For the Storefront, we have chosen to use a pseudo module so that all our administration functionality is contained within the main module.

Implementing the storefront administration area

To implement the administration area of the Storefront, we are going to need to create our pseudo module. To do this, we are going to use a Route, Front Controller plugin, and a Layout Script.

Admin Route

The Admin Route will be added to the Router and will match URLs that point to the admin resources. Add the following to the Bootstrap classes `_initRoutes()` method, while making sure that this route is the first route to be added to the Router.

application/bootstrap/Bootstrap.php

```
// Admin context route
$route = new Zend_Controller_Router_Route(
    'admin/:module/:controller/:action/*',
    array(
        'action'     => 'index',
        'controller' => 'admin',
        'module'     => 'storefront',
        'isAdmin'     => true
    )
);


$router->addRoute('admin', $route);
```

This route is designed to match any URL that has `/admin` as its first segment and then act like the default route, for example, `admin/storefront/catalog/list/`. To define the route, we instantiate a new `Zend_Controller_Router_Route` route, passing in the route definition that defines:

- The first segment must be the string admin
- The second segment will be used to define the module to use
- The third segment will be used to define the controller to use
- The fourth segment will be used to define the action to use
- The fifth segment adds any user parameters from the URL

We also have the following defaults for this route:

- The default module is `storefront`
- The default controller is `admin`
- The default action is `index`
- `isAdmin` is set to `true`

The `isAdmin` variable we set here will be set as a Request parameter if the route is matched. We will use this later when testing whether we should display the Admin layout instead of the default one.

Admin context Front Controller plugin

Now that we have our Admin Route created, we are going to create a Front Controller plugin that will switch the Layout Script for us if the current request is for an admin resource. By doing this, we can have a totally different layout for our administrator users.

Create the following class in the SF library:

library/SF/Plugin/AdminContext.php

```
class SF_Plugin_AdminContext extends Zend_Controller_Plugin_Abstract
{
    public function preDispatch(Zend_Controller_Request_Abstract
    $request)
    {
        if($request->getParam('isAdmin')) {
            $layout = Zend_Layout::getMvcInstance();
            $layout->setLayout('admin');
        }
    }
}
```

The AdminContext plugin hooks into the preDispatch event of the Front Controller and will change the layout script for us. Inside the preDispatch() method, we simply check whether the isAdmin Request parameter is true. If it is, then we retrieve the Zend_Layout instance using the static getMvcInstance() method. Once we have the Zend_Layout instance, we set the layout script to admin using the setLayout() method. This will then make Zend_Layout load the admin.phtml instead of the main.phtml layout script when the Router has matched our Admin Route.

To enable our Front Controller plugin, we will need to update the store.ini config file, while adding the following to the bootstrap section of the store.ini:

```
resources.frontcontroller.plugins.admin = "SF_Plugin_AdminContext"
```

This will then instantiate our new plugin for us and register it with the Front Controller.

Admin layout

For our new `AdminContext` plugin to work, we will need to create the new layout script for the administration area. Create the following view scripts:

`application/layouts/scripts/admin.phtml`

```
<html xmlns="http://www.w3.org/1999/xhtml" lang="en" xml:lang="en">
<head>
    <?= $this->headTitle(); ?>

    <?= $this->headMeta(); ?>

    <?= $this->headStyle(); ?>

    <?= $this->headLink(); ?>

    <?= $this->headScript(); ?>
</head>
<body>
    <h1 class="noDisplay">
        <?= $this->placeholder('Zend_View_Helper_HeadTitle');?>
    </h1>

    <div id="headwrap" class="clearfix">

        <div class="right">
            <?= $this->render('_adminnav.phtml') ?>
        </div>

        <div id="logo" class="left">
            <img src="/images/layout/logo.png" alt="Shop till you
              drop..." />
        </div>

    </div>

    <div id="contentWrap" class="clearfix">
        <?= $this->layout()->content ?>
    </div>

    <div id="footer" class="clearfix">
        <div class="left">
            <span class="rss"><a href="/rss" title="products
                feed">RSS 2.0</a></span>
        </div>
        <div class="right">
            &#169; 2008 Keith Pope
        </div>
    </div>
</body>
</html>
```

The admin layout is very similar to the main layout. However, we are rendering a different main navigation menu and do not include things like the shopping cart. For the Storefront, we are using the same design as the frontend. Remember that this does not have to be the case; we could use a totally different design if we wanted to and only use the same design here for simplicity.

application/layouts/scripts/_adminnav.phtml

```
<h2 class="noDisplay">Main Navigation</h2>
<div class="main-nav">
    <ul class="clearfix">
        <li><a href="<?=$this->url(array('controller' => 'customer',
            'action' => 'list')); ?>" title="Customers">Customers
        </a></li>
        <li><a href="<?=$this->url(array('controller' => 'catalog',
            'action' => 'list')); ?>" title="Catalog">Catalog
        </a></li>
        <li><a href="/" title="Homepage">Store</a></li>
    </ul>
</div>
```

The _adminnav.phtml is rendered by the admin.phtml script and simply displays the available admin sections.

We also need to update the main layout script and add in the admin link. In order to do this, edit the main.phtml file and add the following to the admin anchor tag:

application/layouts/scripts/main.phtml

```
<a href="<?= $this->url(array(
                'controller' => 'admin',
                'action'     => 'index',
                'module'     => 'storefront'
                ),
                'admin', true
            );
        ?>"
        title="administration area">Admin</a>
```

Admin controller

The final part to implementing our administration area is to create the Admin Controller. We had defined this in our Admin Route so we need to create this for everything to work. This controller will be called when a user visits /admin.

application/modules/storefront/controllers/AdminController.php

```
class Storefront_AdminController extends Zend_Controller_Action
{
    public function indexAction()
    {}
}
```

The Admin Controller contains one action index, and this will render the admin index View. You will need to create this View script or copy it from the Chapter 9 | part 1 example files.

Our administration area should now be accessible. If we build the application and visit /admin, we should now get a different layout looking something like the one shown in the following screenshot:

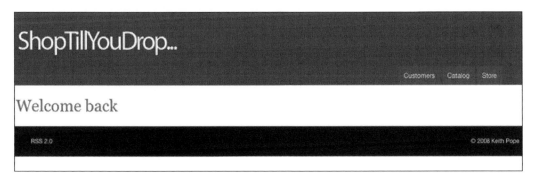

Catalog management

Now that we have our administration area, let's add some administrative functionality to the Storefront. For this, we will add the ability to add products to the catalog. To do this, we will need to install the second part of the example files. This will be our starting point for the rest of this chapter.

In the Chapter 9 example files, we have three directories, Part1, Part2, and Final. To follow the next set of examples you will need to overwrite all the previous code we have created with the code contained within the Part2 directory. We are doing this so that we don't repeat too much code, though you may find it useful to look through the code once we have finished the chapter.

The updated files provide the following functionality:

- Browsing the catalog
- Adding Categories
- Managing Users
- Adding Images to products

This leaves us with the task of implementing the add functionality for products. If we now run a build, then we should be able to log in and browse the catalog products in the admin area, which should look as shown in the following screenshot:

 The default login is me@me.com with a password of 123456.

Adding products

Now that we have imported the updated files, we can start implementing the product creation functionality. To do this, we will need to create a product form, update the Catalog Model, update the Catalog Controller, and create the related View scripts.

Product add form

Just like when we were implementing the frontend customer functionality, we will use the product form to filter and validate data for our Catalog Model. Create the following form class:

application/modules/storefront/forms/Catalog/Product/Add.php

```
class Storefront_Form_Catalog_Product_Add extends SF_Form_Abstract
{
    public function init()
    {
        // add path to custom validators & filters
        $this->addElementPrefixPath(
            'Storefront_Validate',
            APPLICATION_PATH .'/modules/storefront/models/validate/',
            'validate'
        );
        $this->addElementPrefixPath(
            'Storefront_Filter',
            APPLICATION_PATH . '/modules/storefront/models/filter/',
            'filter'
        );
        $this->setMethod('post');
        $this->setAction('');
        // get category select
        $form = new Storefront_Form_Catalog_Category_Select(
            array('model' => $this->getModel())
        );
        $element = $form->getElement('categoryId');
        $element->clearDecorators()->loadDefaultDecorators();
        $element->setRequired(true);
        $this->addElement($element);
        $this->addElement('text', 'name', array(
            'label' => 'Name',
            'filters' => array('StringTrim'),
            'required' => true,
        ));
        $this->addElement('text', 'ident', array(
            'label' => 'Ident',
            'filters' => array('StringTrim','Ident'),
            'validators' => array(
                array('UniqueIdent', true, array($this
                        ->getModel(), 'getProductByIdent'))
            ),
            'required' => true,
        ));
```

```
$this->addElement('text', 'shortDescription', array(
    'label' => 'Short Description',
    'required' => true,
    'filters' => array('StringTrim'),
    'validators' => array(array('StringLength',true,
                        array(1,255))),
));

$this->addElement('text', 'price', array(
    'label' => 'Price',
    'required' => true,
    'validators' => array('Float')
));

$this->addElement('text', 'discountPercent',array(
    'label' => 'Discount %',
    'value' => 0,
    'required' => true,
    'validators' => array('Int'),
));

$this->addElement('select', 'taxable', array(
    'label' => 'Taxable?',
    'multiOptions' => array('Yes' => 'Yes', 'No' => 'No')
));

$this->addElement('textarea', 'description', array(
    'label' => 'Full Description',
    'filters' => array('StringTrim'),
    'required' => true,
));

$this->addDisplayGroup(array(
    'categoryId',
    'name',
    'ident',
    'shortDescription',
    'price',
    'discountPercent',
    'taxable',
    'description'
), 'productInfo', array('legend' => 'Product Information'));

$this->addElement('submit', 'add', array(
    'label' => 'Add Product',
    'decorators' => array('ViewHelper',array
                        ('HtmlTag',array('tag' => 'dd'))),
));
    }
}
```

This will produce a form, as shown in the following screenshot:

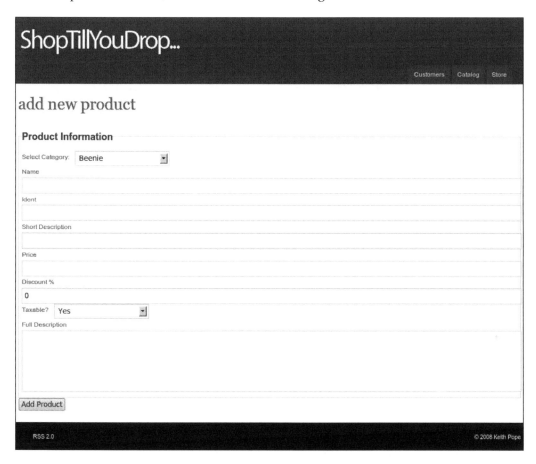

As we can see, the product add form is fairly weighty but most of this has already been covered in our previous forms. However, we have introduced a few new things, so let's have a look at those. Also note that we have not used a base form class for the product form. In a normal application, we would probably use a base class as we would want to use the form for more than just adding context. For now though we will keep it simple.

Sharing form elements

The first difference from our other forms is that we are using another form to create the category drop-down menu for the product form, which is a common requirement as we don't want to duplicate our code. Therefore, we use the other form within our product form while pulling the element we want from that form. Let's have a look at the code:

```
$form = new Storefront_Form_Catalog_Category_Select(
    array('model' => $this->getModel())
);
$element = $form->getElement('categoryId');
$element->clearDecorators()->loadDefaultDecorators();
$element->setRequired(true);
$this->addElement($element);
```

So to share elements from another form, we simply instantiate the form that we want to get the element from, in this case the Catalog_Category_Select form class. We imported this form when we copied the assets folder contents into our application, and it simply queries the Catalog Model and creates an HTML select element for the Storefront categories.

When we instantiate the Catalog_Category_Select form, we also pass in an options array containing the Model to use for the lookup. In this case, this is the Catalog Model which is already registered to the Product Add form ($this->getModel()). Once we have the form instance, we then retrieve the categoryId element from it. This will give us the select element populated with the Storefront categories. We then need to reset the decorators for the element as the categoryId element uses non default decorators. We do this by calling $element->clearDecorators()->loadDefaultDecorators();, which will first clear the element's decorators and then load the default ones for that element. After this, all that is left to do is set the element required and add the element to the form.

If we share elements, then it is important that we document it clearly and try not to overuse this technique. If we do it too often, then we will end up with a mess of interdependencies that will become hard to track. Another way of sharing common elements like this would be to create our own form element class.

Custom filters

The forms **Ident** field uses a custom filter to convert the product ident into a URL friendly format. Using custom filters in forms works in the same way as validators, which we have used before.

```
$this->addElementPrefixPath(
    'Storefront_Filter',
    APPLICATION_PATH . '/modules/storefront/models/filter/',
    'filter'
);
```

Before we can use our custom filter, we need to let the form know where our filters are kept. We do this by using the `addElementPrefixPath()` method. While defining the validator path, we specify a namespace `Storefront_Filter` that our filter classes will be prefixed with, the path to the `filter` directory, and finally the type, which is `filter`.

To create a filter, we need to create a new class within the filter directory that will implement the `Zend_Filter_Interface` interface. This interface defines one method `filter()`, which will be used to return the transformed data.

application/modules/storefront/models/filter/Ident.php

```
class Storefront_Filter_Ident implements Zend_Filter_Interface
{
    public function filter($value)
    {
        $find    = array( '`', '&',    ' ', '"', "'" );
        $replace = array( '',   'and', '-', '',  '', );
        $new = str_replace( $find, $replace,$value);

        $noalpha =
          'ÁÉÍÓÚÝáéíóúýÂÊÎÔÛâêîôûÀÈÌÒÙàèìòùÄËÏÖÜäëïöüÿÃãÕõÅåÑñÇç@°ºª';
        $alpha   =
          'AEIOUYaeiouyAEIOUaeiouAEIOUaeiouAEIOUaeiouyAaOoAaNnCcaooa';

        $new = substr( $new, 0, 255 );
        $new = strtr( $new, $noalpha, $alpha );

        // not permitted chars are replaced with "-"
        $new = preg_replace( '/[^a-zA-Z0-9_\+]/', '-', $new );

        //remove -----'s
        $new = preg_replace( '/(-+)/', '-', $new );

        return rtrim( $new, '-' );
    }
}
```

This filter will take the value of the ident field and transform it from something like my product to my-product. It also removes any invalid characters that would break the URI. To use our filter, we simply need to define it in the filters array for our element. In this case, this is the ident element.

The rest of our form uses functionality that we have already covered and defines all the elements we require to create a valid product. Next, we will use this form in our Catalog Model to validate and filter the input.

Catalog Model

Now that our form is ready, we can add the saveProduct() method to the Catalog Model, edit the Catalog Model, and add the following method:

application/modules/storefront/models/Catalog.php

```
public function saveProduct($data, $validator = null)
{
    if (null === $validator) {
        $validator = 'add';
    }

    $validator = $this->getForm(
        'catalogProduct' . ucfirst($validator)
    );

    if (!$validator->isValid($data)) {
        return false;
    }

    $data = $validator->getValues();

    return $this->getResource('Product')->saveRow($data);
}
```

The saveProduct() method accepts two parameters—$data and $validator. $data should contain an array of the product data, and $validator is an optional parameter that can be used to define the form to use for validation and filtering.

In the method body, we first default the validator to the add form if $validator is null. We then get the form and use it to validate the incoming $data array. If validation fails, then we will return false. Next, we filter the data by retrieving the values from the form using the getValues() method. Once we have the filter data, we can then get the Product Resource and save the data to the database using the saveRow() method.

Catalog Controller

Now that our Model has the ability to save products, we can start putting everything together in our Controller. Edit the CatalogController, and add the following methods:

application/modules/storefront/controllers/CatalogController.php

```
public function addproductAction()
{
    $this->view->productForm = $this->_getProductForm();
}
```

The addproduct Action is used to display the product add form. In this Action, we simply assign the form to the View using the _getProductForm() method.

application/modules/storefront/controllers/CatalogController.php

```
protected function _getProductForm()
{
    $urlHelper = $this->_helper->getHelper('url');

    $this->_forms['addProduct'] = $this->_catalogModel
                ->getForm('catalogProductAdd');
    $this->_forms['addProduct']->setAction($urlHelper->url(array(
        'controller' => 'catalog' ,
        'action' => 'saveproduct'
        ),
        'admin'
    ));
    $this->_forms['addProduct']->setMethod('post');

    return $this->_forms['addProduct'];
}
```

The _getProductForm() method configures and returns the product add form. This is the same technique that we have used previously in our other Controllers.

application/modules/storefront/controllers/CatalogController.php
```
public function saveproductAction()
{
    $request = $this->getRequest();

    if (!$request->isPost()) {
        return $this->_helper->redirector('addproduct');
    }

    if(false === ($id = $this->_catalogModel->saveProduct
                    ($request->getPost())))) {
```

```
        $this->view->productForm = $this->_getProductForm();
        return $this->render('addproduct');
    }

    $redirector = $this->getHelper('redirector');
    return $redirector->gotoRoute(
        array('action' => 'productimages', 'id' => $id),
        'admin'
    );
}
```

The `saveproduct` Action is where the product add form will submit its data to so the Action will create a new product for us. This Action first checks whether the post data is present. If not, then we redirect the user back to the `addproduct` Action. We then try to create the new product by calling the `saveProduct()` method on the Catalog Model. If validation fails, then we re-render the product add form so that the user can correct the missing data. Notice that we also assign the return of the `saveProduct()` method to the `$id` variable. This is done so that if the product is successfully created, we have the insert ID for that product to use later. If the product is created, we then redirect the user to the `productimages` Action. This action was included in the imported example files and allows users to add their images to the product. To perform the redirect, we use the redirector Action Helper's `gotoRoute()` method. This enables us to easily redirect to the `Admin` route and also set the `productId` so that the `productimages` action knows which product to add the images to.

With our Form, Model, and Controller created, we should now be able to add products to the catalog. By using the pseudo admin module, we can see that we have been able to keep all the admin related functionality within the Storefront module. This can help greatly if we want to use our module within another application.

Securing the administration area

The final part we need to look at is security. We need to make sure that people cannot access the admin functionality without the correct permissions. To achieve this, we will use the ACL that we created in the previous chapter, which we added to the default ACL for the storefront module. We will use this Resource as the Resource for our pseudo Admin module. This is because the module does not actually exist, and we need to be able to check if users are allowed access to it.

application/modules/storefront/models/Acl/Storefront.php

```
$this->add(new Storefront_Model_Acl_Resource_Admin)
    ->allow('Admin');
```

Looking at the `Storefront_Acl_Storefront` class, we can see that when we registered the Admin Resource with the ACL, we also allowed access to the Admin Role. This means that only users with the Admin Role are allowed to access the Admin Resource.

As our ACL is already configured, all we need to do is query it in our Controllers when we want to restrict access to a certain Action. However, this does move some of our ACL checking into the application layer of our application, though we will still secure our Catalog Model using the Model ACL implementation a little later on.

ACL action helper

Rather than duplicating our ACL querying code in each Controller, we are going to create an Action Helper to encapsulate this for us. Create the following class in the SF library:

`library/SF/Controller/Helper/Acl.php`

```
class SF_Controller_Helper_Acl extends
    Zend_Controller_Action_Helper_Abstract
{
    protected $_acl;
    protected $_identity;

    public function init()
    {
        $module = $this->getRequest()->getModuleName();
        $acl = ucfirst($module) . '_Model_Acl_' . ucfirst($module);

        if (class_exists($acl)) {
            $this->_acl = new $acl;
        }
    }

    public function getAcl()
    {
        return $this->_acl;
    }

    public function isAllowed($resource=null, $privilege=null)
    {
        if (null === $this->_acl) {
            return null;
        }
```

```
            return $this->_acl->isAllowed($this->getIdentity(),
                              $resource, $privilege);
    }

    public function setIdentity($identity)
    {
        if (is_array($identity)) {
            if (!isset($identity['role'])) {
                $identity['role'] = 'Guest';
            }
            $identity = new Zend_Acl_Role($identity['role']);
        } elseif (is_scalar($identity) && !is_bool($identity)) {
            $identity = new Zend_Acl_Role($identity);
        } elseif (null === $identity) {
            $identity = new Zend_Acl_Role('Guest');
        } elseif (!$identity instanceof Zend_Acl_Role_Interface) {
            throw new SF_Model_Exception('Invalid identity
                provided');
        }
        $this->_identity = $identity;
        return $this;
    }

    public function getIdentity()
    {
        if (null === $this->_identity) {
            $auth = Zend_Auth::getInstance();
            if (!$auth->hasIdentity()) {
                return 'Guest';
            }
            $this->setIdentity($auth->getIdentity());
        }
        return $this->_identity;
    }

    public function direct($resource=null, $privilege=null)
    {
        return $this->isAllowed($resource, $privilege);
    }
}
```

Action Helper work much in the same way as Front Controller plugins. They have three main hooks that we can use, init(), preDispatch(), and postDispatch(). These are called during the dispatch of the Action Controllers. Therefore, init() is called during the Action Controller initialization, preDispatch() is called before the Action Controller preDispatch, and postDispatch() is called before the Action Controller postDispatch.

In the ACL Helpers `init()` method, we load the correct ACL for the module being requested. We do this by getting the module name from the Request object and then instantiating the ACL class. In our case, this will be `Storefront_Model_Acl_Storefront`.

The `getAcl()` method is a simple getter and returns the ACL class stored in the `$_acl` class property.

The `isAllowed()` method will query the ACL for us. It accepts two parameters — `$resource` and `$privilege`. The `$resource` will be a string identifying the resource that we are querying and the `$privilege` will be a string identifying the permission we are querying. The method returns the output of the ACL's `isAllowed()` method. We pass in the identity, resource, and privilege to query the ACL.

The `setIdentity()` and `getIdentity()` methods are simply copied from the ACL abstract class and get and set the identity, defaulting to the identity stored in the `Zend_Auth` session.

Our final method is `direct()`. This is another Action Helper specific method, which is used to proxy calls to the helper of the `isAllowed()` method. This will then allow us to call the `isAllowed()` method directly on the Helper Broker, so that we don't have to get the Helper from the Broker each time we use it.

Once we have created the Action Helper, we need to register it with the Helper Broker. Add the following to the Bootstrap:

`application/bootstrap/Bootstrap.php`

```
protected function _initActionHelpers()
    {
        $this->_logger->info('Bootstrap ' . __METHOD__);
        Zend_Controller_Action_HelperBroker::addHelper(new
            SF_Controller_Helper_Acl());
        Zend_Controller_Action_HelperBroker::addHelper(new
            SF_Controller_Helper_RedirectCommon());
    }
```

To register an Action Helper with the Helper Broker, we simply call the static `addHelper()` method of the `Zend_Controller_Action_HelperBroker` class while passing in a new instance of the Helper. This will then make the Helper available to our Controllers.

We have also registered the `RedirectCommon` Action Helper. This is used to encapsulate common redirects that the application uses, and currently has one redirect that is to the login page. The `RedirectCommon` Helper is included within the files we imported earlier.

Securing the Admin functions

Now that we have our Action Helper, we can secure the Admin functions contained within our Controller. Update the CatalogController methods with the following:

application/modules/storefront/controllers/CatalogController.php

```php
    public function addproductAction()
    {
        if (!$this->_helper->acl('Admin')) {
            return $this->_helper->redirectCommon('gotoLogin');
        }
        $this->view->productForm = $this->_getProductForm();
    }

    public function saveproductAction()
    {
        if (!$this->_helper->acl('Admin')) {
            return $this->_helper->redirectCommon('gotoLogin');
        }
```

Our updated Actions will now check the ACL before they process the Action. We do this by calling the ACL helper and passing in the `'Admin'` string. This will then return `true` or `false` if the current user is authorized to perform the Action. If the user is not authorized, then we use our `RedirectCommon` Helper to redirect them to the login page.

We can now secure all our Actions that are within the pseudo Admin module. We could also reduce the code here by maintaining a list of Actions that should be restricted, and then we can use a `preDispatch` hook to automatically check those Actions before they are dispatched.

Catalog Model ACL

Next we need to update the Catalog Model so that it implements our ACL functionality. Update the Catalog Model with the following (we have removed the other methods for brevity):

application/modules/storefront/models/Catalog.php

```php
    class Storefront_Model_Catalog extends SF_Model_Acl_Abstract
    {
    /** ... */
        public function saveProduct($data, $validator = null)
        {
            if (!$this->checkAcl('saveProduct')) {
```

```
            throw new SF_Acl_Exception("Insufficient rights");
        }

        if (null === $validator) {
            $validator = 'add';
        }

        $validator = $this->getForm(
            'catalogProduct' . ucfirst($validator)
        );

        if (!$validator->isValid($data)) {
            return false;
        }

        $data = $validator->getValues();

        return $this->getResource('Product')->saveRow($data);
    }

    public function getResourceId()
    {
        return 'Catalog';
    }

    public function setAcl(SF_Acl_Interface $acl)
    {
        if (!$acl->has($this->getResourceId())) {
            $acl->add($this)
                ->allow('Admin', $this);
        }
        $this->_acl = $acl;
        return $this;
    }

    public function getAcl()
    {
        if (null === $this->_acl) {
            $this->setAcl(new Storefront_Model_Acl_Storefront());
        }
        return $this->_acl;
    }
}
```

Here we have followed the same conventions we used in the User Model. We first
change the base class that the Model uses to SF_Model_Acl_Abstract rather than
SF_Model_Abstract. Next we need to implement the ACL specific methods, namely,
getResourceId(), setAcl(), and getAcl().

The `getResourceId()` method returns the string Catalog, which will be the identifier for the Catalog Model in the ACL.

The `setAcl()` method configures the ACL for the Model. Here we simply allow the Admin Role access to all actions.

The `getAcl()` method will instantiate the Storefront ACL for us.

The final modification to the Catalog Model is to query the ACL within the `saveProduct()` method. Here we check whether the current user has access to the `saveProduct` action. If not, then we throw an exception.

With all that done, our Catalog Model is now secured from unauthorized access. We can see that with the new Model ACL functionality it is quick and easy to implement the ACL within our Models.

Summary

In this chapter, we have looked at how we can add administrative functionality to an application and the options we have when doing this. Our Storefront is now complete. Although not all the features are included, we have come a long way and hopefully covered many important aspects of the Zend Framework. There are still many features that you can try to implement by yourselves such as adding the ability to edit products. You may find this a good place to start practicing some of the techniques we have covered throughout the book. In the next chapter, we are going to take a look back at the Storefront and cover some aspects that we have not been able to cover in the previous chapters.

10
Storefront Roundup

Now that we have completed the development of the Storefront, we are going to look at some of the topics we did not have time to cover in the previous chapters.

In this chapter, we will cover:

- Using multiple modules
- Sharing elements between modules
- Using Services in modules
- Using Services to extend the Model

Using multiple modules

To start, let's look at how we configure multiple modules. To do this, we are going to use Zend_Application. This makes configuration of modules very easy because all we need to do is create a bootstrap class for each of our modules and then enable the Module's Bootstrap Resource in our configuration file.

Setup

Before we start configuring our modules, we need a new module to work with. Instead of going through the process again, we have included the new module with the example files for this chapter. Therefore, to get started, copy the cms directory in the assets directory of the example files into the modules directory of the Storefront.

We also have a new database table and some data that need to be added to the Storefront's database. Run the following SQL queries to create the new table, and add the default data:

```
CREATE TABLE `page` (
  `pageId` INT NOT NULL AUTO_INCREMENT,
  `title` varchar(200) NOT NULL,
  `body` Text NOT NULL,
  PRIMARY KEY (`pageId`)
) ENGINE=InnoDB  DEFAULT CHARSET=utf8;

INSERT INTO `storefront`.`page` VALUES  (1,'Welcome','Welcome to the
  storefront');
```

Configuring Zend_Application

To configure `Zend_Application` to initialize our new module, we simply need to add in the correct setting to the `store.ini`.

Open `store.ini` and add the following to the bootstrap section:

`application/config/store.ini`

```
[bootstrap]
resources.modules[] =
```

By doing this, we are telling `Zend_Application` that we want to use the Modules Bootstrap Resource plugin. The Modules plugin will load a separate bootstrap class for each of our modules excluding the default module. This is the entire configuration required to get `Zend_Application` working with multiple modules.

Bootstrapping modules

Now that we have enabled the Modules Resource plugin, it will try to load a bootstrap class for each of our modules. Therefore, we need to create a new bootstrap class for the cms module. Create the following class within the cms module folder:

`application/modules/cms/Bootstrap.php`

```
class Cms_Bootstrap extends Zend_Application_Module_Bootstrap
{
    public function _initModuleResourceAutoloader()
    {
        $this->getResourceLoader()->addResourceTypes(array(
            'modelResource' => array(
                'path'      => 'models/resources',
```

```
                        'namespace' => 'Resource',
                    )
            ));
        }
    }
```

The new `Cms_Bootstrap` class will now be loaded and executed during the bootstrap process. The way we name this file is important as the Modules Resource plugin needs to be able to find the class. We must name the file `Bootstrap.php` and name the class using the module name (`Cms`) and `_Bootstrap`. Moreover, as this is a module bootstrap, we also subclass the `Zend_Application_Module_Bootstrap` rather than the `Zend_Application_Bootstrap_Bootstrap`, like we did in the main bootstrap class earlier.

The `Zend_Application_Module_Bootstrap` provides some extra functionality for us to help with the configuration of our modules, this being that it will automatically register our module with the autoloader. If we look back to our main bootstrap class, we can see that we have manually configured the autoloader for the default module.

application/boostrap/Bootstrap.php

```
    protected function _initDefaultModuleAutoloader()
        {
            $this->_logger->info('Bootstrap ' . __METHOD__);

            $this->_resourceLoader = new
                Zend_Application_Module_Autoloader(array(
                'namespace' => 'Storefront',
                'basePath'  => APPLICATION_PATH . '/modules/storefront',
            ));
            $this->_resourceLoader->addResourceTypes(array(
                'modelResource' => array(
                    'path'      => 'models/resources',
                    'namespace' => 'Resource',
                )
            ));
        }
```

The `Zend_Application_Module_Bootstrap` will automatically do the above for us. Now, all that is left for us to do is customize the autoloader for our needs, which we do in the `Cms_Bootstrap` `_initModuleResourceAutoloader()` method.

To customize the autoloader so that it will autoload our Model Resources, we simply get the Resource Loader and call the `addResourceTypes()` method by passing in the Model Resource path and namespace information, just like we did in the main Bootstrap class.

Another important part of the module bootstrapping is the order in which bootstrap resources are executed. Consider the following diagram:

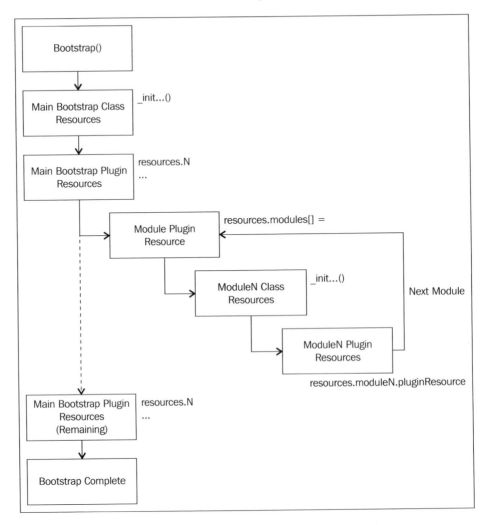

Here we can see the full bootstrap process. The basic flow of this is as follows:

1. The main bootstrap class is called.

2. The main bootstrap class resources are called, for example, `_initViewSettings()`.

3. The main bootstrap plugin resources are called, for example, `Zend_Application_Resource_Frontcontroller`.

4. The modules plugin resource is called. This will iterate over all the modules and call their respective bootstraps—each modules bootstrap class and bootstrap plugin resources are called.

5. The remaining bootstrap plugin resources are called.

6. Bootstrapping is completed.

There are a couple of important things to note about the module bootstrap process:

- The module bootstraps are executed during application initialization and not when the module is requested. A common mistake is to expect the module bootstrap resources to be called only when a module is accessed.

- Because the modules are bootstrapped using a plugin resource within the main bootstrap, this means that if we need one of the main bootstrap resources to be called before the module bootstrap resources, we must put these resources above the `resources.modules[]` = in the `Zend_Application` configuration.

Module specific configuration

When using the Modules Resource, we can also provide module specific configuration. For example, if we have a module that used a different database connection, then we can specify this in the `config` file of our `Zend_Application` using:

```
cms.resources.db.adapter = "MYSQLI"
cms.resources.db.params.dbname = "cms"
cms.resources.db.params.username = "root"
cms.resources.db.params.password = "root"
```

Here we have changed the `cms` modules database adapter to `MySQLI` and the database schema to `cms`.

Sharing common elements

Another common use case when using modules is the ability to share or have global elements. By default, `Zend_Application` will make a lot of elements accessible through the autoloader for us. These are:

- Models
- Forms
- Plugins
- Services
- Model dbtables

The Module Bootstrap Resource plugin will add the above to the autoloader during the bootstrap process, and this means that we can simply instantiate them anywhere in the application. For example, if we are within one of the Storefront modules Action Controllers:

```
$myModel = new Cms_Model_Test();
```

This will now work because the Cms Models are registered with the autoloader.

While Zend_Application can do a lot for us, there are still some things that we need to configure ourselves. One such thing is View Helpers and this need to be accessed on a global basis quite regularly. Therefore, we will refactor our application so that we can have shared View Helpers.

To start, create a new directory in the application directory called views and inside this, another directory called helpers. This is the standard place where views are stored if we are not using modules and it can act as a good place for our global View Helpers. Once we have the directories created, move the BaseUrl.php from application/modules/storefront/views/helpers into the new helpers directory. By doing this, we have now broken our application. If we run it now, then the product pages will throw errors saying that the BaseUrl View Helper was not found. To fix this, edit the Bootstrap class and add the following to the _initView() method:

application/bootstrap/Bootstrap.php

```
    protected function _initView()
    {
        // ...

        $this->_view->addHelperPath(
            APPLICATION_PATH . '/views/helpers', 'Zend_View_Helper'
        );

        // ...
    }
```

Here we have simply added another helper path to Zend_View, which will now tell Zend_View to search this directory for our global helpers. Notice that we have given the namespace here as Zend_View_Helper_, and this means that we also need to rename the BaseUrl class to reflect this change.

```
    class Storefront_View_Helper_BaseUrl
```

Change to:

```
    class Zend_View_Helper_BaseUrl
```

With this done, our application is now fixed and the Cms modules views can now use the BaseUrl View Helper.

In general, anything not globally accessible through the autoloader will need to have extra configuration applied to during the bootstrap process to make them accessible. Another good way of doing this is to add the elements into the library, as the autoloader will be able to load them from there anyway.

Services

We have already used services within the Storefront to provide authentication and taxation functionality. However, Services can also provide an extra important layer to our application from which we can extend and encapsulate additional business logic. Next, we will look at two examples of how services can be used to help us.

Services for cross module communication

When we are using multiple modules, it is very likely that we will need to share the functionality stored in the Models between each module. With Zend_Application, this is very easy as all we need do is instantiate the other module's Models. For example, if we are inside the Storefront module and want to access the Cms module's Models, then we can simply do:

```
$model = new Cms_Model_Page();
```

When we instantiate the Model from within the Storefront module, the autoloader will automatically include the class for us. However, as soon as we instantiate another module's Model, our current module immediately depends on the other, which makes our modules very hard to reuse. We may also want to only provide a limited API to the Model if it is accessed from within another module. Obviously, we can't stop developers from instantiating the Models directly, but we may want to have a convention where developers are told not to instantiate them directly.

To get around these problems, we can use a Service. By using a Service, we can mediate access to the Model's functionality and introduce a layer through which all inter-module communication is handled.

As an example, we are going to create a **Service** that the Storefront can use to access the Page Model of the Cms module. This Model is included within the assets that we imported earlier.

Create the following Service for the Cms module:

application/modules/cms/services/Page.php

```
class Cms_Service_Page
{
    protected $_pageModel;

    public function __construct()
    {
        $this->_pageModel = new Cms_Model_Page();
    }

    public function getPageById($id)
    {
        return $this->_pageModel->getPageById($id);
    }
}
```

The Cms module's Page Service is very simple and essentially composites the Cms_Model_Page class. It has one public method getPageById(), which returns the output of the Page Models getPageById() method.

This Service only uses one Model. However, we could also use a Service to encapsulate many Models from a module. This means that we can group Models from a module together and provide a simplified API to our other modules.

Now that we have our Page Service, we can use it within the Storefront module by simply instantiating it.

```
$pageService = new Cms_Service_Page();
```

This then gives us access to the Page Model. However, by doing this, we are creating an inter-module dependency, and the Storefront module now depends on the Cms module. There is no simple way to get around this dependency. After all, if our Storefront module needs the functionality, then it is always going to depend on it. However, we can add checks to see if the Service exists and then not use it if it's not present.

To do this, we are going to create an Action Helper that will find Services for us:

library/SF/Controller/Helper/Service.php

```
class SF_Controller_Helper_Service extends
Zend_Controller_Action_Helper_Abstract
{
    protected $_services = array();
```

```
public function getService($service, $module)
{
    if (!isset($this->_services[$module][$service])) {
        $class = implode('_', array(
                ucfirst($module),
                'Service',
                ucfirst($service)
        ));

        $front = Zend_Controller_Front::getInstance();
        $classPath = $front->getModuleDirectory($module)
                        . '/services/' . ucfirst($service) . '.php';
        if (!file_exists($classPath)) {
            return false;
        }
        if (!class_exists($class)) {
            throw new SF_Exception("Class $class not found in "
                                        . basename($classPath));
        }
        $this->_services[$module][$service] = new $class();
    }
    return $this->_services[$module][$service];
}


public function direct($service, $module)
{
    return $this->getService($service, $module);
}
}
```

This is our Service Finder (not to be confused with the Service Locator Pattern) and will check if a Service is available for us to use. The getService() method will first check if the Service has already been instantiated. If it has, then it will return the cached instance. If not, then we try to instantiate a new Service instance by creating the class name from the $service and $module parameters. We then use the Front Controller to get the path to the modules directory and check if the Service class file actually exists. We do this because if we just use class_exists, then the autoloader will throw a *not found* exception. We suppress the not found exception because we want to be able to see if the Service is available and do not want exceptions thrown if it does not exist. If the file does exist, then we do one final check to make sure the Service class is within the file and then simply instantiate a new instance of the Service class.

Now that our Service Action Helper is created, we need to register it with the Helper Broker. Edit the bootstrap class and add the following:

application/bootstrap/Bootstrap.php

```
protected function _initActionHelpers()
{
    $this->_logger->info('Bootstrap ' . __METHOD__);
    Zend_Controller_Action_HelperBroker::addHelper(
        new SF_Controller_Helper_Acl()
    );
    Zend_Controller_Action_HelperBroker::addHelper(
        new SF_Controller_Helper_RedirectCommon()
    );
    Zend_Controller_Action_HelperBroker::addHelper(
        new SF_Controller_Helper_Service()
    );
}
```

Our Service Action Helper is now ready to use. To test it, we are going to replace the home page welcome text with text pulled from the **Cms Page Model**. Update the storefront modules IndexController with the following:

application/modules/storefront/controllers/IndexController.php

```
public function indexAction()
{
    if ($service = $this->_helper->service('page', 'cms')) {
        $this->view->page = $service->getPageById(1);
    }
}
```

The indexAction of the IndexController now checks to see if the Page Service exists in the Cms module. If it does, then we use the Service to assign the page data to the View. To see this in action, we also need to update the index.phtml View Script.

application/modules/storefront/views/scripts/index/index.phtml

```
<? if($this->page) : ?>
<h3><?=$this->page->title;?></h3>
<p>
    <?=$this->page->body; ?>
</p>
<? endif; ?>
```

We have removed the static HTML from the View Script and replaced it with the data from the Page Service. Additionally, we have wrapped this in an IF statement so that nothing is rendered if the data is not present.

Now when we visit the home page, the data from the Page Model that is stored in the page table of the database is displayed. If we were to delete the Page Service file from the Cms module, then nothing would be displayed.

By doing this, we have reduced the effects of the dependency between the two modules. We do, of course, have to add each check within our code to check whether the Service is available, but it goes a short way in achieving more portable modules.

Services for extending model behavior

Another great use for a Service is to extend the model's behavior. By using Services, we can easily create many different endpoints that our application can use when the Models are required in different contexts.

For example, our current Models in the Storefront mainly return Objects. However, there are times when we would probably want to have the data returned in a different format. The temptation here is to do the reformatting of the data within our Controllers. However, if we reformat any data within a Controller, we cannot reuse that transformation code, meaning that we will need to duplicate the code whenever we need that format. The second temptation would be to add a method to the Model or extend it to add the extra functionality. However, this could make our Models very large, and by extending we get all the problems associated with inheritance.

To get around this problem, we can move this code into a Service. In this way, we can easily reuse it, and it is using composition over inheritance. A good example of this is when we want to get data using Ajax; consider the following Service class:

```
class Storefront_Service_Cart
{
    protected $_cartModel;

    public function __construct()
    {
        $this->_cartModel = new Storefront_Model_Cart();
    }

    public function getItems()
    {
        $items = array();

        foreach($this->_cartModel as $item) {
            $items[] = array(
                'name'      => $item->name,
                'productId' => $item->productId,
                'lineCost'  => $item->getLineCost(),
            );
        }

        return Zend_Json::encode($items);
    }
}
```

This Service class extends the Cart Models functionality and adds a JSON layer to our application. Now, whenever we need the Cart data in a JSON format, we can use the Cart Service class to output the formatted data. This is a very simple example, but we could be querying many Models within one Service to create highly customized data for our JavaScript layer to use. By doing so, we have cleanly separated this behavior from the rest of our application, which should make maintenance of the code much easier in the future.

Summary

In this chapter, we have covered the use and configuration of multiple modules, how we can use Services to communicate between modules, the problems of cross module communication, and how to use Services to extend Models and add extra Service layers to our application. In the last two chapters, we are going to look at how we can optimize the Storefront and how we can test our application using PHPUnit.

11
Storefront Optimization

An important part of any application is performance. All that we want is to get the best out of our application and where possible, reduce server costs. In this chapter, we will look at how to tune the Zend Framework and improve the performance of the Storefront application. This will include:

- Opcode caching
- PHP optimizations
- Autoloading and Require statements
- Zend Frameworks standard caches
- Caching Model output

General optimizations

To start, we will look at some of the standard ways in which we can improve the performance of our application. These will include both optimizations of the Zend Framework components and PHP in general.

Opcode caching

As PHP is an interpreted language, when we execute a PHP source file, the PHP engine must compile the source file into something that the machine can understand. This something is **opcode**. The opcode has to be generated for every request, meaning that the PHP engine has to do a lot of work, especially for a framework that has many files to compile per request.

To get around this, we can use an opcode cache. This will cache the opcode generated by the first request. Moreover, on subsequent requests, it will run the opcode stored in the cache instead of having to re-compile the source file. By doing this, we can totally skip the compilation step, which can save us a lot of CPU and memory.

There are a few opcode caches available for PHP. For the Storefront, we are going to use **APC (Alternative PHP Cache)**. However, you may want to have a look at the other offerings, which are:

- eAccelerator (`http://eaccelerator.net`)
- Alternative PHP Cache (`http://pecl.php.net/package/APC`)
- XCache (`http://xcache.lighttpd.net`)
- Zend Platform (`http://www.zend.com/products/platform`)
- Zend Server (`http://www.zend.com/products/server/`)

Some of these are Open Source while others are Commercial. You can choose whichever one you like most as they all achieve the same goal.

To use an opcode cache, we must first install it. For us, this is going to be APC. APC is available through PHP PECL (`http://pecl.php.net`) and therefore can be installed easily on most systems. To install it on Linux and OSX, we simply need to install it through the PECL command line tool:

```
pecl install apc
```

This will then download and compile the PHP extension for us. Note that you will need the devel PHP packages that contain the tools to compile extensions. Now, on Windows as compilation can be a headache, the easiest way is to get the precompiled binaries of the `php_apc.dll`. The precompiled binaries for Windows were available at `http://pecl4win.php.net/`, however, this service has now been pulled. The only other place providing precompiled binaries at the time of writing is `http://downloads.php.net/pierre/`. You may need to do some searching to find them otherwise.

Path optimizations

As of PHP 5.1, the paths used to include and require files in PHP are now cached using the `realpath` cache. This cache helps to speed up the file inclusion in PHP. However, to get the most out of it, we need to use absolute paths. Therefore, we can edit the `application.php.dist` file and change our relative paths to absolute ones.

application/application.php.dist

```php
<?php
$paths = array(
    realpath(dirname(__FILE__) . '/../library'),
    '.',
);
set_include_path(implode(PATH_SEPARATOR, $paths));
```

Here we have changed the way we set our include paths. Instead of using relative paths like ../library, we are now using the realpath() function to find the absolute path to the library directory. We have also removed the get_include_path() from the paths array. This is another optimization. The less paths we have in our include path, the quicker PHP can check them. However, this does mean we can no longer use PEAR packages, as the default include path to these has been removed.

Along with the realpath cache, there are also some php.ini directives that we should be aware of. These are:

- realpath_cache_size
- realpath_cache_ttl

The cache size by default is 16k, which is quite small and should probably be increased to 32, 64, or 128. However, I would suggest some trial and error with this to find what works best for your system.

The **TTL (time to live)** of the cache by default is 120 seconds. This can also be increased and again requires some trail and error to get it right. Remember though, this can affect changes to the applications file system. If you move a file, for instance, the cache will have the old path, and this could possibly cause errors! Therefore, it is best to only do this on production systems and remember to restart the web server when deploying changes.

Requires and includes

Along with optimizing our include paths, we also need to optimize our class includes. Traditionally, require_once and include_once are slow in PHP. This was vastly improved after PHP 5.1 but they can still affect performance. The storefront does not use many require statements at all as it uses Zend_Loader_Autoloader to include its resources and is faster than using require_once. Therefore, wherever possible, we want to use the autoloader over require_once or include_once. As we have already done this in the storefront application, the only thing left using require_once is the Zend Framework library itself. This is mainly because it can be used as a component library as well as a fully fledged framework, and therefore needs to be distributed with the require_once statements.

To make the framework use the autoloader, we need to remove all the require_once statements from the library. We are going to use Apache Ant to remove them for us. Add the following to the build.xml:

build/build.xml

```
<target name="deploy">
        <echo message="---- Removing require_once ----" />
        <replaceregexp byline="true">
            <regexp pattern="require_once 'Zend/"/>
            <substitution expression="// require_once 'Zend/"/>
            <fileset dir="${basedir}/library/Zend"
             excludes="**/*Autoloader.php" includes="**/*.php" />
        </replaceregexp>
    </target>
```

This build target will comment out all the require_once statements in the source files contained within the library/Zend directory excluding the Autoloader.php file. This uses the standard replaceregex Ant task that is shipped with Ant. To run the target, we simply need to run the following command from within the build directory:

ant deploy

After doing this, we again need to edit the application.php.dist file so that the Autoloader is included as well as the Zend_Application.

application/application.php.dist

```
require_once 'Zend/Loader/Autoloader.php';
require_once 'Zend/Application.php';
```

With this done, our application should now run as normal. Obviously, we would only ever do this while deploying an application to a live environment, as there is little point on a development machine. However, we can see that Ant is very useful for automating these processes.

Standard caches

Some of the Zend Framework components also provide ways of caching parts of them to improve performance. These standard caches can dramatically improve the performance of the components. The components that have caches are:

- Zend_Db_Table
- Zend_Loader_PluginLoader
- Zend_Paginator

- Zend_Locale

- Zend_Translate

- Zend_XmlRpc_Server

- Zend_Currency

- Zend_Date

All of these components can use caching to improve their performance. We are not going to cover all of them, but generally these components will provide a setCache() method or something similar that can be used to pass a Zend_Cache instance to the component. This will then be used to cache some of the heavier operations that these components perform. For full details on each component's caching functionality, check the online reference manual.

For the storefront, we are going to use two of these standard caches, namely, Zend_Db_Table and Zend_Loader_PluginLoader. The Zend_Db_Table component has to get the table information or metadata for the database table that it is connected to each time we instantiate a new table instance. This means that Zend_Db_Table executes a DESCRIBE SQL statement (or equivalent) every time we use a table class. This, for obvious reasons, can affect our application's performance. The Zend_Loader_PluginLoader is used by many other components to load plugin resources like View Helpers. Internally, the Plugin Loader stores a stack of paths that it will scan to find the file to include. This can affect the performance of our application as the Plugin Loader must iterate over all the paths while checking for the file in each directory.

Plugin loader cache

We have now identified two places in our application where we can improve performance by using a cache. Next, we need to fix this by configuring these components to use a cache and getting rid of some of this heavy work that they are doing. To start, we will enable the plugin loader cache. To do this, add the following to the bootstrap class:

application/bootstrap/Bootstrap.php

```
protected function _initPluginLoaderCache()
{
    if ('production' == $this->getEnvironment()) {
        $classFileIncCache =
            APPLICATION_PATH .
            '/../data/cache/pluginLoaderCache.php';
        if (file_exists($classFileIncCache)) {
            include_once $classFileIncCache;
        }
```

```
Zend_Loader_PluginLoader::setIncludeFileCache(
    $classFileIncCache
);
    }
}
```

Here we have created a new bootstrap class resource called
_initPluginLoaderCache. This method should be **the first method** in the
class as we want it to be called as early as possible. In the method body, we
first have to check to see if the environment is production. Generally, we
only want to cache things in the production environment as caching in the
development environment could cause unpredictable errors.

To configure the cache, we first need to specify the location where the cache file
should be stored. In this case, this is data/cache/pluginLoaderCache.php. We then
check if the cache file already exists. If it does, then we include the cache file using
include_once. The final step is to tell the Plugin Loader that we are using the cache.
We do this by using the setIncludeFileCache() method and passing in the cache
file location as its only parameter.

The Plugin Loader will now write all the files that it includes to the cache file. The
file's contents will look something like this but much longer:

```
<?php
include_once 'Zend/Controller/Action/Helper/ViewRenderer.php';
include_once 'Zend/View/Helper/Doctype.php';
include_once 'Zend/View/Helper/HeadMeta.php';
....
```

As we can see, it is a file that contains PHP include statements. Now when we
include this file in _initPluginLoaderCache(), all the files are automatically loaded
for us, meaning that the Plugin Loader no longer has to do its expensive filesystem
operations to find each file to include.

Db table cache

Now that we have our Plugin Loader using caching, we can move on and address
the issues with Zend_Db_Table. To enable the cache, we are going to need to
configure a Zend_Cache instance and pass this to Zend_Db_Table. Again, we will do
this within the bootstrap class.

application/bootstrap/Bootstrap.php

```
protected function _initDbCaches()
{
    $this->_logger->info('Bootstrap ' . __METHOD__);
```

```
    if ('production' == $this->getEnvironment()) {
        $frontendOptions = array(
            'automatic_serialization' => true
        );

        $cache = Zend_Cache::factory('Core',
            'Apc',
            $frontendOptions
        );
        Zend_Db_Table_Abstract::setDefaultMetadataCache($cache);
    }
}
```

Again, we have created a new bootstrap class resource. This time we have called our resource _initDbCaches(). This resource does not need to be called too early and so does not need to go at the top of the bootstrap like the _initPluginLoaderCache(). In the method body, we again check to see if we are in a production environment because we want any changes to the database tables to be instantly available during development.

Our next step is to configure a Zend_Cache instance. In this case, we have chosen to use APC as the cache backend, and this will store the table metadata in memory. The Zend_Cache has two main elements—the frontend, which controls the cache settings and the backend, which handles the storage of the data. Typically, when configuring a Zend_Cache instance, we would provide two sets of options, one for the frontend and other for the backend. However, APC requires no backend options. Therefore, we only provide frontend options to Zend_Cache. The frontend options we use here turn on automatic_serialization. This tells Zend_Cache to serialize the data before saving it. Serialization will be done using the PHP serialize() function. For more information on this function, check the PHP manual. Once we have our configuration options ready for Zend_Cache, we need to fetch a Zend_Cache instance. To do this, we use the factory method of Zend_Cache. To the factory() method, we pass the type of frontend and backend to use as well as the frontend options, which will give us our configured Zend_Cache instance. We can then instruct Zend_Db_Table_Abstract to use the cache using the setDefaultMetadataCache() static method. This will make all Zend_Db_Table instances use the cache.

Now, when we run the application in production, we have eliminated all the calls for table information that Zend_Db_Table normally makes. We will look at Zend_Cache in more detail later when we implement caching in our Models.

Dispatching optimizations

Next we are going to look at how dispatching can affect performance. By dispatching we mean to dispatch the loop the Front Controller uses to call Action Controllers in the MVC architecture. We first looked at this way back in Chapter 2, so let's just recap on what the dispatch loop does. The diagram below shows the dispatching process for the Zend Framework:

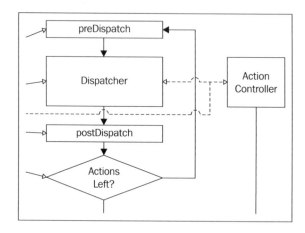

In the previous diagram, we can see the dispatching part of the MVC Request Handling process. It shows us how the Front Controller loops while there are Controller Actions left to call. This looping can affect performance if we overuse it. The more the loops, the longer dispatching will take. So first, we need to understand what parts of the Zend Framework can add loops to the dispatching process. Some of these are:

- The `Action()` Action Helper
- The `_foward()` Action Controller method
- The Action Stack
- Front Controller and Action Helpers that forward the request

We have to avoid these as much as possible when creating our application. The worst one performance-wise here is the `Action()` Action Helper. If we want this type of functionality, then it is best to use the Action Stack instead. However, the Action Stack still adds loops to the Dispatch so we also want to avoid this as well. We have used the Action Stack in the Storefront to populate the main Category menu. Let's refactor this out now.

To eliminate the use of the Action Stack from the Storefront, we are going to use a View Helper instead. Generally this is the best way to create reusable components that need to appear on every page or act as "widgets". Our View Helper will query our Model directly for the Categories. The rule we need to follow here is that View Helpers only have Read access to the Model. They should never write to the Model. Create the following View Helper:

application/modules/storefront/views/helpers/Category.php

```
class Storefront_View_Helper_Category extends Zend_View_Helper_
Abstract
{
    public function Category()
    {

        $catalogModel = new Storefront_Model_Catalog();
        return $catalogModel->getCategoriesByParentId(0);

    }

}
```

Our new View Helper is very simple. It contains a single method `Category()`, which instantiates the `Storefront_Model_Catalog` Model and returns the output of the `getCategoriesByParentId()` method. The `getCategoriesByParentId()` will return a `Zend_Db_Table_Rowset`, which we can iterate over in our layout script. Once we have our View Helper, we can now edit the layout script.

application/layouts/scripts/main.phtml

```
    <h3>select <span>category</span></h3>
        <ul>
           <? foreach ($this->Category() as $category): ?>
               <li><a href="<?=$this->url(array('categoryIdent' =>
                   $category->ident), 'catalog_category', true
                   );?>"><?=$category->name; ?></a></li>
           <? endforeach; ?>
        </ul>
    </div>
```

Now in our layout script, we use the `Category()` View Helper to create the menu instead of the Response Segment we used earlier with the Action Stack. This then avoids the use of an extra dispatch loop that was caused by the Action Stack. The final part of the optimization is to unregister the `SF_Plugin_Action` Front Controller Plugin from the Front Controller. To do this, we simply need to delete the following line from the `store.ini` file:

```
    resources.frontcontroller.plugins.action = "SF_Plugin_Action"
```

We have now successfully eliminated a dispatch loop from the dispatch process. It is always important to think about the cost of dispatching when creating an application. However, the dispatching process is earmarked for some performance optimizations in the 2.0 release of the Zend Framework.

Caching

Now that we have looked at the general aspects of Zend Framework performance optimization, we are going to move on and look at caching. Caching comes in many forms, and there are a variety of tools and techniques that we can employ to add caching at various levels within our application. For the Storefront, we are going to look at caching data produced by our Models. This is one of the many ways to cache data in our application and should give us enough knowledge of Zend_Cache to apply it in other areas.

Before we start, let's first look at some of the options available to us when thinking about implementing caching in general. Basically, there are four types of caching:

- **Full page caching**: This caches the full output of the page. It can be achieved using Zend_Cache by caching the returned Response Object or creating static files (.html) that are served instead of going through the MVC process. There are also many non-PHP tools that can enable full page caching, such as Zend Server (http://www.zend.com/en/products/server/), which can be used to cache pages without doing any code changes to your application.

- **Partial page caching**: This caches part of the page output. We can again use Zend_Cache, but this time we would only cache parts of the Response Object in order to cache only small parts of the page's final output. This would normally happen at the application level inside our Action Controllers.

- **Data caching**: This caches the data. This is what we are going to implement for our Models. As Models represent data in the MVC triad, we will be caching at this level of the application. We add caching to the Model or Domain layer of our application so that we can use the Models and thereby caching outside of the MVC environment.

- **Client-side caching**: This caches data on the user's computer. It is usually performed by the browser and is usually more suited to a client side programming language like JavaScript.

There are of course many other ways to cache data in an application and many techniques to achieve the desired result. It is important to choose a caching strategy that works for your business requirements. The strategies listed here hopefully point you in the right direction.

Zend_Cache

Before we dive in and get started with our Model data caching, let's first get an overview of how `Zend_Cache` works. As mentioned before, `Zend_Cache` consists of a frontend that controls the cache and a backend that controls the cache storage. There are various cache frontends and backends available by default in the Zend Framework. Currently, all frontends extend the `Zend_Cache_Core` class, which provides generic frontend cache functionality such as saving, tagging, and cleaning data.

The frontend types available are:

- **Class**: Caches output for classes methods, and allows proxy calling from cache to class
- **File**: Caches files that are read into PHP
- **Function**: Caches the output of a function call
- **Output**: Caches the output using output buffering, useful for partial caching of output
- **Page**: Caches full page output

The backend types available are:

- File
- APC
- Zend Server
- Zend Platform
- XCache
- Sqlite
- Memcached
- TwoLevels

To use `Zend_Cache`, we need to configure a `Zend_Cache` instance like we did previously for the `Zend_Db_Table` metadata cache. Here is an example of configuring `Zend_Cache` and querying it for data:

```
$frontendOptions = array(
    'lifetime' => 1800,
    'automatic_serialization' => true
);
$backendOptions = array(
    'cache_dir'=> 'my/cache/dir'
);
```

```
$cache = Zend_Cache::factory(
    'Core',
    'File',
    $frontendOptions,
    $backendOptions
);

if (!$data = $cache->load('myCachedData')) {
    $data = 'My test data that is really big';
    $cache->save($data, 'myCachedData');
}
echo $data;
```

Here, we have used the Core frontend and the File backend. We configure the frontend to automatically serialize data and give it a lifetime of 1800 seconds. As the backend is File, we have to configure the cache_dir so the backend knows where to create its cache files.

We check if the data is in the cache using the load() method. We need to pass in the ID of the cache, which we set when we save the data to the cache. In this case, it is myCacheData. If the data is not in the cache or has expired, then the load() method will return false. If this happens, we reload the data and store it in the cache using the save() method. When saving data, we pass in the data and the ID we wish to use in order to retrieve the data later.

We can also provide tags when saving data to the cache so that we can group cached data, making it easy to clear parts instead of the cache when required. To tag data, we simply provide an array of the tags as the third parameter of the save() method.

```
$cache->save($data, 'myCachedData', array('tag1', 'tag2'));
```

We can then clear the tagged parts of the cache using the clean() method.

```
$cache->clean(Zend_Cache::CLEANING_MODE_MATCHING_TAG, array('tag1'));
```

This would then remove any data that has been cached against the tag1 tag. It is important to note that not all backends support tagging like the APC backend does.

Full documentation for the Zend_Cache API is available in the reference manual, which covers all frontend and backend functionality.

Model data caching

Moving on from our basic example, we are now going to look at how to implement caching in our Models. To do this, we are going to use the Class frontend and the File backend. The Class frontend allows us to specify a class to cache. The class methods can then be called through the cache instance and their output cached. This is particularly useful when dealing with Models as all we want to do is cache the output of their public methods. It means that we do not need to change the Model too much to achieve this.

Basic class caching

An example of the basic usage of the Class cache frontend is as follows:

```
class myModel
{
    protected $_name = 'test';

    public function doTest()
    {
        return $this->_name;
    }
}
$frontendOptions = array(
    'cached_entity' => new myModel()
);
$cache = Zend_Cache::factory(
    'Class',
    'File',
    $frontendOptions,
    $backendOptions
);
$cache->doTest();
```

In this example, we have a class, myModel, and we want to cache the output of its public methods. The myModel class is very simple and has one method doTest(), which returns the protected class property $_name. To cache the myModel method output, in the frontend options, we specify the cached_entity option as a new myModel instance. This tells the frontend that we are caching this instance's methods.

Once we have configured a new Zend_Cache instance, we can then call the doTest() method on the cache instance. This call then proxies to the myModel() instance through the cache instance. Zend_Cache will then take care of the caching for us. Therefore, the first time we call $cache->doTest(), the doTest() method will actually be called. On subsequent calls, the data will be pulled from the cache instead.

As we can see, `Zend_Cache` makes it very easy for us to cache class methods. What's even better is that `Zend_Cache` recognizes different parameters passed to the methods. This means that `$cache->doTest(1)` is cached separately from `$cache->doTest(2)`, and we don't get the wrong data returned when the output is based on the parameters given to the method.

Now this is all very good and we could simply place this code within our Action Controllers and our caching would be ready. However, just like with the ACL, if we do this, then we can only use caching in the MVC context. Therefore, we are going to integrate the caching into our base Model class so that we have caching ability outside of MVC.

Model cache integration

Now that we know how to cache class methods, we need to look at how to integrate this within our Models. As we do not want to cache every method of our classes by default, we are going to add a method to our base Model called `getCached()`. This method will return a `Zend_Cache` instance that has been configured to cache the methods of the Models that extend our base Model (`SF_Model_Abstract`). By doing this, we are then able to call methods on our Model like this:

```
$sfModel->getCached()->getSomeData();
```

Here we first call `getCached()`. This then returns a `SF_Model_Cache_Abstract` instance. We then call the Model method that we want to execute. This call is on the `SF_Model_Cache_Abstract` instance, which will proxy to `Zend_Cache` and then back to our Model just like in our previous example.

The abstract cache class

To start the implementation, let's first create an abstract cache class that will be stored by the base Model class and which will handle all the caching functionality for our Models:

`library/SF/Model/Cache/Abstract.php`

```php
abstract class SF_Model_Cache_Abstract
{
    protected $_classMethods;
    protected $_cache;
    protected $_frontend;
    protected $_backend;
    protected $_frontendOptions = array();
    protected $_backendOptions = array();
    protected $_model;
    protected $_tagged;
```

```
public function __construct(SF_Model_Abstract $model, $options,
                           $tagged = null)
{
    $this->_model = $model;

    if ($options instanceof Zend_Config) {
        $options = $options->toArray();
    }

    if (is_array($options)) {
        $this->setOptions($options);
    }

    $this->setTagged($tagged);
}

public function setOptions(array $options)
{
    if (null === $this->_classMethods) {
        $this->_classMethods = get_class_methods($this);
    }
    foreach ($options as $key => $value) {
        $method = 'set' . ucfirst($key);
        if (in_array($method, $this->_classMethods)) {
            $this->$method($value);
        }
    }
    return $this;
}

public function setCache(Zend_Cache $cache)
{
    $this->_cache = $cache;
}

public function getCache()
{
    if (null === $this->_cache) {
        $this->_cache = Zend_Cache::factory(
            $this->_frontend,
            $this->_backend,
            $this->_frontendOptions,
            $this->_backendOptions
        );
```

```
        }
        return $this->_cache;
    }

    public function setFrontendOptions(array $frontend)
    {
        $this->_frontendOptions = $frontend;
        $this->_frontendOptions['cached_entity'] = $this->_model;
    }

    public function setBackendOptions(array $backend)
    {
        $this->_backendOptions = $backend;
    }

    public function setBackend($backend)
    {
        $this->_backend = $backend;
    }

    public function setFrontend($frontend)
    {
        if ('Class' != $frontend) {
            throw new SF_Model_Exception('Frontend type must be
                Class');
        }
        $this->_frontend = $frontend;
    }

    public function setTagged($tagged=null)
    {
        $this->_tagged = $tagged;

        if (null === $tagged) {
            $this->_tagged = 'default';
        }
    }

    public function __call($method, $params)
    {
        if (!is_callable(array($this->_model, $method))) {
            throw new SF_Model_Exception('Method ' . $method . ' does
                not exist in class ' . get_class($this->_model) );
        }
```

```
                $cache = $this->getCache();
                $cache->setTagsArray(array($this->_tagged));
                $callback = array($cache, $method);
                return call_user_func_array($callback, $params);
        }
    }
```

The main purpose of the cache abstract class is to proxy calls to the Zend_Cache instance. It also accepts a number of options that configure the Zend_Cache instance and handles the tagging of the cached data.

The constructor accepts three parameters, which are $model, $options, and $tagged. These parameters set the Model to cache, the options for the cache, and the tag to use when saving data respectively.

Most of the other SF_Model_Cache_Abstract methods are setters and getters that configure its behavior. The setOptions() method will search the class for setters that match the keys within the $options array passed in the constructor. For example, if in the options we pass a key called cache, then getOptions() will call the setCache() method. This way of setting options for a class is common in many Zend Framework components and provides an easy way to override the default settings in a class, making it easier to test.

The next notable method is the setFrontendOptions(). This is a simple setter for the Zend_Cache frontend options array. However, we add in the cached_entity key every time this is called so that the Zend_Cache instance knows to cache the Model instance passed in with the constructor.

The final method and the most important is the __call() method. This is a magic method defined by PHP and will capture any calls to class methods that do not exist. This enables us to proxy calls to the class to another object. In this case we proxy all other calls to the Zend_Cache instance. Inside the method body, we first check that the incoming method call is available in the Model using the is_callable() function. If the method does not exist in the class, then we throw an exception. If the method is callable, we then set up a callback to the Zend_Cache instance and finally call the method using the call_user_func_array() function. We also set the tag to use on the Zend_Cache instance before we execute the callback. This will then call the method on the Zend_Cache instance, which in turn will call the Model method or get the data from the cache.

The concrete cache class

We will also need to create a concrete implementation of the cache abstract so that the base Model can instantiate it.

library/SF/Model/Cache.php

```
class SF_Model_Cache extends SF_Model_Cache_Abstract
{}
```

This class simply subclasses the SF_Model_Cache_Abstract class and requires no further modification.

Model abstract modifications

Now that we have our cache class created, we need to make it available in our Models and add the getCached() method. In order to do this, edit the SF_Model_Abstract class, and add the following methods:

library/SF/Model/Abstract.php

```
public function setCache(SF_Model_Cache_Abstract $cache)
{
    $this->_cache = $cache;
}

public function setCacheOptions(array $options)
{
    $this->_cacheOptions = $options;
}

public function getCacheOptions()
{
    if (empty($this->_cacheOptions)) {
        $frontendOptions = array(
            'lifetime' => 1800,
            'automatic_serialization' => true
        );
        $backendOptions = array(
            'cache_dir'=> APPLICATION_PATH . '/../data/cache/db'
        );
        $this->_cacheOptions = array(
            'frontend'         => 'Class',
            'backend'          => 'File',
            'frontendOptions' => $frontendOptions,
            'backendOptions'   => $backendOptions
        );
```

```
        }
    return $this->_cacheOptions;
}

public function getCached($tagged = null)
{
        if (null === $this->_cache) {
          $this->_cache = new SF_Model_Cache(
              $this,
              $this->getCacheOptions()
          );
        }
        $this->_cache->setTagged($tagged);
        return $this->_cache;
}
```

To the base Model class we have added two new setters, setCache() and setCacheOptions() so that we can override the default cache behavior during testing or for Models that need different settings. We then have two getters, getCacheOptions() and getCached(). The getCacheOptions() method sets up the default cache options for us if we have not already set any. We have decided to hardcode these settings; however, we could easily pull this from a configuration file if needed. The getCached() method is what we will call to get cached results from the Model. It accepts one optional parameter, $tagged, which should be a string that defines the tag in which the result should be stored against. Within the method body, we create a new SF_Model_Cache instance, passing in the Model to cache $this and the cache options. We also set the tag to use and then finally return the cache instance.

All of our Models are now able to access the caching functionality, and we can now start to add caching to our application.

Caching the product listing

With the new additions to our Model ready, we can now start to use them within our Action Controllers when we want cached data. To demonstrate, let's optimize the main product listing and eliminate some of those database calls.

application/modules/storefront/controllers/catalogController.php

```
public function indexAction()
    {
        $products = $this->_catalogModel->getCached('product')
          ->getProductsByCategory(
              $this->_getParam('categoryIdent', 0),
              $this->_getParam('page', 1),
```

```
            array('name')
    );

    $category = $this->_catalogModel->getCached('category')
     ->getCategoryByIdent($this->_getParam('categoryIdent', ''));
    if (null === $category) {
        throw new SF_Exception_404('Unknown category ' . $this
          ->_getParam('categoryIdent'));
    }

    $subs = $this->_catalogModel->getCached('category')
     ->getCategoriesByParentId($category->categoryId);
    $this->getBreadcrumb($category);

    $this->view->assign(array(
        'category' => $category,
        'subCategories' => $subs,
        'products' => $products
        )
    );
}
```

Here we have simply replaced all the calls to the catalog Model with calls that go through the getCached() method. By doing this, the data returned is now cached. For example, to get the products for the category we call:

```
$this->_catalogModel->getCached('product')->getProductsByCategory(
    $this->_getParam('categoryIdent', 0),
    $this->_getParam('page', 1),
    array('name')
      );
```

Notice that we also provide the string 'product' when calling the getCached() method. This specifies the tag under which the data for this method should be stored. We do this so that when we save data, we can easily clear the relevant part of the cache.

Saving new data

Currently, if we save the new cached data, then it will not appear until the cache expires. To get around this, we need to edit our Catalog Model so that it clears the cache every time new data is saved.

To do this, edit the application/modules/storefront/models/Catalog.php file and replace this line:

```
return $this->getResource('Product')->saveRow($data);
```

With this:

```
$primary = $this->getResource('Product')->saveRow($data);

// clear the cache
$this->getCached()
    ->getCache()
    ->clean(Zend_Cache::CLEANING_MODE_MATCHING_ANY_TAG,
        array('product')
    );

return $primary;
```

This modification to the Catalog Model will clear the cache every time we save a new Product. To clear the cache, we first get the SF_Model_Cache instance (getCached()), then we get the Zend_Cache instance (getCache()), and finally call the clean() method on the Zend_Cache instance. When cleaning the cache, we also supply the tag to the cache segment that we want to clear. In this case, we want to clear the product segment.

Fixing Zend_Db_Table_Row exceptions

To complete the Model caching, we need to fix one problem with our implementation where the cache will sometimes store our row objects. When it does, it will serialize them using serialize(). When our row objects are un-serialized, they will become disconnected from the database table and will throw exceptions when we try to use them. To get around this, we need to modify our base row class to automatically reconnect the rows to the table when they are reinstated.

library/SF/Model/Resource/Db/Table/Row/Abstract.php

```
public function __wakeup()
{
    if (!$this->getRow()->isConnected()) {
        $tableClass = $this->getRow()->getTableClass();
        $table = new $tableClass();
        $this->getRow()->setTable($table);
    }
}
```

The __wakeup method will be called every time the row class is un-serialized. Within the method, we check whether the row is indeed disconnected from the table. If it is, then we get the table class name from the row instance and then instantiate a new table instance. Once we have a new instance of the correct table class, we then reconnect the row to the table using the `setTable()` method.

Summary

In this chapter, we have looked at all the general techniques we can use to optimize a Zend Framework based application, from PHP optimizations such as opcode caching all the way to caching data in our Models. It is important to remember though that over-optimization can waste development time. We should only optimize the parts that we really need to and try to avoid micro-optimization. This comes down to a balance between the need for optimization and the speed of development. Micro-optimization may shave a few milliseconds off a request but if you spend a week doing this optimization, you have already lost your gain in performance.

This is also true for some of the benchmark tests you may see against the Zend Framework. While these may be true to an extent, the real performance you gain with the Zend Framework is the speed of development and easy-to-maintain MVC architecture. If you are looking for total performance, then use scripts instead of Object Oriented Programming, and take a hit on the maintainability of your application.

We should also be aware that this chapter covers a very small part of data caching. We have only looked in detail at the caching of Model data. This may not be appropriate for every application, so it is important to consider your options when choosing a caching strategy. You might require full page caching or even a totally separate cache using a third party piece of software. The choice is very application-specific and something that you will need to decide for yourself.

In the next chapter, we are going to start testing the Storefront using `Zend_Test` and `PHPUnit`. These tools allow us to easily test the functionality of our application.

12
Testing the Storefront

When developing an application before we deploy it, we need to confirm that it is functioning as expected. In the past, this may have been a case of manually testing each page/function of the application once we have completed development. However, this manual testing can be very time consuming and is hard to repeat multiple times. To help with this, we are going to look at ways in which we can automate this process and the tools that the Zend Framework provides for this purpose.

In this chapter, we are going to:

- Know what is testing
- Set up the PHPUnit and `Zend_Test`
- Write tests
- Test the Customer Controller

What is testing?

Testing comes in many forms, and the type of testing we use depends heavily on the type of project that we are working on. We can test software in various ways from manually verifying behavior all the way to automated test suites that can be run at will by the developers or stakeholders. The main categories for tests are as follows:

- **Unit testing**: Unit testing happens at the class or low level, where we isolate a single unit of code from the rest of the system to perform the test. You will notice that we have included unit tests for the main Storefront units within the examples in most of the chapters of this book.

- **Integration testing**: Integration testing happens again at a low level. However, it tests the behavior of interacting units and not just one single unit of code.

- **Functional/system testing**: Functional or system testing happens at a much higher level. Here we test the behavior of the system as a whole, involving all the units of code that make up the system. We will be using this type of testing when using `Zend_Test`, as we will be testing the Storefronts functionality at a high level.

- **Acceptance testing**: Acceptance testing happens also at a high level. This type of testing usually happens at the end of a project or development sprint, where the stakeholders confirm that the system works in the way they expect it to and that they accept its behavior.

This list of testing categories is not complete as there are probably more types of testing than we could possibly cover. However, they do mark out the general types of testing that are available to us. On the most basic level, all of these test types do the same thing, that is, they confirm that something works as expected. This is the heart of what testing is.

For the Storefront, we are going to be looking at functional testing. Therefore, we are going to be testing the system as a whole with all elements fully integrated with each other for the tests. For these tests, we aim to create a test suite that can be executed with the least amount of effort. By doing this, we encourage developers to run them as often as possible and hopefully pick up more bugs. Now functional tests do run slower than unit tests as they involve a lot more units of code and usually a database connection. This is why we create a unit test suite as well as a functional test suite. This allows developers to run the unit tests very frequently and functional tests less frequently.

You may have noticed that we already have unit tests created for the example files supplied with most of the chapters. We will not be covering those in this book. However, they still provide an example of unit testing and help make sure that the example files function as expected.

PHPUnit and Zend_Test setup

As with the unit tests, we are going to be using PHPUnit to create the functional tests for the Storefront, so our first step is to create a test suite that will house all of our tests. Inside the Storefront project, we already have one test suite for the unit tests. We could add our functional tests into this suite. However, we want them separated so that we can run them independently of each other. Again this goes back to the speed of the tests, as we want our unit tests to run as fast as possible!

PHPUnit setup

To start, we need to create an `AllTests.php` file that will act as the main endpoint for the PHPUnit test runner.

tests/application/AllTests.php

```php
<?php
if (!defined('PHPUnit_MAIN_METHOD')) {
    define('PHPUnit_MAIN_METHOD', 'SF_Application_AllTests::main');
}

require_once dirname(__FILE__) . '/TestHelper.php';
require_once 'controllers/indexControllerTest.php';

class SF_Application_AllTests
{
    public static function main()
    {
        PHPUnit_TextUI_TestRunner::run(self::suite());
    }

    public static function suite()
    {
        $suite = new PHPUnit_Framework_TestSuite(
            'Storefront Application Tests'
        );
        $suite->addTestSuite('IndexControllerTest');
        return $suite;
    }
}

if (PHPUnit_MAIN_METHOD == 'SF_Application_AllTests::main') {
    SF_Unit_AllTests::main();
}
```

The `AllTests.php` file contains some PHPUnit specific code that is used to configure a test suite. It also contains the main `SF_Application_AllTests` class, which loads and runs the individual tests that we will create later.

To tell PHPUnit which class and method to use when running the tests, we have two IF statements at the top and bottom of the file. The first one defines the `PHPUnit_MAIN_METHOD` constant which defines the method that should be called for this suite, and the second checks for the constant and runs the suite.

Inside the class, we have two methods:

- `main()`: This method calls the `PHPUnit_TextUI_TestRunner::run` method passing in the returned value of the `suite()` method.

- `suite()`: This method creates a new `PHPUnit_Framework_TestSuite` instance defining the name of the test suite. Once the suite is created, we can then add our tests using the `addTestSuite()` method.

Currently the `Storefront Application Tests` suite only has one test `IndexControllerTest`, which will test the Index Controller.

Next, we need to create a Test Helper for our suite. This will be used to set up some common settings that will be used by all the tests.

`tests/application/TestHelper.php`

```php
<?php
require_once 'PHPUnit/Framework.php';
require_once 'PHPUnit/Framework/IncompleteTestError.php';
require_once 'PHPUnit/Framework/TestCase.php';
require_once 'PHPUnit/Framework/TestSuite.php';
require_once 'PHPUnit/Runner/Version.php';
require_once 'PHPUnit/TextUI/TestRunner.php';
require_once 'PHPUnit/Util/Filter.php';

error_reporting( E_ALL | E_STRICT );
date_default_timezone_set('Europe/London');

$root  = realpath(dirname(__FILE__) . '/../../');
$paths = array(
    get_include_path(),
    "$root/library",
    "$root/tests",
    "$root/application"
);
set_include_path(implode(PATH_SEPARATOR, $paths));

defined('APPLICATION_PATH')
    or define('APPLICATION_PATH', realpath(dirname(__FILE__)
              . '/../../application'));

require_once 'ControllerTestCase.php';

Zend_Session::$_unitTestEnabled = true;
Zend_Session::start();

PHPUnit_Util_Filter::addDirectoryToFilter("$root/tests");
PHPUnit_Util_Filter::addDirectoryToFilter("$root/library/Zend");
```

Our test helper first includes some of the PHPUnit classes that are required to run the suites, then we set the error_reporting level and the default time zone. These will be set in the bootstrap. However, it is always a good practice to include them anyway. Next, we set up the include paths by adding the library, tests, and application folders. We also set the APPLICATION_PATH constant to the application folder.

With all the main configuration options created, we then include the ControllerTestCase.php class file. This class will act as a base class for all of our tests and will contain some common setup methods that each of our tests will use. Next, we configure Zend_Session to run in its unit test state by setting the $_unitTestEnabled property to true. This setting stops common errors when testing with Zend_Session.

For our final piece of code, we will add some PHPUnit filters to the PHPUnit test runner. This is so that the code coverage reports do not include the directories we specify. Therefore, we are effectively blacklisting the classes in these directories from being included in the PHPUnit statistics.

Zend_Test setup

Now that we have our test helper and our main test suite, we need to create a base class from where all our individual tests will extend from. This is not absolutely necessary, but it saves a lot of time when creating our tests, as it provides a place for all our common test code to live.

tests/application/ControllerTestCase.php

```php
<?php
require_once 'Zend/Application.php';
require_once 'Zend/Test/PHPUnit/ControllerTestCase.php';

class ControllerTestCase extends Zend_Test_PHPUnit_ControllerTestCase
{
    public $application;

    public function setUp()
    {
        $this->application = new Zend_Application(
            'test',
            APPLICATION_PATH . '/config/store.ini'
        );

        $this->bootstrap = array($this, 'appBootstrap');
        parent::setUp();
    }
```

```
public function tearDown()
{
    $this->resetRequest()->resetResponse();
    $this->request->setPost(array());
    $this->request->setQuery(array());
}

public function appBootstrap()
{
    $this->application->bootstrap();
}
}
```

The `ControllerTestCase` subclasses `Zend_Test_PHPUnit_ControllerTestCase`. This provides all the functionality required to test our application's controller actions. This in turn subclasses the PHPUnit test case class that defines the PHPUnit API. Our new base test case will be used to set up the test environment for each of our tests. If we did not use a custom base test class, then we would need to include the above code in each of our tests.

The test case class defines two special methods that are part of the PHPUnit API—`setUp()` and `teardown()`. These methods are called between every test, so when a test starts, the `setUp()` method is called, and when a test finishes the `tearDown()` method is called. This provides us with a way to reset our environment before running each test. This is very important as we need to be sure that the environment is exactly the same for each test. If it changes each time, then we cannot confirm the behavior accurately.

The `setUp()` method needs to configure our environment. For `Zend_Test` to work, we need to provide a bootstrap method that configures the application just like in our normal application setup. Therefore, we use `Zend_Application` to provide the bootstrapping for us. We instantiate a new `Zend_Application` instance by passing in the environment of `test` and the path to the `store.ini` configuration file. This will make `Zend_Application` configure the application for the `test` environment. This is currently the same as the production environment but may not always be the case. `Zend_Test` is not tied to using `Zend_Application` so we need to provide it with a callback to our bootstrapping method or instance method. To do this, we simply set the callback array on the `bootstrap` class property. The callback we provide in this case is `array($this, 'appBootstrap')`. This will make `Zend_Test` call the `appBootstrap()` method on the current instance of the test case. The final call in the `setUp()` method is to `parent::setUp()`. This is very important as we need to call the `setUp()` methods in the parent classes for everything to work properly.

The `tearDown()` method is used to reset our environment. Here we tell `Zend_Test` to first clear the Request and Response objects, and then we clear the Post and Query arrays. This will stop any unexpected results caused by adding a test's data to these objects.

Our final method is `appBootstrap()`. This is the callback target we specified in `setUp()` and simply calls the `bootstrap()` on the `Zend_Application` instance we created earlier. Now this executes the full bootstrap. There may be times when we have certain parts of the bootstrap we do not want to call. If this is the case, then we need to bootstrap the individual bootstrap resources. For example, we may only need database and routes. Therefore, we could only bootstrap these using:

```
public function appBootstrap()
{
    $this->application->bootstrap('db')->bootstrap('routes');
}
```

Handling the database

One other important aspect of the test environment setup is the database. We need a database to test against and ideally it needs to be in the same state to start with for each test. The way we do this depends greatly on what type of database we use. If we are using something like SQLite, then we can easily load the database into memory for each test. However, with something like MySQL, this is harder to achieve.

For the Storefront, we are going to simply import the database and data into a test schema before we run the tests. To do this, run the following commands:

```
mysql -uroot -p storefront_test < structure.sql
mysql -uroot -p storefront_test < data.sql
```

We then need to edit the `store.ini` and change the database schema for the test environment.

```
[test : bootstrap]
resources.db.params.dbname = "storefront_test"
```

Here, we simply override the default schema with the test, so that our tests do not use the live database.

Setting up the test database in this way is not ideal, as we need to do this every time before we run the tests. For the Storefront, as we have a small database, this is not such a big deal. However, for more complex databases, it would become very tiresome. Also, what we really need to achieve is the database to reset before each test, and not the whole test suite. Therefore, ideally we would reload the database in the `setUp()` method.

The way we achieve this is beyond the scope of this book as it is very project and database dependent and would either involve third party libraries or the creation of scripts that reload the database and data for each test. PHPUnit supports database fixtures, though it can be hard to get it to work with zend_Test. The doctrine project (www.doctrine-project.org), a database Object Relational Mapper, supports both database migrations (tracking database changes) and fixtures. This is a very good tool.

Writing tests

Okay, now that we have everything set up it is time for the fun part, which is writing our tests. To start, create the following test class:

tests/application/controllers/indexControllerTest.php

```php
<?php
class IndexControllerTest extends ControllerTestCase
{
    public function testIndexAction() {
        $this->dispatch('/');
        $this->assertController('index');
        $this->assertAction('index');
        $this->assertModule('storefront');
    }
}
```

This is the most basic test we can write. We create a class called IndexControllerTest that subclasses our ControllerTestCase and adds a single method testIndexAction(). The testIndexAction() method is our test. By prefixing the method name with test, we tell PHPUnit that this is a test within the IndexControllerTest case or suite. We can add as many tests as we want to a test suite by adding more test methods.

Inside the IndexAction test, we have our test code. Every test that we create needs to make some sort of assertion. By this we mean a test needs to verify some behavior. The IndexAction test makes three assertions:

- The Controller should be index
- The Action should be index
- The Module should be index

So this is the behavior that we are confirming with the test. However, to make the assertion, we need to make our application do something. We do this by using the dispatch() method. This is part of the Zend_Test API and will make the Front Controller dispatch to the URL we specify. In this case, we dispatch to the root of the application (/). When we call the dispatch() method, Zend_Test does not use a browser to make the request. Instead, Zend_Test does everything using PHP. This is a great feature of the Zend Framework as previously we would have had to launch a browser to do this kind of testing.

Now the assertions we make are all provided by Zend_Test and PHPUnit. Both provide a whole host of different assertion methods for us to work with. We will be covering a lot here but it is worth checking the documentation for both. In our test, we use three different assertion methods, namely, assertController(), assertAction(), and assertModule(). All of these are actually provided by Zend_Test and confirm the Controller, the Action, and the Module called respectively. Every assertion either fails or succeeds. So in our test, if we dispatch to /catalog/hats instead of /, the test will fail as the assertions are not met.

Running tests

Now that we have our first test created, we need to run it. The simplest way to do this is from the command line change into the tests/application directory, and run the following command:

```
phpunit AllTests.php
```

This will now run the test suite for us and show the result. It should look something like the following screenshot:

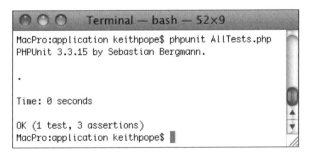

Here we can see that the tests passed and that we ran one test with three assertions. If we now edit our test and change the dispatch() from / to /catalog/hats/ and re-run the test suite, then our tests will fail and output something like this:

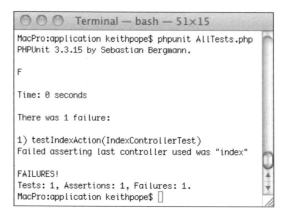

Here we can see that our test has now failed. The output tells us which test has failed and in which suite. It also tells us why the assertion has failed.

Adding tests to the build

Running our tests like this can be a little tiresome. Therefore, we can add this to the Ant build so it is easier to run, and we can provide some extra options.

To do this, add the following to the build.xml file:

build/build.xml

```
<target name="testapp" depends="getProps">
    <exec dir="${basedir}/tests/application"
          executable="phpunit${script-suffix}" failonerror="true">
      <arg line="--colors --report ${basedir}/build/report
          --log-xml ${basedir}/build/logs/phpunit.xml
          --log-pmd ${basedir}/build/logs/phpunit.pmd.xml
          --log-metrics ${basedir}/build/logs/phpunit.metrics.xml
          --coverage-xml ${basedir}/build/logs/phpunit.coverage.xml
          AllTests.php"/>
    </exec>
</target>
```

This new build target simply runs the same command we ran earlier. However, we pass in more options this time. These new options will produce code coverage and metrics for our project.

Now, if we change into the build directory and run the following command:

```
ant testapp
```

Ant will run the tests for us with all the extra options we need, saving us a lot of typing! The output will now look like this:

```
MacPro:build keithpope$ ant testapp
Buildfile: build.xml

getProps:
     [echo] ---- Build Properties ----
     [echo]
     [echo] OS is Mac OS X
     [echo] Basedir is /Users/keithpope/Sites/book_trunk2
     [echo] Property file is /Users/keithpope/Sites/book_trunk2/build/ant.properties
     [echo] Script-suffix is
     [echo]
     [echo] ---- Storefront Properties ----
     [echo]
     [echo] Environment is development

testapp:
     [exec] PHPUnit 3.3.15 by Sebastian Bergmann.
     [exec]
     [exec] F
     [exec]
     [exec] Time: 3 seconds
     [exec]
     [exec] There was 1 failure:
     [exec]
     [exec] 1) testIndexAction(IndexControllerTest)
     [exec] Failed asserting last controller used was "index"
     [exec]
          FAILURES!
          Tests: 1, Assertions: 1, Failures: 1.

     [exec] Writing code coverage data to XML file, this may take a moment.
     [exec]
     [exec] Writing metrics report XML file, this may take a moment.
     [exec]
     [exec] Writing violations report XML file, this may take a moment.
     [exec]
     [exec] Generating code coverage report, this may take a moment.

BUILD FAILED
/Users/keithpope/Sites/book_trunk2/build/build.xml:39: exec returned: 1

Total time: 15 seconds
MacPro:build keithpope$
```

Again our test fails, as we haven't fixed the `indexControllerTest`. You may want to change that back now for later. We also see that once the tests are complete, PHPUnit writes code coverage XML, metrics XML, violations XML, and generates a code coverage report. The XML files are not of any use to us. However, they can be used by other programs such as **phpundercontrol** to provide us with more detailed reports. We won't cover that here as it's far beyond the scope of this book. We leave them in here for good practice. Now, the coverage report is of use to us. This is an HTML report of the code lines that were executed during the test. If we open the `index.html` file within the `build/report` folder, then we can browse to see what was executed.

Storefront Application Tests

Current file: /Users/keithpope/Sites/book_trunk2/application/modules/storefront/models/Catalog.php

Legend: executed   not executed   dead code

	Classes		Coverage Functions / Methods		Lines	
Total	100.00%	1 / 1	33.33%	5 / 15	26.26%	26 / 99
Storefront_Model_Catalog	100.00%	1 / 1	33.33%	5 / 15	26.26%	26 / 99
public function getCategoriesByParentId($parentID)			100.00%	1 / 1	100.00%	2 / 2
public function getCategoryByIdent($ident)			100.00%	1 / 1	100.00%	1 / 1
public function getCategories()			0.00%	0 / 1	0.00%	0 / 1
public function getProductById($id)			0.00%	0 / 1	0.00%	0 / 2
public function getProductByIdent($ident)			0.00%	0 / 1	0.00%	0 / 1
public function getProductsByCategory($category, $paged = false, $order = NULL, $deep = true)			100.00%	1 / 1	90.91%	10 / 11
public function getCategoryChildrenIds($categoryId, $recursive = false)			100.00%	1 / 1	100.00%	9 / 9
public function getParentCategories($category, $appendParent = true)			100.00%	1 / 1	33.33%	3 / 9
public function saveCategory($data, $validator = NULL)			0.00%	0 / 1	0.00%	0 / 10
public function saveProduct($data, $validator = NULL)			0.00%	0 / 1	0.00%	0 / 16
public function saveProductImage(Storefront_Resource_Product_Item $product, $data, $validator = NULL)			0.00%	0 / 1	0.00%	0 / 14
public function deleteProduct($product)			0.00%	0 / 1	0.00%	0 / 11
public function getResourceId()			0.00%	0 / 1	0.00%	0 / 1
public function setAcl(SF_Acl_Interface $acl)			0.00%	0 / 1	0.00%	0 / 6
public function getAcl()			0.00%	0 / 1	0.00%	0 / 4

```
 1        : <?php
 2        : /**
 3        :  * Storefront_Catalog
 4        :  *
 5        :  * @category    Storefront
 6        :  * @package     Storefront_Model
 7        :  * @copyright   Copyright (c) 2008 Keith Pope (http://www.thepopeisdead.com)
 8        :  * @license     http://www.thepopeisdead.com/license.txt      New BSD License
 9        :  */
10      1 : class Storefront_Model_Catalog extends SF_Model_Acl_Abstract implements Zend_Acl_Resource_Interface
11        : {
12        :     /**
13        :      * Get categories
14        :      *
15        :      * @param int $parentID The parentId
16        :      * @return Zend_Db_Table_Rowset
17        :      */
18        :     public function getCategoriesByParentId($parentID)
19        :     {
20      1 :         $parentID = (int) $parentID;
```

Here is an example of one of the pages outputted by PHPUnit. It shows us a table with all the statistics for what has been executed, as well as showing the source of the file with the lines colored to indicate which ones were executed. This tool can be very useful, as we generally want to try to get as close to 100 percent code coverage as possible, and it shows us what we need to do to achieve this.

Testing the Customer Controller

We are now ready to start writing some more tests. In this section, we are going to test the Customer Controller. In these tests, we are going to confirm the following behaviors:

- Registered users should be able to log in
- Invalid login credentials should not allow the user to log in
- When logged in, a user should have access to their profile
- Admin users can access the admin area
- Non-Admin users cannot access the admin area

To start, we are going to create our test class and a helper method that logs a user into the Storefront, which will save us from repeating the login code in each test:

tests/application/controllers/customerControllerTest.php

```php
<?php
class CustomerControllerTest extends ControllerTestCase
{
    public function login($email, $passwd)
    {
        $this->request->setMethod('POST')
                      ->setPost(array(
                          'email' => $email,
                          'passwd' => $passwd,
                      ));
        $this->dispatch('/customer/authenticate');
        $this->assertRedirectTo('/customer');
        $this->teardown();
    }
}
```

We have now created our basic structure for our test case. The `login()` helper method will be used by the test methods to authenticate with the Storefront. Inside the method body, we configure the request object. We set the request method to `POST` and add a new post array containing the `email` and `passwd` fields that are required for authentication. Once we have the request object configured, we then tell `Zend_Test` to dispatch to `/customer/authenticate`. This will execute the authentication process on the Storefront, just as if we had submitted the login form manually. We then make an assertion that the application will redirect us to `/customer` if the login is successful using the `assertRedirect()` method. Our final call is to the `tearDown()` method which will reset the test for us, clearing all the request data.

If we run this test case now, nothing would happen. This is because we have not yet added any test methods. Therefore, we need to now add our tests. We will start by adding a test to make sure a valid user can log in.

```
public function testUserCanAuthenticate()
{
    $this->login('me@me.com','123456');
}
```

For the `testUserCanAuthenticate` test, we simply call the login helper method, passing in a valid login for the Storefront. This will be enough to confirm our intended behavior as the `login()` method contains an assertion already.

Next, let's make sure invalid users cannot log in to the system. For this, add the following test method:

```
public function testFailedLogin()
{
    $this->request->setMethod('POST')
                  ->setPost(array(
                      'email' => 'me@me.com',
                      'passwd' => 'asdasdasdasdasd',
                  ));
    $this->dispatch('/customer/authenticate');
    $this->assertQueryContentContains(
        '.error', 'Login failed, please try again.'
    );
}
```

For the `testFailedLogin` test we do not use the `login()` method, as this expects a valid login. Instead, this time we manually configure the request, passing in an incorrect password and dispatching to `/customer/authenticate`. This will cause the login to fail and the login form to be displayed, showing the error to the user. We therefore need to confirm this behavior. To do this, we use the assertQueryContentContains() assertion. This assertion uses Zend_Dom and can be used to search an HTML document using CSS3 style selectors. In this case, we search the contents of all elements that have the CSS class error for the value Login failed, please try again.

The assertQueryContentContains assertion supports all the main CSS3 selectors. Here are some example queries:

- input: selects all input elements
- input[type=text]: selects all input elements with the text type attribute
- #myelement: selects the element with the ID attribute of myelement
- div > h1: selects all h1 elements that are descendents of a div

As we can see, this is a powerful and simple way to query the HTML content of our application. Moreover, most web developers are already familiar with this type of selector. If you are not familiar with CSS, then there are plenty of CSS selector tutorials on the net and more examples in the Zend_Dom page in the reference manual.

Our next test will confirm that once a user has logged in, their profile is displayed, which they can update using the form on that page.

```
public function testUserHasProfileAccessWhenLoggedIn()
{
    $this->login('me@me.com','123456');
    $this->dispatch('/customer');
    $this->assertQuery('form');
    $this->assertXpath('/html/body/div[2]/div[2]/form');
}
```

To see our profile, we need to log in first. Therefore, we use the login() helper method to log in before we continue with the rest of the test. Once we have successfully logged in, we then dispatch to /customer. This is where the customer's profile is located. The first assertion we make is using assertQuery('form'). This confirms that there is a form on the page and uses CSS selectors like before. Our second assertion actually makes the same assertion as the first but using a different query method, Xpath. The assertXpath() and assertXpathContentContains() work in exactly the same way as the Query assertions, using Xpath as the query language. Here we have a choice to use whichever we are most familiar with.

Our final two tests test the security on the administration area. These probably would be best suited in a different test case as they are not strictly associated with customers. However, they serve as good examples for now.

```
public function testAdminAreaRoute()
{
    //authenticate admin user
    $this->login('me@me.com','123456');
    $this->dispatch('/admin');
    $this->assertRoute('admin');
}


public function testUnauthenticatedUserCannotAccessAdmin()
{
    $this->dispatch('/admin');
    $this->assertQueryContentContains('p','Access Denied');
}
```

The testAdminAreaRoute test confirms that an authenticated user can access the administration area. We first log in using the login helper and then dispatch to /admin. To check that the user has the correct access, we assert that the current route being used is the admin route, using the assertRoute() assertion.

The testUnauthenticatedUserCannotAccessAdmin test simply dispatches to /admin without first logging in. This should give an access denied error to the user. We confirm this by using the assertQueryContentContains() and searching the content of all p tags for **Access Denied**.

Running the Customer Controller test

To run the Customer Controller test case, we need to add the test to the test suite. Edit the AllTests.php file, and add the following highlighted lines:

```
require_once 'controllers/indexControllerTest.php';
require_once 'controllers/customerControllerTest.php';

$suite->addTestSuite('IndexControllerTest');
$suite->addTestSuite('CustomerControllerTest');
```

Now, we can run the tests just like before using Ant.

Common problems

Sometimes, when writing tests, we will face situations where we need to debug failing tests. This can be hard but there are a few little tips that we should be aware of:

1. Make sure all `_forward()` and redirects calls within Controllers return. For example:

   ```
   public function indexAction()
   {
    return $this->_forward('myAction');
   }
   ```

2. Never use `$_POST`, `$_GET`, `$_SESSION` globals. Instead, always use the Request object.

3. Never use `header()` to do redirects. Use the redirector Action Helper or use the Response object for other headers.

4. Never output anything in your Controllers. Always use the Response object.

5. To debug errors, use `var_dump()` to view the contents of the Request and Response objects. If dumping the full objects produces too much data, then you can access specific parts. For example:

   ```
   var_dump($this->request->getPost());
   var_dump($this->response->getException());
   ```

Summary

In our final chapter, we have looked at how we can test the Storefront to confirm that it is functioning as expected, by using functional testing. We have also looked at the different types of testing available to us such as unit testing and acceptance testing. We have created a test suite using PHPUnit and `Zend_Test` that can be easily executed through Apache Ant and is repeatable. For individual tests, we have looked at the API provided by `Zend_Test` that allows us to make assertions based on the output of the application to confirm specific behaviors.

This is the final chapter, so I hope that you have found this book a useful resource and that it has shown you how flexible and powerful the Zend Framework is. I have certainly enjoyed putting this book together and would highly recommend the Zend Framework to anyone—and I see it growing further in the future.

Installing Supporting Software

In the book we use various supporting software tools to help work with the Zend Framework, these tools help us maintain, test, and debug our applications. In this chapter, we look at how to install these tools on various platforms.

Installing PHPUnit

The book's examples use PHPUnit for testing. You will need PHPUnit installed to run these tests. PHPUnit can be installed using PHP's PEAR interface and using the following commands:

```
pear channel-discover pear.phpunit.de
pear install --alldeps phpunit/PHPUnit
```

Running this command will automatically install PHPUnit for you. The version used in the book is 3.3.6 although later 3.x versions should also work. You can find more information about PHPUnit at http://www.phpunit.de.

To test your installation, you should be able to run the tests included in one of the example packages using:

```
cd tests
phpunit AllTests.php
```

PHP memory limit

You may need to increase the memory limit of PHP to install PHPUnit and run the tests. This can be done by editing the php.ini and changing the memory_limit directive. Typically, I use between 64M and 128M.

Installing Xdebug

Xdebug is a PHP extension that helps with the debugging of PHP applications. The reason we use it in the book examples is mainly for its code coverage analysis, which is used by PHPUnit to produce various metrics for us. If you have not already come across Xdebug, then I would strongly advise installing it, as it has many great features for debugging and profiling your applications.

The installation of Xdebug can be a bit troublesome sometimes, especially on Windows systems, as you need to compile the extension.

Windows installation

Luckily for Windows, there are precompiled Xdebug modules available on the Xdebug home page at `http://www.xdebug.org`. If you are on Windows, I suggest downloading the correct dll for your PHP version and dropping it in your extensions directory.

Linux based installation

On any Linux system, the compilation of the extension can be done through the PECL interface. To install, run the following from your shell:

```
pecl install Xdebug
```

Hopefully, this will download, compile, and install the extension for you. If not, then you may need to download it and compile it manually. For more information on compiling Xdebug, go to `http://www.xdebug.org/docs/install`.

OSX Installation

OSX installation can be somewhat troublesome; if you are using the Macports version of PHP you can easily install it using the ports command using:

```
sudo port install php5-xdebug
```

If you are using MAMP, the best way to get the Xdebug binary is to download the precompiled one from the ActiveState website, `http://aspn.activestate.com/ASPN/Downloads/Komodo/RemoteDebugging`. Select the correct PHP Remote Debugging package for your system and then copy the `xdebug.so` file for your PHP version to:

```
/Applications/MAMP/bin/php5/lib/php/extensions/no-debug-non-zts-
20050922/xdebug.so
```

Also, if you have fully configured PHP on your OSX system you should be able to use the `pecl` command like on Linux. However, this is not possible on a default OSX install.

Configuration

Once you have the module installed, you need to activate it in your `php.ini`. Edit your `php.ini` and add the following at the bottom:

For Windows:

```
zend_extension_ts="c:/php/modules/php_xdebug-4.4.1-2.0.2.dll"
```

For Linux:

```
zend_extension="/usr/local/php/modules/xdebug.so"
```

Remember, you need to change the path and version numbers to match your environment settings!

Installing Apache Ant

We use Apache Ant to automate some tasks that configure the application. This is not essential, but I use this on all my projects and so thought to include it as I personally find it very useful. There are other alternatives such as Phing (`http://phing.info`). You can use either, but all the examples in this book have used Ant.

To run Ant, you will need the Java Runtime installed and the Java JDK 6. It is best to get the Sun version from `http://java.sun.com/javase/downloads/index.jsp`. Once you have that installed it, you can download Ant from `http://ant.apache.org/bindownload.cgi`. Get the latest version 1.6.

Windows installation

Unpack the downloaded Ant package to `C:\ant`.

Once the package has been extracted, we need to set some environment variable so that we can run Ant from the command line and so that Ant knows where Java is located.

Open: `My Computer | Advanced System Properties | Environment Variables`.

Then add the following variables:

- `ANT_HOME C:\ant`
- `JAVA_HOME C:\java\bin`

You may already have the JAVA_HOME variable set. If so, then leave it as it is. Also remember to change the JAVA_HOME path given above to match your system's Java `bin` directory.

We then need to edit the PATH variable and add the path to the Ant `bin` directory. We do this by adding the following to the end of the PATH string:

`; C:\ant`

We should now be able to open the command prompt and run the Ant command.

Linux installation

As Ant is widely used, you should be able to install it through any of the distributions package managers such as `apt-get` or `yum`. So you should be able to run something like:

`apt-get install ant`

On Linux, it is important to make sure that you are using the Sun version of Java and that the JAVA_HOME and ANT_HOME environment variables are set. These should be set by your package manager anyway.

Index

E

environmental checking methods, HTTP Request object
isDelete () 75
isFlashRequest () 75
isGet () 75
isHead () 75
isOptions () 75
isPost () 75
isPut () 75
isSecure () 75
isXmlHttpRequest () 75
environment specific configuration, Zend_Application 93
error handling 38, 39
Escape() 33

F

fat controller
about 117
product controller 117
product model 117
product model, disadvantages 118
fat model
about 118
product controller 118
product model 118
product model, advantages 119
Fat Model Skinny Controller
about 117
fat controller 117
fat model 118
Fat Model Skinny Controller principle 192
fetchAll() method 148
filter() method 279
filters, user forms
using 211, 212
find() method 149
findDependentRowset() rowset method 152
firstname element
about 207
Alpha validator 207
creating 207
filters, passing 207
required option, passing 207
StringLength validator 207

StringTrim filter 207
validators, passing 207
first view
creating 30
first view, creating
URL View Helper 35
view, creating 31-33
view customization 37
view directories 31
view helpers 35
formatAmount() method 236
Form elements
about 200
decorators 200
description, decorators 200
errors, decorators 200
HtmlTag, decorators 200
label, decorators 200
ViewHelper, decorators 200
Front Controller
about 45
actions 48
controllers 48
default behavior 46
default objects 46
default plugins 47
design 45
employing 47
invocation parameters 47
methods 51
modules 48
modules, using 49-51
MVC component customization 51
options 48
plugins 52
Front Controller, methods
setDefaultAction(String $name) 51
setDefaultControllerName(String $name) 51
setDefaultModule(String $module) 51
setModuleControllerDirectoryName(String $name) 51
Front Controller, methods for handling invocation parameters
clearParams(String | Array | Null $name) 48
getParam(String $name) 48
getParams() 48

P

partial page caching 310
password verification validator
about 210
creating 210, 211
path optimizations 302
persist() method 222
PHP optimizations 302
PHP settings, Zend_Application 90
phpundercontrol 334
PHPUnit
installing 341
PHPUnit installation 341
PHPUnit setup
about 325
main() method 326
suite() method 326
Plugin Loader 211
populate() method 191
preDispatch() method 270
preg engine 58
preg library 59
prepend (string $name, string $content)
method 77
product add form
about 275
creating 275, 276
custom filters, using 279, 280
form elements, sharing 278
ProductImage Resource Item
about 155
creating 155, 156
Product Model Resource
about 149
creating 149-152
Product Resource Item
about 152
creating 152-155
products, adding to catalog
catalog controller, editing 281
catalog model, editing 280
product add form 277
product add form, creating 275, 276
project structure
creating 11, 13

creating, Zend_Tool component used 11
public directory, hellozend directory 14

R

RedirectCommon Action Helper 285
regex matching 58
registerPlugin(Zend_Controller_Plugin_Ab-
stract $plugin, Optional Int $stackIn-
dex) method 52
registerUser() method
about 185
using 186
removeItem($product) method 222
request, Zend Framework MVC 42
request dispatching, Dispatcher 67
request handling, Zend Framework MVC
about 42, 43
process 44
Request object
about 70
Apache404 Request object 71
design 71
employing 71, 72
getActionName() 72
getControllerName() 72
getDispatched() 72
getModuleName() 72
HTTP Request object 73
methods, for accessing parameters 72
setActionName() 72
setControllerName() 72
setDispatched() 72
setModuleName() 72
Simple Request object 71
request object 26
Request object methods, for accessing
parameters
getParam() 72
getParams() 72
getUserParam() 72
getUserParams() 72
setParam() 72
setParams() 72
required option 207
reset() method 152

Thank you for buying
Zend Framework 1.8
Web Application Development

Packt Open Source Project Royalties

When we sell a book written on an Open Source project, we pay a royalty directly to that project. Therefore by purchasing Zend Framework 1.8 Web Application Development, Packt will have given some of the money received to the Zend framework project.

In the long term, we see ourselves and you—customers and readers of our books—as part of the Open Source ecosystem, providing sustainable revenue for the projects we publish on. Our aim at Packt is to establish publishing royalties as an essential part of the service and support a business model that sustains Open Source.

If you're working with an Open Source project that you would like us to publish on, and subsequently pay royalties to, please get in touch with us.

Writing for Packt

We welcome all inquiries from people who are interested in authoring. Book proposals should be sent to author@packtpub.com. If your book idea is still at an early stage and you would like to discuss it first before writing a formal book proposal, contact us; one of our commissioning editors will get in touch with you.

We're not just looking for published authors; if you have strong technical skills but no writing experience, our experienced editors can help you develop a writing career, or simply get some additional reward for your expertise.

About Packt Publishing

Packt, pronounced 'packed', published its first book "Mastering phpMyAdmin for Effective MySQL Management" in April 2004 and subsequently continued to specialize in publishing highly focused books on specific technologies and solutions.

Our books and publications share the experiences of your fellow IT professionals in adapting and customizing today's systems, applications, and frameworks. Our solution-based books give you the knowledge and power to customize the software and technologies you're using to get the job done. Packt books are more specific and less general than the IT books you have seen in the past. Our unique business model allows us to bring you more focused information, giving you more of what you need to know, and less of what you don't.

Packt is a modern, yet unique publishing company, which focuses on producing quality, cutting-edge books for communities of developers, administrators, and newbies alike. For more information, please visit our website: www.PacktPub.com.

Symfony 1.3 web application development

Design, develop, and deploy feature-rich, high-performance PHP web applications using the Symfony framework

Tim Bowler   Wojciech Bancer   PACKT

Symfony 1.3 Web Application Development

ISBN: 978-1-847194-56-5   Paperback: 250 pages

Design, develop, and deploy feature-rich, high-performance PHP web applications using the Symfony framework

1. Create powerful web applications by leveraging the power of this Model-View-Controller-based framework

2. Covers all the new features of version 1.3 – many exciting plug-ins for you

3. Learn by doing without getting into too much theoretical detail – create a "real-life" milkshake store application

4. Includes best practices to shorten your development time and improve performance

CakePHP Application Development

Step-by-step introduction to rapid web development using the open-source MVC CakePHP framework

Ahsanul Bari   Anupom Syam   PACKT

CakePHP Application Development

ISBN: 978-1-847193-89-6   Paperback: 332 pages

Step-by-step introduction to rapid web development using the open-source MVC CakePHP framework

1. Develop cutting-edge Web 2.0 applications, and write PHP code in a faster, more productive way

2. Walk through the creation of a complete CakePHP Web application

3. Customize the look and feel of applications using CakePHP layouts and views

4. Make interactive applications using CakePHP, JavaScript, and AJAX helpers

Please check **www.PacktPub.com** for information on our titles

1101338R0

Printed in Great Britain by
Amazon.co.uk, Ltd.,
Marston Gate.